MUSEUMS AND THE FIRST WORLD WAR

For Eric and Margaret Coles

MUSEUMS AND THE FIRST WORLD WAR

A SOCIAL HISTORY

Gaynor Kavanagh

LEICESTER UNIVERSITY PRESS
LONDON AND NEW YORK

DISTRIBUTED IN THE UNITED STATES AND CANADA
BY ST MARTIN'S PRESS

Leicester University Press
A division of **Pinter Publishers Ltd**
25 Floral Street, Covent Garden
London WC2E 9DS, United Kingdom

First published in 1994

Distributed exclusively in the USA and Canada by St. Martin's Press Inc., Room 400, 175 Fifth Avenue, New York, NY 10010, USA.

British Library Cataloguing in Publication Data
A CIP catalogue record for this book is available from the British Library

ISBN 0 7185 1713 X

Library of Congress Cataloging-in-Publication Data
A CIP catalog record for this book is available from the Library of Congress

Set in Monotype Bembo by Ewan Smith
48 Shacklewell Lane, London E8 2EY
Printed and bound in Great Britain by Biddles Ltd
Guildford and King's Lynn

CONTENTS

LIST OF ILLUSTRATIONS

LIST OF TABLES

INTRODUCTION

THE First World War 1914–1918 altered everything, and everything that came after it somehow bore its mark. The lives we lead today carry many legacies, and those of this war are not the least. Its memory provokes emotions rather than facts: sorrow, bewilderment, pride. It is not that we are short of facts and statistics – they are available in substantial measure – but it is the feelings that rise to the surface first. The nation coped, struggled, endured for four years the best it could. It then left its people to grieve, forget or remember as best they could. Armistice day is not about a nation glorifying its wars, but about individual people, in their own right, mourning their dead.

The cold statistics of the war are available in plenty and they could not be more stark. Between 1914 and 1918, in the World War conflict centred on Europe, ten million people, mostly men, were killed and twice as many seriously wounded. Five million wives became widows, nine million children became orphans. Ten million people became refugees (Marwick 1974: 2). These are the global figures, which can only be approximations. It is impossible to put accurate statistics together. How can any statistician accurately count the dead of the battlefield, those who died much later of their injuries, and those who lost their lives in accidents behind the lines or in factories and munitions works, and be sure none has been forgotten or overlooked?

In Britain, somewhere between 723,000 and 745,000 men were killed – the greater proportion young and non-commissioned – and 1,700,000 returned wounded. As a result, 160,000 wives lost their husbands and over 300,000 children lost their fathers. Women serving the war effort as nurses, Red Cross, VAD (Voluntary Aid Detachment) or St John's workers suffered the worst casualties of all women on national service, with over 400 lives lost. The home front had its deaths too. Hundreds of men and women were killed or seriously injured in industrial accidents, many in the munitions and other war industries. In 1921, the Government was distributing 3.5 million pensions, by 1928 this had risen to 4.2 million, as more men succumbed to their war wounds (Bourne 1989: 178; Griffiths 1991: 8; Marwick 1965: 290; Wilkinson 1991: 38; Winter 1986: 74).

As the war dragged on, few lives remained untouched or unchanged by it. The number of casualties and what increasingly became an absence of justification for such a huge loss of life led to a profound sense of futility. But it was not a war totally without reasons. There were both long- and short-term causes for the war, rooted in rapid industrialization, empire-building and rivalry. The catalysts, arguably, were 'the fears and ambitions of the governing élite of Imperial Germany' (Bourne 1989: 2). The Great War, as it came to be called, did not happen by accident. Nor, when the events of 1914 conjoined, was it – in the minds of the Government – avoidable. But the decision to go to war was taken by a Cabinet which was truly not aware that it was committing Britain to a total war, a war of attrition, one which would last four awful years. The price was paid even by members of the Government: Asquith lost one son, Bonar Law, two.

Historians have paid considerable attention to the political and military history of the war, and the literature in this area is now extensive. Since the publication of Arthur Marwick's book *The Deluge* in 1965, more study has been devoted to understanding the history of the home front and the domestic scene, and their relationships with the war fronts. This is a hugely important area, revealing the experiences of ordinary people dealing with bewildering and traumatic events. Even so, many avenues of research have not as yet been taken.

All historians working on this period are faced with a problem of language. The immense impact of the war on people's lives was such that at times words fail. Much of what was experienced and witnessed in the war, especially on the battle fronts, was often literally beyond verbal description (Fussell 1975). Historians have long sought suitable adjectives and similes that might appear apposite and meaningful. Words such as 'horror', 'folly', and 'comradeship' can be employed, as can the imagery of 'armageddon', but they now sound hollow and insufficiently expressive.

The more deeply eloquent expressions of the war experience are to be found not so much in the histories, but in the contemporary accounts of first-hand experience, the poetry, art and music that sprang from it, and the private ephemera of memory, such as the sepia photographs of young soldiers, or young nurses and VADs, their futures so uncertain. Even more poignant, perhaps, are the war memorials erected in the years after the war that list brothers, cousins and friends who did not return. Towns and villages experienced their losses in many ways, although most publicly they measured it in the slate, granite or marble of their war memorials. Even the smallest of villages found more than one name for its list of 'the fallen'. Behind each of these accounts, paintings, poems, photographs and memorials were countless individual testimonies to the sacrifice, anger, endurance and courage the four years exacted.

The war and the war effort demanded and brought about unparalleled change. Every individual was expected to be active, and to be part of the nation's effort, whether at home or in the forces. For four years, private, quiet, ordinary lives ceased to be possible. Similarly, institutions and public services reformed themselves, or were reformed compulsorily: a full and dedicated contribution was expected. The state had to be served, the war machine maintained. Further, this was modern warfare: it was not a distant affair. Rather, it was fought on two fronts – the war front and the home front; civilian morale was critical to the ultimate success of the British forces.

The inter-dependence of battle front and home front was quite complex. Only a small proportion of the soldiers were regular soldiers. The substantial proportion of the five million men who joined up or were called up were ordinary working-class men, they were 'citizens in uniform'. On a practical level, they depended on the home front for their supplies, equipment and armaments. They needed the workers at home to be co-operative and efficient. But of equal importance, they retained their emotional ties with home and needed the security of knowing they were remembered and cared about. Fundamentally, they needed to be certain beyond doubt of the approval at home for their actions. Without this, as was proven by the American forces in Vietnam, morale would have been totally undermined and victory impossible. The home front and the war fronts were therefore deeply connected, yet oddly a world apart (Bourne 1989) – so much so that when the soldiers returned, they found conversations about the war impossible with those who had not experienced it first hand. Robert Graves recorded how he found that 'the civilians talk a foreign language' (quoted in Glover and Silkin 1989: 316). Later, he was to describe how two different Britains had been created out of the war, the 'Fighting Forces' and the 'Rest' (Graves and Hodge 1940: 10).

This book is concerned with how, during four demanding, dislocating and world-changing years, that most Victorian of institutions, the museum, was forced or prompted to meet the extraordinary test of war on the home front. Museums were no more immune from the pressures of war than any other institution and the changes in museums during this period, some long term others transitory, do much to explain the nature and character of museums in Britain today. Their history reveals and reflects the broader history of the home front, and the willing, stumbling, confused efforts to do the right thing at the right time. They were far away from the fighting, the despair and degradation of the battlefields; but they were in some measure not only close to but part of a society at war.

The discussion will principally cover the progress of museums from just before the advent of war in August 1914 to the immediate post-war period, 1920 or thereabouts; although this will be set in the context of museum developments before and after this span of time. Museums will be considered in relation to the tensions and prevalent conditions of this period. Further, the nature and effect of the experience on them and the public services they provide, in both the long- and short-term, will be considered.

There is an argument that if we wish to understand the 'forgotten years' of 1914–1918, we should not look back on them with a view that is inevitably obscured by subsequent experiences. Any, even tentative, understanding of the experience of war, whether on the home or battle fronts, has to begin with an open mind, some humility, and the personal accounts of those who endured, who fought and died (Munson 1984). This advice could not be followed absolutely, however acknowledgement in full is given to its wisdom.

This book is based upon an MPhil. thesis, successfully submitted at Leicester University in 1985. It grew out of an interest in the First World War, brought about long ago by a combination of listening to the stories my great aunts and uncles told of such times, and the reading of Vera Brittain's *Testament of Youth* (1933). When I began studying the history of museums, I was drawn to this period. I wanted to know whether museums were used effectively during this time, and if they made a valid contribution to the war effort. I also wanted to find out if the subsequent development of museum provision and practice was affected or influenced by the experience of serving a society at war.

The study of museum history is very much in its infancy. Much that has been written has sought, not necessarily consciously, to lay before the reader a story of progressive and healthy development. As the authors of such works have been museum curators, perhaps this is not surprising. I admit to an enthusiasm for museums and hold deep convictions on their potential. This has, no doubt, influenced the way I have approached this subject. However, I hope that the work, through attention to primary sources, will expose fairly the complexities, problems, achievements and even absurdities of museum provision within the time-span 1890–1930.

All historians are conscious of the limitations of the sources they use and the history of museums offers no exceptions in this regard. The sources used here are very varied and need a brief comment. The records of provincial museums are particularly problematic. Their survival is, to say the least, haphazard. Ironically, those institutions that are concerned with 'heritage' are not always even conscious of their own. Acquisitions registers, letter books, and bundles of correspondence are too frequently purely chance survivals. Minutes of council meetings, a principal source for these years, can be detailed and enlightening where they can be found. But they can also be frustratingly vague or sketchy, referring to reports no one bothered to keep. Annual reports are important and useful, where they exist. Overall, I became aware of how much of the record had been lost.

The records of the national museums and art galleries appear better kept and are more accessible. As their annual reports are published as Parliamentary Papers, they are readily available on microcard for research. Most of the national museums have a designated officer who can advise on their institution's archives. Working papers and other documentary sources can be consulted. Many museums – national and municipal – postponed the publication of their annual reports until after the war, due to paper shortages. These retrospective accounts bear all the hallmarks of being prepared in peacetime: with hindsight and an eye on the future. Newspaper cuttings, official reports and references in contemporary literature have been most helpful, although care has had to be exercised in their use. There is no such thing as a neutral source.

Of prime importance to this research have been the records of the curators themselves. These give insight into how they perceived their tasks in wartime and how they accounted for their experiences. The most obvious publication in this regard is the *Museums Journal*. Produced every month, without fail, under the astute editorship of W.R. Butterfield (Curator of Hastings Museum), the journal published verbatim accounts of important meetings and conferences; articles written by curators and academics; news of current museum developments; and continuous discussion of what museums were doing, or should be doing, during the war period. Even so, the opinions aired were, quite clearly, those of a small, prominent group. There can be no proof that their opinions and experiences were typical. Besides the *Museums Journal*, there were a number of pamphlets and papers published independently by curators and others with an interest in museums, who wished to air their views either to a wider audience or with a degree of detachment from the Museums Association.

Secondary sources on museum history are few and deal only slightly with the war experience (such as Lewis 1984). The exception to this is the extremely useful account of the official art collections amassed during the war, given in Meirion and Susie Harries' book *The War Artists* (1983). Until very recently museum histories, whether about a broad sweep of museums or about individual institutions, neglected not only the more difficult primary sources but also the social and political contexts in which museums were positioned. Arguably, this neglect robbed the histories of the layers of meaning one needs to understand museum development. This is already undergoing some change, however. Refreshing new views and more rigorous styles of enquiry are emerging (for example, Bell 1991; Condell 1985; Moore 1991; Skinner 1986).

The referencing style adopted warrants explanation. It is a requirement of the Leicester University Press that the Harvard (author/date) system be used by all authors. All references to published sources are given in this way, with full references in the Bibliography. References to material published in the

Museums Journal where the author is not recorded, are cited in the text through the journal name, volume number and page references. This will be sufficient for any reader wishing to locate the material and a fuller reference will therefore not be given in the bibliography. Such material is in the form of either brief notes or verbatim accounts of meetings. This approach has been adopted to avoid an extremely lengthy and tedious list of the works by that prolific writer, Anon!

Although the pedigree and flexibility of the Harvard system is well known, it is unsuited to the referencing of unpublished material and parliamentary papers. In Britain, historians rarely use it. The British Standard Recommendations for the citation of unpublished documents (BS 6371: 1983) recommends instead the use of running notes and warns that the Harvard system is 'the least satisfactory'. The documents used in the research for this book come from many diverse sources; many are without the benefit of unique call numbers. The referencing of such material presents serious difficulties. Therefore, the Harvard system has had to be abandoned for all primary source references, and the more acceptable running numbers system used in its stead, with full citations in the chapter notes. Similarly, all references to Parliamentary Papers are given in the chapter notes, to avoid the use of complex command and volume numbers in the text. I accept that some may see this as unconventional, but hope that the results will be a smoother text with increased ease of access for readers wishing to pursue any of the references used.

The museum world has changed considerably since the years of the war. In finalizing the text, one of the most startling and obvious differences between then and now is in respect of the Natural History Museum. This was once an integral part of the British Museum, whose founding collections, those of Sir Hans Sloane, were predominantly natural specimens. The Natural History Museum, in organisation, spirit and provision, is now a world away from the British Museum and the old British Museum (Natural History). I have used the titles the museums had within the period under discussion.

Finally, I appreciate that the geographic coverage of museums in this book is somewhat uneven. I have tried to balance this out with the use of published sources, but a bias inevitably remains. There is certainly not enough material on Scotland in this book. The history of Scottish museums in this period deserves a volume in its own right.

During the course of research, the production of the thesis and now the production of this book, I received help, encouragement and hospitality from a number of people. I am particularly grateful to my colleagues at the Department of Museum Studies, especially its Director Professor Susan Pearce. Their support and encouragement have been invaluable, as have their sense of humour and commitment to museum studies. The original work was supervised by G.D. Lewis, formerly Director of the Department of Museum Studies. Very wise advice and much encouragement were given at the outset by Professor G.H. Martin, formerly Keeper of the Public Records and my history tutor during my undergraduate years at Leicester University. Dianne Condell at the Imperial War Museum was especially helpful over the developments at the Imperial War Museum, which was a joint area of interest for us, although our work covered the ground in rather different ways. Special thanks are due to Philip Reed, Deputy Keeper, Department of Documents, Imperial War Museum, for being as always a great help, kind host and the best of friends.

Gilbert Bell kindly gave me permission to use his research on museums founded as local war memorials after 1918. This comes from the fourth chapter of his unpublished masters degree dissertation 'Museums as memorials' (University of Leicester 1991). His research has led him to uncover the many ways in which museums over the last two centuries have been used as memorials, to the rich, the learned and the dead. Peter Thwaites gave me permission to use his research on the Royal Signals Museum. I have drawn on the first chapter of his unpublished masters degree dissertation 'From Corps collection to public museum: a history of the Royal Corps of Signals Museum of Army Communication 1920–1992' (University of Leicester). I am very glad to acknowledge the help given by Bryan Stitch on the history of Hull Museums. Tom Hodgson kindly provided me with the sources relating to the history of The Royal East Kent Regimental Museum.

Stephen Price and Dr Stuart Davies, formerly of Birmingham Museum and Art Gallery, now of the Priests House Museum, Wimborne and Kirklees Museum Service respectively, and Timothy Ambrose, Scottish Museums Council, not only made useful suggestions, but also helped track down archives no one else could locate. Janet Wallace and Christopher Date were particularly helpful in their advice about the British Museum's archives. Lyn Thomas, Ann Sarson and Jo Lyons saw through the worst of the typing, for which I am more than grateful. Timothy Ambrose and Elizabeth Frostick read and commented on an early draft. Their thoughts and comments on the work have been well judged and much appreciated. The final text and the faults therein, however, have to be seen as mine.

The Imperial War Museum, the British Museum, Norfolk County Museum Service, Hull City Museums and Art Galleries, Punch Publications, the Museums Association and the Museums Documentation Centre in Zagreb generously gave permission for their photographs to appear in this book.

The Coles and Kavanagh families supported the preparation of this work in ways too numerous to mention. Edmund helped as best he could, and Terry Cavanagh provided unfailing encouragement. With love, I thank them.

CHAPTER I

MUSEUMS AND PRE-WAR BRITAIN

IN 1920, Britain had 424 museums, just over half of which (215) had been founded or built between 1890 and 1914. One-hundred and fifty-eight of these museums were run by local councils (Teather 1983: 147). In 1913, Elijah Howarth,[1] Curator of Sheffield Museum, had been able to claim that 255 towns and villages outside the capital cities possessed museums.[2] His count included university and private society museums, as well as municipal ones. On the eve of war, therefore, most major towns and cities in Britain boasted a museum. A significant proportion of these had been established in the previous two decades. By anyone's standards, this was a substantial growth in museum provision, of a kind not to be seen again until the heady days of museum expansion in the late 1970s. The museum boom of the 1890s and 1900s laid the essential structure for museum provision in Britain. The provision of museums in the towns and cities of Britain was a measure of the extent to which Britain had, in 1914, become a primarily urban and industrial society, rich enough to support museums and willing to entertain the idea that such institutions would benefit the populace, 78 per cent of whom now lived in towns.

One hundred years before this, in 1814, there were very few public museums in existence. London could boast the British Museum which was founded in 1753 and was struggling with its premises – Montagu House in Bloomsbury – and the newly established Dulwich Art Gallery, but little else. Private and society collections were increasingly evident, but had not yet effectively met the emergent philosophy of public access and education. However, it would be wide of the mark to suggest that the nineteenth century was a period of smooth and triumphant progress for the development of the public museum. That they developed at all has to be ascribed to a combination of political expediency, social need, economic expectation and moral pressure. Occasionally, the additional vital ingredients were: civic pride; the availability of interesting but redundant collections; and, most crucially, industrialists and entrepreneurs with both money and a yen to have their names remembered.

National museums and galleries and their influence

In 1753, the British Government passed the British Museums Act and brought into public ownership the Sir Hans Sloane collection, principally natural history specimens, to be added to the Cottonian Library, which included the Lindisfarne Gospels, and the Harleian collection of manuscripts, which the nation already owned. The British Museum became the first corporate museum in the world (Wilson 1989:13). A house and land in Bloomsbury were bought to accommodate both the collections and the museum's curators and servants. By the turn of the century, the museum had substantially enlarged its collections, especially of Greek and Roman antiquities, through such important purchases as the Hamilton collection of Greek vases (1772). The future direction of the British Museum was being established, and its influence would be extensive. Its aim of building universal, encyclopaedic collections, with emphasis on the antiquities of Greece and Rome, fine art, ethnography and natural history, coupled with a commitment to allow free access to all interested visitors, set a pattern which later museums were to follow. In time, few museums anywhere in Britain were felt to be complete without some stuffed birds, at least one Egyptian mummy (or a piece thereof) and a good few cases of Roman remains.

In 1824, the Government yielded to pressure and purchased the Angerstein collection of paintings, so that the National Gallery could be founded. In 1838, the National Gallery was installed in the building, designed for it by William Wilkins, on the north side of what is now Trafalgar Square. The National Gallery provided the model for public art collections elsewhere, although none could emulate the quality and range of paintings its inspired curators drew together in the middle decades of the nineteenth century.

The success of the British Museum and National Gallery in the first half of the nineteenth century was clear to see. It must have surprised some, for neither institution had the wholehearted support of Parliament. Arguably, both were founded not for any high-flown motives of public good, but because the Government of the day had been largely manoeuvred into a position where it could do no other but allow the founding Acts to go through. But the meanness of spirit showed. The British Museum was founded not out of the public purse (there was much reluctance to do this), but out of a lottery (notorious in its day and since) which raised £95,194 8s 6d. Both the British Museum and the National Gallery endured decades of neglect, administrative confusion and under-funding until they reached the point in the public consciousness where no government could deny them what they needed, which in the first instance was proper housing. The history of these museums echoes through the histories of later museums, not least in this respect (Caygill 1981; and Minihan 1977).

Not only did the British Museum and the National Gallery help lay a blueprint for museum provision elsewhere, but they also provided a testing ground for the social benefits museums might bestow. Both the Select Committee on Arts and Manufactures, which met in 1835 and 1836, and the Select Committee on National Monuments and Works of Art, which met in 1841, gathered evidence on the popularity of museums and the behaviour of visitors. The concern that museums might be at risk from potential visitors, especially the new urban working classes, was central to these inquiries. One witness was asked for his observations of visitors to the National Gallery:

> ...you see a great number of mechanics there, sitting, wondering and marvelling over those fine works, and having no feeling but of pleasure and astonishment; they have no notion of destroying them.

The committee asked him to specify the class of people to which he referred. He answered 'men who are usually called "mob", but they cease to become mob when they get taste' (quoted in Minihan 1977: 89).

Through the Select Committee Reports, the Government was sufficiently convinced of the efficacy of museums to pass the Museums Act in 1845. This was the first Act which formally allowed local authorities to establish museums. Its principal significance was that it witnessed the willingness of the Government to put museums on the political agenda. Regrettably, they did not stay there for long. Only six museums were established as a result of it[3] and in 1850, many of the powers it established were modified or revoked in the Public Libraries and Museums Act 1850.

The time was not yet right for the provision of local museums. Local government was not sufficiently empowered to take on such a task. Furthermore, there were greater priorities and more urgent necessities, including the provision of adequate sanitation and housing for a rapidly growing and very unhealthy urban population. In many towns and cities, the voluntarily run antiquarian societies and philosophical institutions provided a focal point, engaging in the kinds of activities museums were later to promote: local study, lectures, scientific experiments, archaeological excavations, and the display and study of collections. These societies and institutions, as diverse as the Antiquarian Society of Newcastle-upon-Tyne (founded in 1813) and the Penzance Natural History and Antiquarian Society (1839) had prodigious energy and often access to private wealth. They played an important role in facilitating learning and debate amongst the middle classes and, in many instances, the rising artisan class.

Official interest in museums remained tempered. Doubts about the population's readiness for such cultural institutions were considerable. In the same year that the Museums Act was passed, 1845, the Government also passed the

Protection of Works of Art and Scientific and Literary Collections Act. This was passed in the wake of one of the British Museum's greatest treasures, the Portland Vase, embarrassingly on loan at the time, being reduced to 200 pieces by a young man wielding a conveniently placed 'inscribed stone of considerable weight'. The Act established a severe penalty for the destruction or damage of museum collections: six months imprisonment with hard labour. It signalled that the Government was not prepared to take any risks with museums or their property, the collections. The 'hungry forties' was a turbulent decade and on one further occasion at least, museum collections were protected at Government insistance. In 1848, the Government sent a group of Chelsea Pensioners to guard the British Museum during the Chartist protests.[4]

A number of themes had run through the arguments of those still prepared to support the cause of museums, and by the mid-century, these were well developed. Adequate provision for the arts, in which museums held a central place, was a credential of a civilized state: they were instruments and evidence of national honour and glory. Arts and museums would be an antidote to the brutalizing effects of mechanization, industrialization and urbanization. People could be led to a higher social order through them. Moreover, museums could help promote a partnership between art, science and design, which would in turn create better products for Britain to make and sell. Greater wealth would result. Further, the study of science, and science in relation to art, would provide a means of understanding the God-given order in life.

Such thoughts underpinned the development of the South Kensington museums. These were established in 1852 following the Great Exhibition, which had given final proof that the working classes were capable of being interested in and enjoying art and exhibitions without rioting. The profits from the exhibition, topped up with Government funds, had bought 86 acres of land at Brompton, later referred to as South Kensington because it sounded better. Four elegant streets were laid out – Exhibition Road, Cromwell Road, Queensgate and Kensington Gore – which were in time to bound an extraordinary complex of buildings and institutions devoted to the study of the arts and sciences. This land, in time, was part occupied by the Victoria and Albert Museum and the Science Museum, which grew out of the original South Kensington Museums; the British Museum (Natural History), moved from the parent museum to South Kensington in 1880; and the Museum of Practical Geology.

The South Kensington museums particularly stressed the central educational role of museums and organized their activities around this. Their development through the second half of the nineteenth century was based on the philosophy which Henry Cole, so instrumental in their establishment and development, made clear:

> a museum presents probably the only effectual means of educating the adult, who cannot be expected to go to school like the youth, and the necessity for teaching the grown man is quite as great as that of training the child. By proper arrangements, a Museum may be made in the highest degree instructional. If it be connected with lectures, and means are taken to point out its uses and applications, it becomes elevated from a mere unintelligible lounge for idlers into an impressive schoolroom for everyone. (Quoted in Minihan 1977: 112)

To these ends, the South Kensington museums provided free entry, set days aside for the museums to be used by students, and opened regularly in the evenings. Collections which could be sent to other venues were developed. Thus, those who might not be able to visit the museums could at least have a chance to see some of the collections.

It took the whole of the second half of the nineteenth century for the South Kensington Museums to evolve into the Victoria and Albert Museum and the Science Museum. Just as the natural history collections in the British Museum had been the poor cousin, until housed separately, the science collections at South Kensington were similarly marginalized until separate directorships, as late as 1893, at last allowed coherent development. Consistent with a growing lack of interest in the sciences, evident elsewhere but particularly in the teaching offered in schools, the Science Museum's collections were brought together in the early days more by luck than judgement. The taking over of the Board of Trade's Patents Museum, a white elephant in its time, was a godsend to its collections.

The emergence of local authority museums

By the 1870s, the political agenda had changed. In this, there had been little choice. The industrial boom that had brought about what Disraeli called 'a convulsion of prosperity' had peaked by the mid-nineteenth century and had ended by 1875. The years ahead were ones of increasing uncertainty. Failure to plan, invest and renew had exacerbated both the appalling social conditions under which the majority of the population lived, and the capacity of British industry to compete effectively in the world market. Private philanthropy and individual initiatives were not enough. Increased state involvement in national life was both inevitable and vital for survival. From the 1870s onward, Parliament passed legislation which established the welfare state, with all that implied for a just and open society. As one liberal politician said 'we are all socialists now', meaning that the middle classes could no longer simply ignore the situation, especially the poor, and leave every social problem to market forces (Ford 1992: 7).

Through this legislation, both the powers of local government and the role of education were strengthened considerably. During this period, the arts and museums were beneficiaries of several public health enactments extending the power of local government over recreation and entertainment. Cricket and football grounds, gymnasiums, music halls and public parks, were all encouraged under new legislation. Parliament also enabled local authorities to enlarge their jurisdiction over museums: towns and cities were empowered to establish museums. This led to the museum boom period of the 1890s and 1900s. The most important pieces of legislation during this period were the Museums and Gymnasiums Act 1891 and the Public Libraries Act 1892, which further enabled urban authorities to provide and maintain museums in England, Wales and Ireland, but excluded London until 1901.

However, it was not a simple matter of the provinces founding museums because they wanted them. A whole range of forces came into play, not least of which was the availability of collections. The learned societies that had worked so well in the first half of the nineteenth century had lost their momentum. Whereas it might have been possible to maintain interest and funding over one, possibly two, generations of enthusiastic local people, it was not possible to sustain many of the societies for more than this. By the 1860s, many were already in serious difficulties; others had gone under. The collections had to be safeguarded somehow. Some became the founding collections of new local authority museums. In 1887, a British Association Report noted that of the 211 museums outside London, one-half originated from local society collections, one-quarter from private collections. A number of societies managed to strike up a partnership arrangement with the local authority, which provided accommodation for both the collection and themselves and bore most of the costs.

The existence of legislation and collections on which a museum might be established, were not always significant in themselves for many municipal authorities. The vital ingredient often needed was the gift of funds or land for the building of a museum and art gallery. Philanthropic providers, including Andrew Carnegie, Passmore Edwards and Henry Tate, did much to ensure public museums and libraries had suitable homes and firmly established the notion that art and culture were not 'merely the ornament of a privileged élite' (Ford 1992:15). Whether the wealth to found museums came from one source or several, there was much meaning in the inscription of the memorial stone at Birmingham Museum and Art Gallery: 'By the gains of industry, we promote Art'.

The public museums built from the 1880s onwards by town and city councils, were sources of great pride, as the grandeur of their buildings suggests. Along with the new town halls, concert halls, and libraries, muse-

1. The Municipal Museum, Hull, c. 1907, typical of many provincial museums at this time
Source: Hull City Museums and Art Gallery

ums were statements of a new civic order. The chaos of the old days was being replaced by a new way of life and living, cleaner, healthier and more enlightened. The path would be a long one.

Further development of the national museums and galleries

By the turn of the century, the national museums were also moving on and again confidence was expressed through the creation of new buildings and new administrative arrangements. In 1896, the National Portrait Gallery moved into its own building and a year later the National Gallery of British Art, financed by funds from Sir Henry Tate and containing his collections, opened on Millbank. In 1900, the Wallace Collection was opened in a house provided as part of the bequest; and in May 1914, the Edward VII galleries were officially opened at the British Museum. The development of national museums was not confined to London. The Edinburgh Museum of Science and Art became the Royal Scottish Museum in 1904; and the foundation stone of the National Museum of Wales was laid in Cardiff in June 1912.

In 1898 the Science Museum entered the last phase of its struggle to be a national museum in its own right, when a select committee recommended that a new building should be erected for it behind the British Museum (Natural History), which did not want it there. A long controversy followed, only to be resolved in 1911. New buildings were begun for it and for the Geological Survey and the Museum of Practical Geology. Most construction work stopped because of the First World War and it took a long time for the building to be completed. Although the framework of the building was more or less complete in 1918, the walls were only temporarily clad. Much remained to be done and there was to be quite a long wait. The official opening of the Science Museum's Eastern Block took place in 1928.

In all this activity and growth, however, some rather fundamental questions remained not only unanswered, but unasked. How were museums to be operated to fulfil the goals that had long been set for them? It was one thing to have a high sense of idealism, yet another to achieve and prosper. The development of museums, once established, fell to an emergent group of museum workers: salaried (as opposed to honorary) curators.

The museums profession

The museums profession was just one of the many new self-styled professions which had emerged through the nineteenth century as a result of the specialization of management and the growth of both national and local government.[5] In 1889, they were sufficiently self-aware to establish a professional

2. Museum curators – a year away from war – at the annual meeting of the Museum Association, Hull 1913

Source: Museums Journal

body, the Museums Association. In time, this assumed the trappings expected of such a body: a hierarchy of honorary officers, committees and associates, an annual meeting and a range of publications. Analysis of the Museums Association's early papers makes clear what a diverse set of people these early curators were and how narrow were their attitudes towards the museums they controlled (Kavanagh 1991). These papers, especially the Museums Association's founding 'list' of interests, read more like those of a gentlemen's club, than an association of public servants seeking to enhance their professionalism and the quality of public service. The list contains no mention of the visitor, nor any reference to how the profession might be regulated in terms of entry qualification or training.

Those engaged in museum work had very different experiences of it. In 1894, James Paton of Glasgow Museum observed how the museums profession was divided into two great classes:

> the specialist who belongs to the great public and nationalist museums, and the provincial curator who must be everything and do everything in his own much-embracing institution. (Paton 1894: 97)

It is little wonder the profession had, and still has, a crisis of idenity! Curators in the national museums saw their task as paralleling the great universities and the work attracted experienced and often gifted academics. Curators in large provincial museums modelled themselves on the national museum staff. Here the work attracted well-meaning enthusiasts, some of whom were graduates; many were also librarians, attempting to run both a library and a museums service. Curators in small museums did the best they could with whatever they had to hand. In such museums, the positions were often unsalaried and were occupied by local people, in retirement or benefiting from unearned income, dedicated to the study of the collections.

The profession, therefore, came to establish itself as a broad church ranging from the national expert and the elevated town hall clerk to the amateur enthusiast. The absence of training and of an entry requirement had far-reaching consequences, which became more evident and detrimental to museums as the decades passed. It was one of the reasons why curatorial salaries remained low, often without the promise of a pension. It may well have also been the reason why, in these important years, it was difficult to recruit people of talent to non-national museums. Writing about curatorial staff in provincial museums in the late 1920s, Sir Henry Miers noted:

> The important factor in making a museum good or bad is the influence of the curator, depending upon his energy and his qualifications ... .
>
> In a great number of museums, curators are appointed in middle age, without any previous training and experience. This applies to nearly all those cases where librar-

ians have undertaken the duties of curator. Fortunately many of them have made up by enthusiasm much of what they lack in experience. (Miers 1928: 19–20)

The first generation of professional museum curators were still very much in place when war broke out in 1914. Many of them had both experienced and been part of the excitement of establishing new museum ventures in the 1880s and 1890s. Now in the 1900s, they were faced with the dilemma of how to move museums forward. The collections in so many museums were indeed glorious, instructional and sometimes controversial. The potential of the museums was embedded in their effective use.

Museum provision and services

The more enlightened curators became increasingly conscious of the educational potential of museums. The pervading attitude towards education at the time was that it was a means of creating dutiful social conformity in the young. Even secondary and higher education, reorganized under the Education Act 1902, had tasks that were distinctly social (Briggs 1983: 249). Museums were seen as being able to provide social improvement through giving visitors the opportunity to see and reflect upon treasures of the highest order.

Elijah Howarth made plain his own enthusiasm when he said that for museums education 'in its widest significance' had become 'the cult of the day' (Howarth 1913: 42). This enthusiasm was not confined to municipal museums. A successful campaign, organized by Lord Sudeley, had put pressure on the national museums to provide specialist guides to explain the collections. The British Museum in 1911, the British Museum (Natural History) in 1912 and the Victoria and Albert Museum in 1913 had each for the first time appointed demonstrators to work in the galleries interpreting the collections to the public (Stearn 1981: 101; *Museums Journal* 14: 185–6). Significantly, Henry Leonard, the guide at the BMNH, was a graduate with teaching experience.

Outside London, the educational viability of the museum was being addressed in a variety of interesting, though relatively isolated initiatives. Museums, including Liverpool, Salford, Sheffield and the Ancoats Museum in Manchester had developed a variety of provision for schools use of collections (Harrison 1985; Hooper-Greenhill 1991). Some of the work was highly imaginative. For example, Sunderland Museum was engaged in education work with blind children in 1912. Not all curators, however, were equally keen on the development of educational activities in their museums. Frank Leney, curator of the Castle Museum, Norwich, in 1909 described how 'it seemed at one time as if a lecturer on 'Nature Study' would be added to the museum staff ... Happily for the Museum, I think, it was found that funds would not permit the appointment' (quoted in Lewis 1989: 21).

In spite of the reservations of some curators, overall, the situation in 1914 showed promise. A survey of 134 museums undertaken by the British Association revealed that instruction was given by teachers alone in 28 museums, by teachers with some assistance from curators in 24 museums and in 16 museums instruction was given by museum staff only. Most museums received sketching parties or individual students (British Association 1920: 269–70). These figures do not reveal the extent, quality or relevance of the work undertaken, nor do they throw any light on what the hundreds of other museums were doing in this regard. All that can be said is that a number of museums were experimenting with educational work and most intended this to contribute to the 'improvement' – moral and social – of the child.

Not only was the functional base of museums developing (however sporadically), but also the disciplines represented. A number of prominent museums, for example museums devoted to anthropology or natural history such as the Pitt-Rivers Museum in Oxford (Van Keuren 1984) and the British Museum (Natural History) in South Kensington (Stearn 1981), still held a strong position within their academic fields. These museums were seen as companion establishments to universities, both in terms of the scholarship and the facilities for study they could offer. The degree to which this position was still secure by 1914 is open to question. On the eve of war, a gradual distancing of academic trends from certain museum practices and directions had begun, perhaps within some disciplines more than others.

In 1914, there were museums addressing the subjects of anthropology, archaeology, natural sciences and the broad sweep of art. Technology had established a foothold, but as a means of explaining technical advances and design development, rather than as a means of recording work or work practices. There were no museums that considered popular or cultural history in ways which were already well established in the folk museums of Sweden, Norway and Denmark (Rasmussen 1966; Higgs 1963). Nor were there regimental museums or war museums, as we have now come to understand them. There were, however, three important armoury collections, the Royal Artillery Collections at the Rotunda Museum, Woolwich, the Royal United Services Institution collection at the Banqueting House, Whitehall, and the Armouries at the Tower of London (Westrate 1961).

There is little evidence that, outside the regiments, war or military action were commemorated at a local level through a museum or public collection. An exception was a small collection of mementoes of the Crimean War and the Indian Mutiny, held in rooms in Bristol. Here, 'benevolent gentlemen' had made provision for Crimean War and Indian Mutiny veterans: principally, a little extra pension, a room to meet in, free tobacco and a fire. The men brought to the room things 'they had got at Balaclava, Sebastopol, and elsewhere', which in time transformed it into a museum of 'relics'. It was still very much in use in 1917 (Bolton 1917: 94).

The development of militaristic and patriotic mentality from the turn of the century and the social tension of the pre-war years have been much discussed (for example Marwick 1965; Taylor 1969; Bond 1983). The papers in the *Museums Journal* shed a curious light on the disposition of the profession in this context. The case for a national history museum, that is a British Folk Museum, was made frequently in its pages, confirming a distinctly nationalistic (although essentially English) line evident elsewhere. Yet the anti-German feelings which grew in intensity in the years before the war are not evident in professional comment until the war began, after which F.A. Bather of the BMNH, struck a particularly jingoistic line. In the pre-war years, for example, the *Museums Journal* printed reviews derived from the German professional journal, *Museumskunde*. Moreover, Professor Dr Frederich Rathgen, Chemist to the Royal Museums, Berlin, was invited to speak at the annual conference in 1913. His standing as the leading expert in the evolving field of scientific conservation was well recognized in Britain by this time. His work had been translated into English in 1905, and was the basis of scientific conservation in Britain for many years (Oddy 1992). His conference paper was published subsequently in the November 1913 edition of the *Museums Journal*: his professional standing meaning much more to curators than his nationality. Such detachment continued in the editorial style of the *Museums Journal* in the first two years of the war. Deaths of German and Austrian colleagues were noted.

Other than letters to the press and comments made in meetings by those with vested interests such as local government councillors, there is no direct evidence on which to draw to gain some idea of how museums were regarded by the public. No visitor surveys exist to indicate who visited museums in the years before the war and what their occupations and social backgrounds might have been. Further, museums did not conduct any form of evaluation to find out how well their exhibitions and services worked. On these fundamental areas of interest, other than in the bald statistics of monthly and yearly visitor figures, there is silence. What is clear is that many thousands of people in the capital and in the provinces visited museums (see Chapter 7).

The national museums in particular were organized to promote and facilitate public access. Evening opening to 8 or 9 pm was commonplace. Students were encouraged with free entry on study days and all visitors could enjoy free entry at weekends. It can only be suggested that museums appealed to an interested public and that this was drawn from a cross-section of society, but no categorical proof can be provided. In a period when the middle class, now taken to be the typical museum audience, made up only

25 per cent of the population of 44 million, it seems unreasonable to assume they were the only audience. From the 1830s social reformers had worked assiduously for the provision of museums, particularly for the benefit of the skilled worker, the artisan. In a country still committed to self-improvement and all-embracing social reform, the spirit of the times would suggest that some, if not a significant proportion, of the museums were enjoyed by an audience drawn from more than one social group. Protests over the closure of museums in 1916 (see Chapter 3) appear to carry at least the tenor of this argument.

On the eve of war, then, there was a pattern of museum provision, both at national and municipal levels, which had seen at least one generation of curators. The museum as a credential of civic status, scholarship or civilized nationhood still appeared to hold good, if investment in museum developments can be taken as an indicator, although museums were beginning to slip from the agenda of liberal politics. Museum development had come to depend upon the skills and attitudes of the museum curator and there were individual, sometimes isolated, initiatives to find a role for museums, especially within the field of education. However, with the outbreak of war the very worth and purpose of museums were tested and met a response as diverse as the museums themselves.

CHAPTER 2

MUSEUMS AND COLLECTIONS AT RISK

THE declaration of war in 1914 was greeted in a spirit of euphoria, even of ecstasy. In that hot summer month, there was a surge of patriotism and a tremendously heightened sense of national unity (Bond 1983: 100). Then, as the weeks passed, those on the home front ineligible for enlistment settled down to an existence summed up in the contemporary catch-phrase 'business as usual', in the full expectation that war would be over by Christmas (Marwick 1965: 39–44).

Museums, suffragettes and women visitors

In August 1914, the fabric and contents of museums were seen to be more at risk from militant suffragettes than from the Germans. The activist tactics of the Women's Social and Political Union had begun in 1910 and were an expression of outrage at the stalemate reached over the suffrage issue (Marwick 1977: 25). The suffragettes engaged in extremist activities which destroyed property and disrupted the peace. Besides chaining themselves to railings and breaking windows, the suffragettes damaged or burnt down railway stations, churches and, in Scotland, three castles. A small bomb damaged the Coronation Chair in Westminster Abbey. In addition, 'art galleries were much favoured' (Fulford 1957: 294). As a result, many galleries and museums in London and the provinces closed or denied women access to them.

The British Museum (Natural History), closed for a short time in 1912, 'because of the activities and threats of the suffragists'. When it opened again, muffs, parcels and umbrellas, 'their usual weapons' had to be left with cloakroom attendants (Stearn 1981: 105). The National Gallery was a prime target. On 10 March 1914, serious damage was caused to Velazquez' *Rokeby Venus*. The Gallery was closed for a fortnight. On 22 May, five pictures by Gentile and Giovanni Bellini were damaged: this time the National Gallery closed for three months.[1] Other art galleries had similar experiences. Sargent's portrait *Henry James* and Herkomer's portrait the *4th Duke of Wellington* were both slashed within days of each other at Burlington House.

Butchers' cleavers were the favoured weapon. One was used by a suffragette to damage the portrait of Thomas Carlisle by Sir J.E. Millais at the National Portrait Gallery. The NPG closed for a fortnight after the attack and, when reopened, access to the galleries was restricted.[2] A similar weapon was used by Bertha Ryland to damage a painting by George Romney, *Master Thornhill,* at Birmingham Museum and Art Gallery on 9 June 1914. Her handbag had been carefully examined at the turnstile, but the chopper, concealed under her coat, was not detected. As a result of the attack, Birmingham Art Gallery and Aston Hall were both closed. Further, on 20 July, the Museum and Art Gallery Committee postponed a loan of Rossetti drawings because of 'suffragette outrages in London'.

Suffragette activity and the threats it posed to the national museums in London caused such concern that in April 1913 the President of the Board of Education hurriedly called together a conference of national museum directors at which the Commissioner of the Metropolitan Police was present. The directors were against the closure of the museums and, on the advice of the Commissioner, it was decided that the museums' regular warding staff should be supplemented by plain-clothes policemen[3]

In March 1914, the Director of the British Museum asked for Treasury sanction to continue this arrangement and also asked the Commissioner to supply officers familiar with the appearance of prominent suffragettes. Women who had been convicted for participation in 'suffragist outrages' were to be excluded from the museum. However, these arrangements were not sufficient. On 9 April 1914, a woman who later gave the alias of 'Mary Stewart' broke a number of panes of glass in the Asiatic Saloon by means of a chopper which she carried concealed about her person. The cost of the damage amounted to £22, plus an additional £6 for three Chinese porcelain cups damaged by falling glass. Her behaviour was described as 'contumacious' by the magistrate presiding at the Bow Street Police Court and she was committed for trial.[4] Following a further incident in June, when two suffragettes broke glass in the Egyptian Room, women were required to obtain 'vouchers of good behaviour from responsible persons' before being allowed into the galleries[5]

The advent of war precipitated a change in attitude on behalf of both the militant suffragettes and the authorities. Many suffragettes expressed doubts about the war at the outset. Some remained pacifist throughout. But the perceptible change in attitude in the majority was such that an amnesty was granted to suffragette prisoners and similar offenders (Marwick 1965: 87). In September 1914, the *Museums Journal* recorded that the London Museum was reopened on 17 August, the National Gallery and the Tate on 20 August. Restrictions on the admission of women to the British Museum also lapsed on 20 August and from the end of September plain-clothes policemen ceased patrolling the galleries, although regular inspection of handbags continued for some time. 'Thus' commented the editor tartly 'great events from trifling causes spring' (*Museums Journal* 14: 120).

Understanding the risks

The Government was swift to introduce emergency legislation, yet slow to use it. The most important measures enacted were through the Defence of the Realm Acts. The first Defence of the Realm Act (DORA) came into force on 18 August 1914. Additions were made in a second DORA on 28 August and amendments and revisions in the Defence of the Realm Consolidation Act on 27 November. Further modifications were made in 1915 and 1916. Through the Defence of the Realm Acts, the Government gave itself almost unlimited powers and traditional freedom was signed away at the stroke of a pen (Williams 1972: 23). In spite of these powerful legal rights behind the Government, no scheme emerged in 1914 to place the country on a war footing. While thousands of men enlisted in 'Kitchener's Army', the social and economic organization of the country experienced a conspicuous continuation of pre-war trends.

A month after war was declared, the Museums Association held its annual conference in Swansea. Delegates were prepared to discuss the risks to collections as a result of the war, and the insurance available to cover such risks. Clearly, the effects of a total war on museums had not even been imagined by curators at this time. Their discussions were based on a peacetime understanding of the word 'risk' with emphasis on prevention of risk rather than compensation. E. Rimbault Dibdin,[6] President of the Museums Association, later acknowledged that it was with this attitude that museums went into the war:

> I don't suppose it ever entered into our heads before to consider what precautions were necessary against any dangers to the contents of museums, art galleries and libraries other than those offered by the forces of nature, and debased human nature – accidental fire, theft, public riots, and those more insidious and deadly agents of Time's effacing finger: dust, damp, and destructive microscopic organisms. (Dibdin 1915: 33–4)

In the national museums, although directors such as Kenyon were prepared to entertain the notion that there might be some new risks to collections, this did not extend to all staff. In response to a memo from Kenyon, Sir Hercules Read, Keeper of the Department of Mediaeval Antiquities and Ethnography at the British Museum, replied on 12 November that the only step he had taken to safeguard precious objects in his Department was to 'remove to temporary store in my studies practically the whole of the Waddesdon Bequest and the Royal Gold Cup'.[7]

3. E. Rimbault Dibden, President of the Museums Association1915–18,
and director of the Walker Art Gallery, Liverpool, until 1918.
Source: Museums Journal

Black-out regulations and civil defence were, in the early years of the war,
the responsibility of the local military authorities. There was no early warning system, nor were there any co-ordinated procedures for advising the populace. On 11 September 1914, the lights of London were lowered for the first
time. Museums with roof-lit galleries, such as the Science Museum, had to
close them at dusk, thus ending the evening opening of museums. But, the
standard of preparedness for air attack varied considerably.

With the reckless prediction that 'there is little likelihood that more of our
coast towns will suffer bombardment', the *Museums Journal* in April 1915,
advised museums of the correct protective sign that should be employed to
denote a museum building, for the information of the enemy. The sign was
a 'large stiff rectangular panel divided diagonally into two pointed triangular
portions, the upper black and the lower portion white'. This should be placed
prominently on the exterior of the building. The sign had been approved at
the Hague Conference of 1907. The Appendix to the Conference stated that,
among others, buildings devoted to art, science and literature, and historic
monuments, would be spared as far as possible in bombardments, 'provided

that they are not being used at the time for military purposes'. Clearly, the ramifications of aerial bombardment, its random, destructive chaos and essential lack of precision, had not been considered when this advice was drawn up.

In September 1915, the *Museums Journal* reported an announcement made at 'a special court of the London Hospital'. Information had been received from the War Office to the effect that agreement had been reached between the British and German governments for the protection of 'specific buildings, including museums'. The need to mark museums with the protective sign was reiterated. The basis of this report is somewhat vague and its contents seem quite extraordinary. If there had been such an agreement, official communication of it surely would have been made to museum authorities, and at least a hint of it would exist in the *Museums Journal* and in museum authority archives, but this is not the case. Instead, the information appears to have been relayed to the profession at least third-hand. Although it reinforced the case for using the protective sign, scepticism rightly remained, at least among some museum staff.

Air attacks, particularly using incendiary devices, escalated in the summer of 1915. Criticism of the 'protective' sign was voiced in the pages of the *Museums Journal*. In November 1915, 'A Provincial Curator' who 'had seen more results of air raids than most curators' wrote:

> having regard to the great reverence the Germans have already shown for 'specified buildings' including museums, surely the one thing we should *not* do in this country would be specifically to mark the museums with a so-called 'protective sign' as such a 'protective sign' would certainly be looked upon as a target for the air raiders (*Museums Journal* 15: 184).

In his postscript, the 'Provincial Curator' cited the German destruction of Malines, Antwerp and Lierre, as evidence of the level of respect given by the enemy to monuments and art treasures. The Editor's reply defended the use of the sign on the grounds that it was the necessary and obvious step a curator should take to protect both museums and collections. He suggested that if the sign were not displayed curators could be indicted for negligence. The Editor concluded: 'whether a museum be marked or left unmarked, it is important that the curator safeguard himself: and the obvious thing to do is for him to consult his committee, and to leave the decision and the responsibility with that body'. The Editor's reply was interpreted by the 'Provincial Curator' as a suggestion that he was neglecting necessary precautions. In a further letter, he not only defended his position and the decision taken by his committee, 'prominent citizens, broad-minded business men' not to use the sign, but also enquired whether the sign was in use at the Editor's museum, Hastings. No reply was published.

Practical precautions

A serious air raid in London on 18 June 1915 prompted the police to make a list of suggestions on appropriate behaviour in an attack. Precautions taken by museums in the capital and elsewhere intensified. At the British Museum (Natural History) buckets of sand were placed in 'convenient positions' to extinguish 'any conflagration which might be caused by an enemy bomb'. A layer of gravel and sand was spread over the roof of the building used for storing the spirit collection. The windows of rooms containing specimens of special value were sand-bagged. Members of staff were issued with instructions defining action to be taken in the event of an air raid, including the treatment of the general public. Ambulances, first-aid equipment and fire appliances were held in readiness.[8]

In 1915, a Government white paper was published on air-raid insurance. A scheme came into operation with insurance companies acting as agents for the Government.[9] A survey published in 1916 revealed that, in general, air-raid insurance had been taken up by museums and the collections were kept on exhibition rather than removed to safety. For example, Leicester Museum took out air-raid insurance and in 1915 paid a premium of £57, a not in-considerable sum. Consideration of all risks insurance was deferred.[10] However, Sheffield Public Museums Sub-Committee decided not to take out insurance cover, even though they must have realized that the city with its munitions industries could be a prime target.[11]

Some curators remained unconvinced and sceptical of the real risks of war. W. B. Barton of the Preston Museum, considered that:

> ... the pureness of air, the subjection to the right amount of light, the freedom from damp, the regulated temperature, and the accessibility to inspection, followed by opportunities of cleaning and of giving other necessary attention, might all be more or less lost by removing pictures to places inaccessible to bombs which after all may never arrive. The question may be asked, is it advisable to avoid a bad but remote risk, by incurring other risks, which might be quite bad enough to deprive the pictures, in a greater or lesser degree of the pre-eminent qualities for which they are prized? (Quoted in Dibdin 1916: 34)

This attitude did change however. As the war intensified, more rigorous precautions became essential.

In preparing places of safety for collections in event of air attack, the type of devastation to be expected from bombing was taken more seriously into consideration. In the early part of the war, it was anticipated that bombs would explode before they penetrated solid floors. Thus lower galleries and basements were considered safe. By August 1916, the President of the Museums Association cautioned that:

... all the wise devices of sandbins in the galleries and the removal of exhibits to cellars are utterly futile. The high explosive and incendiary shells dropped from Zeppelins are much too efficient to be evaded: the former are just as likely to explode in the basement as on the roof, and in the case of fire there is more hope of saving pictures hung on the walls than those packed away in the cellar. (Dibdin 1915: 35)

The fears of air attack were compounded by fears of submarine attacks, 'the activities of German agents tolerated in our midst, and all the furtive methods of warfare, so suitable to Teutonic genius'. The very exchange of ideas and experiences was warned against, although it was conceded that curators could 'help each other in more private fashion'. Dibdin recounted how one curator, having made provision for the security of the museum collections, informed his committee that plans had been made. The curator refused to give details, even to the chairman:

'I should certainly not tell you', he said, 'for you don't know how to tell a lie if you wanted to, and if the Crown Prince or some other German connoisseur came treasure-seeking in our city, you are naturally the first person to whom torture would be applied in order to elicit information as to the hiding-place of our best possessions, of which he would, no doubt, bring a complete list with him. (Dibdin 1915: 35)

In spite of the security and the secrecy that at the time surrounded the movement of collections, details of precautions taken by museums have emerged. In the early stages of the war, Birmingham Museum and Art Gallery kept a significant proportion of its principal paintings on exhibition. However, in the event of an air raid, paintings which should be rescued before others, were indicated by a red disc. In the later stages of the war, parts of the museum were appropriated for other purposes. The National Service Medical Board took over the space occupied by the Industrial and Decorative Art Department. This necessitated the removal of cases and objects. In June 1918, the Keeper, Sir Whitworth Wallis,[12] reported that large proportions of these had been placed in the picture galleries. Two privately owned Oriental collections and other collections were stored in the balconies of the Central Hall. The keeper's report recorded that 'the removal and storage of these thousands of objects is a very serious matter representing the contents of 75 glass cases including glass, porcelain, ivories etc.' The movement of the collections was seen as 'the only solution to a very difficult problem'. [13]

Hull Museum, like Birmingham, found that movement of collections was necessary when buildings were required for alternative uses. In November 1918, Tom Sheppard, Curator of Hull Museum published, with his known wry humour, 'Notes on packing and removing a Museum of Geology and Antiquities in war time' (Sheppard 1918). His experience involved the removal of a private collection bequeathed by Colonel Clarke from its original home at Driffield to a large house in the city rented by the Museum Committee. The move was necessitated by 'an enormous influx of American visitors' requiring accommodation. Sheppard explained that 12 hours' notice was given of their need for the building. He also described the necessities of documentation; problems of moving large, weighty or fragile objects; choices of packaging materials and means of freighting; and the final dismantling of cases and plinths. He must have been giving details of an experience shared by other museum curators at this time.

Removal of the major collections to places of safety

The care of collections at the national museums received little publicity. The Science Museum simply recorded that measures were taken to protect collections.[14] This involved consultations with the Admiralty and the Home Office. The use of Science Museum premises by Government Departments meant that collections not moved out were brought together in whatever space was available. Congestion of collections in the available galleries was mentioned several times in subsequent reports.[15] Similarly, the Victoria and Albert Museum gave little information on precautions taken. In the museum's report for 1917, it was simply noted that with the increased possibility of air attacks by hostile aircraft, further measures were taken for the protection of objects in the museum. A very large number of objects were withdrawn from exhibition and stored in places of safety.[16]

Much more detail is available on the precautions taken at the British Museum (Natural History)[17] and the British Museum (Kenyon 1934). At the BMNH, the most extensive removal was that of the majority of type specimens of mammals, together with a large number of the more valuable small mammals from the remainder of the study collection, to Exeter where accommodation was provided by the Royal Albert Memorial Museum. This collection was accompanied by the museum's mammal curator, M.R. Oldfield Thomas FRS, and an articulator. A number of the most valuable specimens of meteoric stones and many type specimens of plants were removed to the museum at Tring, where Lord Rothschild 'very kindly' found room for them. Also moved to Tring were the Sloane and other ancient Herbaria, most of the collections of original botanical drawings, and manuscripts and certain books from the Botanical Library. The most valuable mineral and geological specimens were stored in sand-bagged rooms in the basement. Many of the office records including the Minute Books, most of the zoological registers and a number of valuable books from the Zoological Library were also placed in what were recorded as the safest portions of the basement. Study collections were moved to what were considered safer parts of the building. In addition, more detailed instructions were issued on necessary action in the event of an air raid.

The Director of the British Museum, Sir Frederic Kenyon,[18] in a lecture given at the University of Glasgow in 1934, described how the collections of the British Museum were cared for during the war period (Kenyon 1934). He compared the experience of staff at the British Museum with that of officers at the Louvre, who had to remove their chief treasures with only around 24 hours' notice, 'when the Germans were nearly at the gates of Paris'. Between August and October 1914, the British Museum took several important measures to safeguard collections. Objects of special value from the upper galleries were removed to the supposed safety of the ground floor and basement. The closing of a temporary exhibition in the new wing (opened only three months before the war began) gave space for the Waddesdon Collection and parts of the china, glass and mediaeval collections. Valuable prints and drawings from the top floor went to the sub-ground floor and some of the Egyptian papyri and Assyrian cylinders and tablets were stored in cases in the basement. A small room on the south-west back staircase was prepared for important small objects, in particular 'the choicest Greek and Roman vases'. Strong-room provision was increased and safes procured for the most precious printed books and manuscripts. The advice of the London Fire Brigade was sought. Lights in and about the museum were reduced and screened. Improvements were made both to the high-pressure water supply and electric lighting. Staff and firemen were retained on night duty at the museum.

The British Museum extended its plans for protecting collections when it was recognized that the war was going to be much longer in duration than initially envisaged and that a lengthy conflict would have added risks for collections. The Parthenon Marbles, some of the Assyrian bas-reliefs and the principal sculptures in the collections were seen to be particularly at risk. The Director of the British Museum received unsolicited and singularly inappropriate advice on the protection of the collections and the museum as a whole; for example, it was suggested that the Elgin Room should be entirely filled with sand, the weight of which would have caused the collapse of the whole building! A suggestion was also made that the roof should be covered with sand-bags – impractical as many of the roofs were glass. Similarly, a proposal that wire netting should cover the entire building was rejected. Instead, sculptures which could not be moved were sandbagged where they stood or packed around with slag-wool. Objects that could be moved were placed in strong rooms in the basement.

With the closure of the British Museum in March 1916, following the Retrenchment Committee's recommendations (see Chapter 3), there was no reason why better provision for collection security should not be made. The most valuable contents could be removed from the museum premises altogether. The apparent incongruity that the Government could close the national museum without a coherent plan for the subsequent care of collections was pointed out by Sir Sydney Colvin in his presentation to the Prime Minister, as part of a deputation appealing against closure. He said 'the proposed economy has the double drawback of making the collections for the present useless and at the same time of doing nothing efficient, nothing serious, for further protection' (*Museums Journal* 15: 321). In the absence of any centralized plan, museums made what provisions they could.

In December 1917, with the advance warning of heavier and considerably more destructive air raids, provision was made for the removal of the greater proportion of all collections from the British Museum. New buildings of the Library of Wales, Aberystwyth had been offered to the British Museum in June 1917. The British Museum responded and the transfer of collections took place in February 1918. A special train of six coaches was provided by the London and Northern Western Railway. The first consignment consisted of 21 cases of printed books and manuscripts, 19 cases of office records and 580 parcels of prints and drawings. A similar consignment was sent on 1 March, and a third and smaller one on 15 May. The Keeper of Prints and Drawings, Mr Campbell Dodgson, went to Aberystwyth to take charge.

Objects that could not be moved from the British Museum were protected by whatever means seemed most suitable. Statues were removed from pedestals, laid on the floor and covered by sandbags; glass and porcelain were packed with protective materials in cases.

The best of the removable antiquities and coins were lodged in a most remarkable refuge, a new section of underground railway. This was a line coinciding with Holborn and Oxford Street, which had originally been intended to be used by the Post Office's parcel service. Forty to seventy feet below the surface, it was certainly safe from air attack, but there was great risk from damp and the problems of packing and transportation had to be considered. It was prepared to receive the collections of the British Museum by the installation of floors, a lift, ventilation apparatus, electric radiators, hygrometers and thermometers. The delay in their provision allowed time for the books and manuscripts to be despatched to Aberystwyth.

The underground line provided the museum with considerable storage space. Kenyon described it as 'two parallel tubes, about 170 ft in length with a diameter of 25 ft, and smaller tubes projecting from each of the larger tubes, giving in all four lengths of about 225 ft with a diameter of 14 ft'. Much of the work of packing was done by 'a voluntary corps of ladies'. The antiquities collections were moved to the underground in the fortnight beginning 2 April 1917. Kenyon's list gives some idea of the enormity of the task:

The Department of Egyptian and Assyrian Antiquities sent 333 cases, including the Rosetta Stone, the head of Amenemhat III and other sculptures, all the limestone stelae that could be moved, the entire collections of Babylonian and Assyrian tablets (about 118,000 in number), the bronze gates of Shalmaneser, the statue of Ashurnasirpal and many of the bas-reliefs of this king. The Greek and Roman antiquities contributed 422 cases, including the slabs of the Parthenon frieze, about 95 per cent of the objects in gold, silver, ivory and porcelain, and of the gems, about 75 per cent of the bronzes and bases of the best period, including the Portland Vase, and about 50 per cent of the other vases, the terracottas, and the contents of the room of Greek and Roman life .... The contingent from the British and Medieval Department was smaller, since the Ceramic Collections were considered too fragile to move ... the whole collection of Coins and Medals was removed in the cabinets in which they stood in the Medal Room'. (Kenyon 1934: 32–3)

The collections in the underground were protected from April onwards by a permanent patrol, consisting at any one time of two museum clerks. One of the keepers of antiquities visited it at least once in every 24 hours. A telephone was arranged from underground to the British Museum, and an alarm bell to the Post Office overhead was installed. The Post Office canteen provided meals. The men on duty had a small stove on which to boil a kettle. Kenyon noted 'the service was dull but not onerous, and none of the anticipated dangers was realised in practice'.

A proposal to arm the men was rejected even though an appeal was made that weapons would be useful in dealing with rats. The National Gallery's collection was also housed underground, in a section of the Aldwych tube, and the guards in that instance *were* armed with revolvers which Lionel Earle, H. M. Office of Works, considered a 'wise precaution'.[19]

Damage, return and repair

It is difficult to gauge whether museums in London or elsewhere sustained any damage from air attack. There is no mention of any incident in the *Museums Journal*. However, information is available of damage at the British Museum (Natural History) and the British Museum. One or two bombs fell in the immediate neighbourhood of South Kensington and one fell within the museum grounds, although the building itself was not struck. Slight damage was caused by anti-aircraft guns and fragments of shrapnel penetrated the roof of the museum in several places. No damage was occasioned to any of the specimens. No real damage was caused to the British Museum building in Bloomsbury, although there was one instance of damage to the collections: on 7 June 1917 a fragment of shell from one British gun fell through the glass roof of the main book store, flaying 'the backs off two unimportant German books'. As it turned out, falling fragments from British shells were the main risk. One hit the roof of one of the porter's lodges. Kenyon kept it as a memento.

4. *Removing sandbags in the Northern Egyptian Gallery* by Henry Rushbury, 1919.
Pencil and water-colour.
Source: Imperial War Museum

The frequency of the raids created an unforeseen use of museum space. A long series of passages in the south-east basement of the British Museum became an air raid shelter. Accommodation was provided for 200 persons, although 250 people used it on 21 October 1917. The basement of the British Museum (Natural History) was similarly used. Both museums were concerned about the risks to their security from these arrangements. At the BMNH, a museum officer slept in the immediate neighbourhood, so as to be able to come on duty promptly and take charge in the event of a night raid.[20]

The return of museum collections to peacetime conditions of care has gone largely unrecorded, though Kenyon detailed the experience in his Glasgow lecture. He paid credit to those who had packed, removed, returned and unpacked the collections, adding that 'A few objects had come to pieces along the lines of old fractures and a few mummy cases had collapsed under pressure'. He described the total damage as 'infinitesimal'; and none of it was irreparable. Moreover, a cuneiform tablet thought for some years to have been lost, turned up in the unpacking. Kenyon commented modestly on the experience: 'If a museum official had been asked whether he could dismantle the whole museum without considerable injury to its contents, he would probably have hesitated to undertake it' (Kenyon 1934: 36).

Although the nation's collections had been successfully secured from bomb damage and returned safely, this had been achieved at a cost to the well-being of some of the collections. Kenyon recorded that the damage had been slight, but admitted that there was deterioration in the condition of some objects because of the environmental conditions in the Tube. In fact, much of the deterioration was both rapid and unexpected, and perhaps more extensive than Kenyon was prepared to admit. Andrew Oddy, the current Keeper of Conservation at the British Museum, gives us some idea of the scale of the problem:

> Archaeological iron was rusting, and covered with droplets of a dark brown liquid; archaeological bronzes had developed spots or patches of loose green powdery corrosion (christened 'bronze disease'); some pottery and some stone objects were covered in growths and salt crystals; organic objects were affected by moulds; and many works of art on paper had acquired a rash of brown spots, known as foxing. (Oddy 1992)

Swift action had to be taken. The Trustees requested the Government's Department of Scientific and Industrial Research to report on the condition of the collections and offer assistance in restoration and preservation. Dr Alexander Scott FRS agreed to direct investigations and put forward a proposal for a laboratory in the British Museum. This was sanctioned as a short-term experiment for three years and work began on stabilizing the damaged collections. In 1922, a laboratory was set up in 39 Russell Square. Not until 1931, did it become a formal part of the British Museum. Scott was succeeded by Dr H.J. Plenderleith in 1933 (Caygill 1981: 49–50). The British Museum since this time has been at the forefront of scientific conservation, especially within the field of antiquities.

But the British Museum was not the only national institution which in the post-war years began applying scientific understanding to the well-being of its collections. The National Gallery's collection had also fared poorly in the damp conditions of its temporary store underground. It too established scientific conservation facilities after the war and like the British Museum, is now a world leader in the understanding of conservation within its field.

CHAPTER 3

CLOSURES AND
TAKE-OVERS

By early 1915 conditions had changed so much that state involvement in the home economy was called for to avoid the collapse of the war effort. The Government dropped its endorsement of 'business as usual' and began undertaking a number of new initiatives. But until mid-1916, when the strain of the war really began to tell, the Government had little idea about whether and indeed how best to lead public opinion. Propaganda at home was not an immediate concern. An operation based in London at Wellington House, Buckingham Gate, was established by the Cabinet in the early days of the war to address opinion about the war abroad, especially the neutral states. It cultivated strong ties with the press, but had no brief for propaganda at home, which until early 1917 was left to voluntary agencies and the press (Masterman 1939).

The support of the press was particularly crucial. Rarely did the newspapers strike a directly critical, unpatriotic note; they denied a platform to those who would argue against the war. The resilience of civilian morale was due in no small part to the role played by the press which persisted in believing in the justice of Britain's cause and continuously reminded the public of the underlying values of British society.

Without a propaganda agency at home, attuned to public opinion, the Government in 1915 and 1916 blundered into a number of political gaffes which with hindsight were avoidable. They demonstrated how out of tune the Government was with public opinion. Even though some of the decisions made may have been right and appropriate, in terms of the war effort, their handling created as many problems as they solved. Not least among these was the decision in March 1916 to close all the national museums and galleries in London, not for the safety of the collections or the public, but for a saving of £26,000.

A lesson in economy

By 1915, it was obvious that the war was costing more than the Cabinet had anticipated at the outset. The figures kept on mounting. Lord Middleton speaking at a meeting in Sheffield, on the subject of 'national thrift', laid out the financial position of the country:

> Even the Government themselves did not know what the war was costing us. In May 1915, the deficit for the year was put at £865,000,000. In July, we were told £960,000,000. In December, despite immense increases of taxation it had risen to £1,200,000,000. For next year, it would be far larger. (*The Times* 19 January 1916)

In 1915, in recognition of the mounting difficulties, the press insisted on the need for thrift and the voluntary agencies established a number of anti-waste campaigns. The Government was obliged to be seen taking some form of action. A Retrenchment Committee was appointed to 'inquire and report what savings in public expenditure, in view of the necessities created by the war, can be effected by the Civil Departments without detriment to the interests of the state.'" Through its early reports, the Committee recommended economies in the Post Office, local government and the civil service, and advised on how expenditure might be cut on the war bonus scheme and on Ireland.

The Committee's third report, prepared under the chairmanship of E.S. Montagu, Financial Secretary to the Treasury, dealt exclusively with 'the question which appears to us to deserve separate treatment, viz: the closing of museums and picture galleries etc'.[2] An elaborate set of reasons were given for the recommendation for closure.

First, there was the matter of savings. For the financial year 1915–16, the cost of running the museums was £300,000, and there were additional costs covering the maintenance of buildings and the provision of other services. The Committee anticipated that closure of the museums would provide a saving of £26,000 a year. This would be found through curtailing expenditure on lighting, cleaning and heating. However, the greatest part of the saving was to be achieved by cutting the policing of the museums. This was an additional security measure that museums had long used, in addition to warding by their own staff. In theory, the closure of the museums would set free not only their employees for military service and war work, but also their buildings for war purposes. However, the records make clear that the majority of men eligible for war service had left the national museums by this time. One critic of closure pointed out that the policemen engaged in this work were all over military age and would otherwise be pensioned off (*The Times* 27 January 1916). In further support of their recommendations, the Retrenchment Committee pointed to the drop in visitor figures. The reasons for the reduction were not given in the report, but were attributed to the absence of American and other tourists and the closure of the museums during the evenings. The Committee considered that admission charges could not be used to raise sufficient revenues to keep the museums open. The Committee also argued that 'the closing of (national) museums and galleries would be a valuable lesson in economy and would point the way to similar economies in local museums and galleries'. This would show that economies had to made.

The final argument was clear and unequivocal and perhaps got to the heart of the issue: 'all museums, galleries etc., should be closed forthwith and placed at the disposal of Government'. The Committee was able to cite as an example the National Portrait Gallery, which had been taken over by the War Office 'for the duration' in December 1915. The NPG's galleries had been converted to offices for the War Separation Allowances Department.[3] The extent to which this indicates an underlying agenda, or is simply a style of report writing is open to question. But it was a fact that museums were centrally situated, in stoutly constructed buildings, with a great deal of floor space. The administrative unit behind the war effort in 1916 had become the largest in the British Empire, after the London County Council (Bourne 1989: 177). Furthermore, the various non-governmental bodies supporting the war effort, industry and the financial institutions, all needed more office space. Prime sites in the capital cities were ideal for their purposes.

Public reaction

The first indication that economies on museums were under way came in the speech given in Sheffield by Lord Middleton, a member of the Retrenchment Committee, and published in *The Times* on 19 January 1916. He ridiculed museums and the expectation that they should remain open, especially as 'all museums were shut in Paris'. He made an emotionally-charged case:

> Lloyd George told them we had been too late with munitions. Sir Edward Carson said the same about men. Let the country see to it that they were not too late checking expenditure.

The relative scale of the proposed economy was not spelt out. However, the speech was sufficient to begin a public debate on the value of the museums, which intensified with the formal announcement of the committee's recommendations and ended with the closing of the public galleries in the national museums in March 1916.

At first, *The Times* gave the kind of support the Government expected of it. But this grew more cautious as the weight of protest became evident. By 22 January, *The Times* was commenting:

> Should museums be closed? If the Government is satisfied that a really substantial sum of money can be saved by the closing of museums throughout the country, the sooner they are closed the better. If we are to win the war rapidly, we must econo-

mize at once, and in every possible direction. At the same time we are fully awake to the disadvantages of narrowing, at this time of all others, the intellectual life of the nation.

Criticism of the decision was less muted in other journals. Both *Punch* and a contemporary paper, *The Passing Show*, published satirical cartoons, on 9 and 12 February respectively (see Illustrations 5 and 6). *Punch* added a poem:

INTELLECTUAL RETRENCHMENT

Fetch out your padlocks, bolt and bar the portals,
That none may worship at the Muses' shrine;
Seal up the gifts bequeathed by our Immortals
To be the birthright of their ancient line;
At luxury if you would strike a blow,
Let art and science be the first to go.

Close down the fanes that guard the golden treasure
Wrung by our hands from Nature's hidden wealth;
Treat them as idle haunts of wanton pleasure,
Extremely noxious to the nation's health;
Show that our statesmanship at least has won
A vandal victory o'er the vandal Hun.

And when her children whom seas have sent her
Come to the Motherland to fight her war,
And claim their common heritage to enter
The gate of dreams to that enchanted shore,
To other palaces we'll ask them in,
To purer joys of 'movies' and of gin.

But let us still keep open one collection
Of curiosities and quaint antiques,
Under immediate Cabinet direction –
The finest specimens of talking freaks,
Who constitute our most superb Museum,
Judged by the salaries with which we fee 'em.

o.s.

The Times received 'an unusual number of letters' about the closure, almost without exception, protesting against the decision. The *Museums Journal* also carried vociferous complaints. Petitions were drawn up and the Museums Association organized a deputation to the Prime Minister, H.H. Asquith (*Museums Journal* 15: 325–9, 332–3).

Objections were made on a variety of grounds. Lord Bryce of the British Academy, was not alone in arguing that the national museums were seen as

5. 'Economies in luxury' *Punch*, 9 February 1916.
Source: Punch Publications

A NASTY ONE.

THE PRIME MINISTER: "M'yes, most interesting in peace time. ·Full of ancient
    survivals and funny old relics of bygone times, but a most expensive and
    extravagant luxury in time of war, you know!"
COLONIAL (in London for the first time): "*I see, Sir. Very much like the House of
    Commons, eh?*"

6. 'A nasty one', *The Passing Show*, 12 February 1916. One of the objections made to
the closing of the national mueums was that it denied servicemen from the British
Empire the opportunity to visit them.
Source: Natural History Museum Central Archives

a credential of nationhood and to close them would offer a propaganda initiative to the enemy (*Museums Journal* 15: 318). Robert C. Witt, Secretary of the National Art Collections Fund, was later able to provide evidence that the German and Austrian press had commented on the closure, calling it an act of 'moral bankruptcy which threw a strange light on the economic conditions of England and on the mentality of its people' (*Museums Journal* 15: 322).

Arguments against closure were raised in *The Times* and in the House of Commons on the effects it would have on research and on the general education of the public. Many reasoned that the museums were of considerable importance for the nation's leisure and recreation. Singled out as having a particular need for the museums were British and colonial soldiers on leave, the war-wounded and convalescent, the poor, the weary and women. The moral well-being of these groups was seen to be in jeopardy if access to museums was denied and they had to fall back on music hall, theatre and cinematographic shows for their entertainment (*The Times* 29 and 31 January 1916; *House of Commons Debates* 27 January 1916).

As a form of entertainment, cinema was seen as a source of moral danger. It was, in Marwick's words, 'freely attended by both sexes' and took place in the dark. The National Council of Public Morals, in a report published in 1917, cited a common though misplaced belief that the increase in delinquency was linked to the cinema (Marwick 1965: 141). Only towards the end of the war was the cinema effectively used for propaganda. In 1916, an entertainment as popular yet morally dubious as the cinema was seen as a regrettable alternative to the 'improving' medium of the museum.

Pertinent arguments were also made on the value of the war-related research being carried out at the British Museum (Natural History) and the special wartime exhibitions housed at a number of the national museums (*The Times* 4 February 1916). Furthermore, the proposed level of savings was held with some scepticism, a matter much confused by the use of figures ranging from £26,000 to £60,000. Sir Sydney Calvin, representing the National Art Collections Fund, was able to point out to the Prime Minister that an economy of between £50,000 to £60,000 had already been made 'since the beginning of the war by the withholding of the usual grants for purchases, furniture and fittings etc' (*Museums Journal* 15: 320). This was confirmed after the war by Sir Frederic Kenyon when he pointed out that £53,000 had already been saved on British Museum estimates before the Retrenchment Committee's decision, and a further £11,400 could have been saved without closing the galleries.

The announcement of the closure of the national museums and the subsequent debate created confusion in the museums profession. The position of the provincial museums had not been made totally clear; so the Museums

How to Save.

It is estimated that by closing the museums the nation will save £50,000. This would pay for the war for *very nearly a quarter of an hour!*

7. 'How to save', *Evening News and Evening Mail*, 29 January 1916. This cartoon draws comparison between the virtues of a free, but closed, British Museum and a new form of entertainment – the cinema.
Source: Natural History Museum Central Archives

Association's delegation was relieved to receive Asquith's assurances that the decision was in no way meant to include provincial museums over which the Government had no direct authority. Moreover, even in respect of the national museums, it was not clear to what extent the Committee on Public Retrenchment had meant 'closure'. Ultimately, it was taken to mean the closure of all public galleries, rather than the whole premises and operation of the museums. Most of the museums managed to retain some form of curatorial function throughout the war period.

The final and most effective argument for closure was given by the Prime Minister:

> ... we are at war. That is the governing consideration at this moment. It takes first place, and must take first place, both in the mind and the action of those who are responsible for the Government of the country (*Museums Journal* 15: 336).

So the closures were brought into effect. This was achieved by withholding the vote, that is the annual funds for the national museums, a prerogative which the House of Commons held 'to exercise control of bodies which otherwise it could not control' (*House of Commons Debates* 2 March 1916). Concessions were made. The British Museum Reading Room was kept open, but a charge was made to readers. The British Museum (Natural History) was partially exempted from closure.

The national museums and galleries were closed to the public in early March 1916, although this was not the final word. Several museums attempted to keep at least one gallery open. The Victoria and Albert Museum, which had gained support by accommodating the British Industries Fair in February and March 1916, was allowed to remain open, so that encouragement might be given to British industries through similar exhibitions and education work. In a matter of months, it too was partially closed.

Repercussions

Museums committees in the provinces gave consideration to the possible savings that could be achieved by a similar move. Sir Whitworth Wallis presented a detailed report to the Birmingham Museum and Art Gallery Committee which indicated that only small savings were possible. His arguments that the collections, valued at £250,000, needed constant care and attention and that visitor attendance was significant, helped sway his committee and the museum remained open (see Chapter 7).

Similarly, much discussion was held on the possibility of closing the City and County Museum in Lincoln. On 5 February 1916, Councillor Milner drew attention to the museum accounts for the previous three months which amounted to £86 5s. He questioned the 'impertinence' of asking the council to sanction the payments 'at the present time'. The museum's times and hours of opening were reduced (*The Lincolnshire Leader* 5 February 1916).

This was not reported in the *Museums Journal* even though its Editor, W.R. Butterfield, was punctilious in the gathering of news from all possible sources for dissemination to colleagues. By early 1916, censorship, the sheer volume of information made available from the fronts (regardless of its relevance or completeness), the increasing concern for how the home front should be contributing, and the length and harrowing regularity of casualty lists, meant notices about provincial museums were a *very* low priority in the press. Without official notification from museums threatened with closure or in the process of being closed, Butterfield was not in the position to gauge the number of museums involved or make useful comment in the *Museums Journal*.

When information was received, the Museums Association through the President, E. Rimbault Dibdin, and the Hon. Secretary, E.E. Lowe, made representations to the governing body. An instance of this is the closure of the Whitechapel Museum and the Nature Study Museum in Stepney. News of the Libraries and Museums Committee's proposal had been given by the *East London Observer* on 19 February 1916. Alerted by this, the Museums Association appealed to the Mayor of Stepney, in a letter dated 12 May 1916, 'not to adopt so retrograde a policy' (*Museums Journal* 15: 300).

In July 1916, E. Rimbault Dibdin published in the *Museums Journal* an assessment of the effect of the war on museum activities based on a questionnaire sent to eighty-two 'art museums': 12 in London, 62 in the provinces, 5 in Scotland and 3 in Ireland. Sixty-five replies were received (Dibdin 1916: 29–46). This was a subject on which he had personal experience as Curator of the Walker Art Gallery, Liverpool, where the annual art exhibition had been saved only through the generosity 'of a few citizens who undertook all liability'.

Dibdin revealed that in London the British Museum Print Room, the Tate, the National Portrait Gallery and the Wallace Collection were closed 'for Government purposes' and their grants had been suspended. The Victoria and Albert Museum was partly open and had experimented with variations in opening hours. The National Gallery was open, although most of the 'important pictures' were no longer on view. The Guildhall Gallery was still open, as was the Whitechapel Art Gallery. The Dulwich Gallery was believed to be closed. No replies had been received from the galleries at Peckham and Bethnal Green. Dibdin concluded: 'London, in short, is practically denied the use of its great museums'. As for the provinces, he recorded that only one art gallery had been closed. He was not prepared to say where this was situated other than its being 'in a centre which has more than any other, been scourged by Zeppelin visitations ... the museums of that town remain open as usual'.

Alternative uses of museum buildings

By 1916 schools, country houses, hotels, department stores and a variety of other buildings were transformed into hospitals or accommodation for official departments. Centrally situated and large museum buildings were increasingly seen as being of more use when dedicated to any wartime purpose. Their role as accommodation for collections and curators was of little interest to officals trying to run the war effort.

Sir Frederic Kenyon recalled how:

> A further consequence of the interruption of ordinary museum life, innocent at first but subsequently becoming serious, was foreshadowed in February of this year (1916) when the Office of Works intimated that in pursuance of Treasury instructions, they were considering how to use museums and other kindred buildings for the housing of various official activities. (Kenyon 1934: 18)

Following approaches to the Trustees, the British Museum became host to three forms of 'official activities'. In April 1916, the statistical branch of the Medical Research Committee, which kept health statistics for the entire army, was installed. This was a purely non-combatant service. By the end of its occupation, the committee occupied nearly the entire sub-ground floor of the new wing. The British Museum was also host to the effects of interned Germans from the Cameroons and other captured German dependencies. Space was found in the northern portion of the basement of the new wing, beneath the forecourt.

Kenyon observed that 'for the remainder of the war, and a considerable time afterwards, this space resembled nothing so much as the "left luggage" office of a London terminus'. The Registry of Friendly Societies became, according to Kenyon 'the last intruder, and the most difficult to get rid of'. They were allocated part of the galleries belonging to the Egyptian Department where, it was said, they were troubled by the 'spirit of the notorious wicked mummy'[4] (Kenyon 1934: 18–19).

Aylesbury Museum was an early example of a provincial museum used for alternative purposes. In 1914, as the War Office had taken over the local schools for hospitals, the museum buildings were taken over to be used by the schools (*Museums Journal* 14: 214). Brabazon Museum, Sedlescombe, near Hastings, was later utilized as a workroom 'where the village women and girls made articles of winter-wear for our fighting forces' (*Museums Journal* 15: 213). Although Nottingham Museum remained open during the war, the roof of the castle, from May 1916, was used as an observation

8. Part of the British Museum was turned into a store for the property
of prisoners of war.
Source: Imperial War Museum

post by the military authorities. Part of the castle was used as a military hospital.[5]

By 1917, the growth of the bureaucratic machine was such that there was considerable pressure for office accommodation in both the capital and the provinces. In that year, practically the whole of the Walker Art Gallery, Liverpool, and part of Birmingham Museum and Art Gallery were used by the Food Controllers for those areas (*Museums Journal* 18: 91). By 1918, two museums and six of the galleries in Birmingham were used by the War Office for its departments dealing with prisoners of war and much of the remaining space was taken over by the Office of Works for the National Service Board.[6] The Ferrens Art Gallery in Hull was taken over for military medical purposes. Wimbledon Museum was closed and used as officers' quarters (*Museums Journal* 18: 92).

In May 1917, the Prime Minister, David Lloyd George, gave notice to H.A.L. Fisher, President of the Board of Education, that the Victoria and Albert Museum would have to be occupied by the Board of Education staff, themselves displaced by the War Office and the Admiralty (*Museums Journal* 17: 13–14). The Museums Association protested but to no avail. The Iron-work Gallery and the exhibition galleries to the north of them were therefore closed to the public and became offices.

The British Museum and the Air Board

At the end of 1917, the British Museum was again under threat. Sir Frederic Kenyon referred to it as 'the great crisis in the fortunes of the Museum' (Kenyon 1934: 23). In December 1917, a confidential communication from the Government warned that heavy air attacks could be expected in the spring and that the bombs would be of a type more destructive than had been used hitherto, '... no buildings could be considered proof against such bombs'. This was sufficient for the Trustees to begin plans to move the collections to places of safety, which it did in February 1918 (see Chapter 2).

Information was also received at about the same time that the Air Board was in search of larger premises. The clearance of the museum was required so that the Office of Works could hand the building over to the Air Board. The Trustees recorded 'their conviction of the impropriety of establishing a combatant department in the museum, and instruct the Director to resist any such proposals'. On 11 December, the Director received the Air Board's formal application and duly answered with a strong letter of protest. Sir Frederic Kenyon was invited to attend a meeting of the War Cabinet on 20 December to discuss this matter. He was able to record, some years later:

> ... with one exception, the members of the War Cabinet showed complete indifference to the interests of the museum or to the effect which the proposed action would have on the good name of the country. The Air Minister had said he wanted the museum, and if so, he must have it. (Kenyon 1934: 24)

Two days later the War Cabinet's decision to grant the application was communicated. The Trustees vigorously protested against the decision which would result in a combatant department being housed in the museum and, in Kenyon's words, 'thus make it a most legitimate target for air attack'.

With this issue, as with the Retrenchment Committee's insistence on closure in 1916, there were grounds for effective protest. Yet again it could be argued that it showed an indifference to the cultural and spiritual interests of the nation and that such indifference was admirably suited to the propaganda purposes of the enemy. Public opinion was again mobilized, beginning on 1 January 1918 with a powerful letter of protest from Sir John Sandys in *The Times*. For the next ten days, correspondents in the press, but particularly in *The Times*, debated the Government's stand. *Punch* added a cartoon to the debate on 9 January 1918 (see Illustration 9).

Both the arguments expressed, and the tone employed, repeated those used in the controversy over closure in the early months of 1916. Arthur Evans, President of the British Association and a trustee of the British Museum, called the Government's endorsement of the Air Board's application a 'crowning outrage' (*The Times* 2 January 1918). He argued that 'the removal of collections to accommodate the Air Board would create chaos

PUNCH, OR THE LONDON CHARIVARI.—January 9, 1918.

THE LATEST AIR-RAID.

Scene—*Luxurious Restaurant of Capacious and Eligible Hotel.*

First Indispensable. "I SEE THERE'S BEEN SOME TALK OF COMMANDEERING THE BRITISH MUSEUM FOR THE AIR BOARD."
    Second Ditto. "WELL, WHAT ABOUT IT? THEY MIGHT HAVE TAKEN A PLACE THAT REALLY MATTERS—LIKE THIS."

9. 'The latest air-raid', *Punch*, 9 January 1918. When the Air Board attempted to take over space in the British Museum at the end of 1917, it met strong protest as its presence would have made the building a legitimate target.
Source: Punch Publications

which a generation would fail to set in order', and moreover, 'by occupying the British Museum they would legitimate the dropping of German bombs on what is the largest roof in London'.

The issue was settled at a meeting of the War Cabinet on 8 January. The Air Board had reconsidered and were being advised on alternative accommodation by the Ministry of Works. This change of heart may be attributed to Sir Frederic Kenyon's discussions with the Air Board and Office of Works. One officer, having been shown the premises was heard to say that they were 'd … d unsuitable' (Kenyon 1934: 26). On the following day, 9 January, Lord Curzon announced in the House of Lords that it was no longer necessary to appropriate the British Museum for the accommodation of the Air Board. It was also announced that, due to the difficulties involved in clearing the British Museum (Natural History), it was deemed to be unsuitable for conversion into public offices. *The Times* published this announcement with an air of victory. Sir John Sandys subsequently printed an instructive 'Summary of the Public Agitation', for circulation among MPs. The summary, re-entitled 'A Nine Days Wonder' was published subsequently as a pamphlet.

However, the matter did not end there. Subsequent debate drew attention to the legal status of the British Museum and the right of the Government to make such decisions. On 16 January 1918, in a debate in the House of Commons on the allocation of accommodation, the First Commissioner of Works, Sir Alfred Mond,[7] was asked under what authority he would have acted to use the British Museum. He replied with some firmness: 'the building of the British Museum is a Government building. It is under my department, and is not vested in the Trustees; and, obviously, the War Cabinet has the power of overruling the trustees of any museum' (*House of Commons Debates* 16 January 1918).

Sir Henry Haworth, a Trustee of the British Museum, personalized Mond's statement and wilfully mis-reported it, claiming Mond had asserted 'he was the real Master of the museum and could do as he pleased with it' (Haworth 1917). Mond later had to concede, in a Commons debate on 24 January 1918, that 'the building as well as the contents of the British Museum are invested in the Trustees', but went on to affirm that the property was administered by his department 'in consultation with them'. He expressed regret at his earlier reply. Haworth interpreted this as 'establishing the independent status of the British Museum' (Haworth 1917: 118). In fact, a full reading of the debate reveals that during this period the British Museum was no more independent than any other individual or institution. Mond clearly and correctly stated that had the proposal been proceeded with, it would have been carried out under the Defence of the Realm Regulations. The legal status of the museum, therefore, would have had little relevance.

Museums and galleries in use again

The end of the war did not give museums back to their visitors. In January 1919, the Science Museum was reopened, although its new building was not finally completed until 1928. The Victoria and Albert Museum and the British Museum had also succeeded in opening some exhibition space to the public, although this was very limited (*Museums Journal* 18: 136). In the same month, the *Museums Journal* passed on to its readers the assurance that: 'The Office of Works is doing everything possible to secure the speedy evacuation by various Government departments of the National Gallery, the British Museum, Hertford House (the Wallace Collection) and the Victoria and Albert Museum'. But the release of the National Gallery, Hertford House and the British Museum was to be delayed by at least 18 months. 'The great hotels are likely to be liberated first – the art galleries and museums will follow'.

In fact, the evacuation of the museums in both the capital and the provinces was extremely slow. In the immediate post-war years, there was much difficulty in returning a society so geared to war to one able to cope with peace. Many enlisted men were not demobilized until 1920 and this caused much frustration. Questions were raised in both Houses of Parliament and letters appeared in the press expressing concern over the length of time then being taken to release the museums. But the Office of Works, which had responsibility for the buildings, was dealing with competing priorities and huge demands on resources in this wind-down period. The release of museum space was just one of its problems and took time to resolve. Birmingham City Council was one of many authorities to protest officially, but to no avail.

The last 'guest' to leave the British Museum was the Registry of Friendly Societies in March 1920. Kenyon considered that it was not until 6 March 1922, when the Medal Room was opened in its new quarters, that the recovery of the Museum from the war was accomplished (Kenyon 1934: 37–8). Indeed, it was not until 1922 that many museums were able to operate an unrestricted service.

CHAPTER 4

DUE SHARE AND DEFENCE
OF THE REALM

THE Editor of the *Museums Journal* in April 1915 wrote patriotically:

> ... it must not be supposed ... that we consider museum men to be, by their position, absolved from taking their due share in the active defence of the realm. They are, we rejoice to think, doing so, and will doubtless continue to do so in no less proportion than members of other callings!

The 'due share' that museum men took in the 'defence of the realm' received a rather inadequate record. It came not only in the form of active service, but also in the research in which the science museums and curators became engaged.

The due share

The *Museums Journal* began publishing the names of enlisted men from museums in 1915, but the reports became intermittent as it became more and more difficult to gather information. Proportionally, more men enlisted from non-curatorial grades, that is technicians and warding staff, than from curatorial grades.

For many museum curators, active war service was out of the question. This was an ageing group of professional people. Even in 1918, when the Military Services Act extended conscription to all males between 18 and 51, most curators were well beyond the age limit. Elijah Howarth at Sheffield celebrated his 40th year in that city's museum service in 1918 and must have then been in his early sixties. Ben Mullen at Salford Museum was 52 in 1914, Charles Madeley at Warrington Museum was 65, E. Rimbault Dibdin at the Walker Art Gallery, Liverpool, was 61, and Whitworth Wallis at Birmingham Museum was 59.

Where a curator was eligible for service, he was replaced somehow. The curator of the Hancock Museum, in Newcastle-upon-Tyne, E. Leonard Gill was replaced by his father Joseph J. Gill who delighted in the work, especially educational activities. His son contributed with advice, as best he could, with at least some papers 'composed amidst the roar of big guns a little behind the firing line' (*Museums Journal* 18: 16). James Paton, who had retired from the

10. Elijah Howarth was Curator of the Public Museum and Mappin Art Gallery, Sheffield, between 1876 and 1928. A former President of the Museums Association, his visionand wisdom did much to enrich museum opinion and practice during the war.

Source: Museums Journal

directorship of Glasgow Art Galleries and Museum at the age of 71 in 1914, was brought back when his succesor, Gilbert Ramsey joined up. Ramsey was killed when serving in the Dardenelles and Paton therefore remained in charge until 1919, when a new appointment, T.C.F. Brotchie, was made (*Museums Journal* 20: 242).

The role of the older generation in keeping museums going was keenly felt. In September 1918, the editor of the *Museums Journal* reflected:

> ... the older men of the museums and art galleries are carrying on today because they know that what they are doing is worth doing for the nation, symbolising in a sense the cause for which the nation is at war; they will continue to carry on, because it is for them (alas! for them alone in too many cases) to hand on their traditions to a generation as yet scarcely born. (*Museum Journal* 18: 54)

There were curators who were prepared and able to undertake war service from the beginning, and others who later became eligible for the forces under the arrangements for conscription. Frederic Kenyon, director of the British Museum, was 51 in 1914 and immediately went into war service (see below). In contrast, E.E. Lowe, Curator at Leicester Museum, 37 years old in 1914, somehow gained exemption from war service. In October 1916, the chairman of that museum's committee agreed to appeal for Lowe to be exempted from war service; a further appeal was made in April 1917. It was confirmed in October 1917. Not all museum staff enjoyed such support from their committee. John Piggott was the foreman attendant at Sheffield Museum and had been specially trained in fire-fighting. In May 1916, Howarth appealed to the museum committee to propose his exemption, but was defeated. The threat to the museum from incendiary bombs was recognized, but the best the committee could do was to propose that two of its members should come to the museum in the event of fire.

The experience of museum staff on active service has gone without coherent record. For the greater part, only fragments of evidence remain. For example, when writing to protest at the closure of the national museums, Percy Gardner recorded how at the Ashmolean Museum in Oxford:

> Out of a small staff of the Ashmolean there have come four officers (one killed), a sergeant-major, and two or three privates. Even the elderly men and invalids who remain have done some bits of war work. (*The Times* 3 February 1916)

The annual report of the Castle Museum Norwich in 1917 recorded that four members of the museum staff were 'serving King and Country'. They were: Donald Payler, Assistant Curator; F.N. Chasen, Junior Assistant; W. Martins, Carpenter; and J. Fuller, Fireman.

The record of the war service given by staff from the British Museum, was, however, provided in detail by Kenyon in 1934. The Trustees of the

British Museum had encouraged staff to join the Territorial Army in the years prior to the outbreak of war, and those who joined, or were members of the Army Reserve, were mobilized and joined their battalions at the outbreak of war. The Director, five assistants (higher grade officers) and 24 other members of staff from the British Museum and six assistants and ten others from the British Museum (Natural History) automatically moved into the forces. Kenyon was one of the first to be mobilized. On 2 August 1914, he and three other officers from his battalion, the Inns of Court OTC, were sent to France for service with the Expeditionary Force. He returned a month later and for the war years combined his military and museum duties, conducting the latter through periodic visits and correspondence. Kenyon's military duties were in connection with the training of officers in his battalion at Berkhamsted.

In the early stages of the war, the British Museum placed no obstacle in the way of any volunteer, as there were sufficient older members of staff to provide for the custody of the collections. By the end of 1914, 61 members of staff from the British Museum and 32 from the BMNH had enlisted. By June 1915, 118 members of staff at the British Museum were on naval or military service, with four more sent to other Government departments. The Derby Scheme, introduced in the autumn of 1915, was the first effort at conscription, and brought radical changes. In January 1916, out of a total male establishment of 570 in the two museums, 253 were of military age. Of these, 152 were serving or had served and been discharged; 50 had attested under the Derby Scheme; 33 had been medically rejected; leaving a balance of 18, some of whom, though of military age, were 'incapable of service' (Kenyon 1934: 8).

During this year, several more men were made available for the services, even though Kenyon believed the museum was functioning with the minimum number of staff feasible for such a task. Twenty-six certificates of indispensability were issued. The enquiry carried out by the Manpower Distribution Board in October 1916 revealed that there were only two men between the ages of 18 and 25 at Bloomsbury, both of whom had been rejected, and three at South Kensington of whom two had been rejected and the third medically categorized as C3, the lowest health classification.[1]

The demand for more men intensified in 1917. Government departments were surveyed with 'a fresh and more elastic medical examination'. The British Museum was, in consequence, called upon to supply an additional three men after a given date. It was possible for Kenyon to reply that more than this quota had already enlisted since the date given. When, in early 1918, the Ministry of National Service began withdrawing exemption certificates from all civil servants who were under 24 and fit for service, it was found that there was no man of this description at the British Museum. Indeed there was only one fit man under 36 and he was a fireman who could not be dispensed with because of the risks from air raids.

In his résumé of the war service at the British Museum, Kenyon recorded that 137 staff undertook military or naval service and 44 were lent to other departments. In addition, at the BMNH, 12 men joined the Volunteers, and six formed a museum detachment of the London Ambulance Column.[2] There was one conscientious objector at the British Museum[3] and one at the BMNH: both were allowed to accept work of 'national importance'. Ten men from the British Museum were killed or died of disease on active service; 23 were wounded. From the BMNH, 8 were killed and 14 wounded. From March 1917 onwards, the British Museum wrote letters of condolence to the families of men from the museum killed on service. It also wrote letters of congratulation to all those that had won honours or been promoted.

The experience of the British Museum must have been paralleled in other institutions throughout the country. Yet it is difficult to arrive at any conclusion on the extent and nature of staff enlistment and conscription. Numbers were occasionally published in the *Museums Journal* up to 1916, but rarely names or positions. It can only be suggested that, as a significant proportion of curatorial staff were too old for enlistment, the numbers quoted at the time and since refer to attendant, clerical, technical and junior curatorial staff. Unlike the National Union of Teachers, the Museums Association did not publish a Roll of Honour.

Women, volunteers, old men and invalids

One thing is certain, the much reduced staffing levels between 1914 and 1918 necessitated the use of alternative forms of labour. C.S. Peel described Britain in 1917 as 'a country of women, old men, boys and children, with a sprinkling of men in khaki' (Peel 1929: 105). Therefore, some flexibility was required in finding assistance. By 1917, the British Museum was employing disabled or discharged men and some women. Moreover, a few attendants who had reached or passed the age of retirement were retained or recalled for service. Other museums, including the Museum of Practical Geology, were in a similar position.

Women were taken on in various curatorial and other capacities in a number of museums. For example, at Leicester Museum, three members of the curatorial staff attested in 1916 under the Derby Scheme and were replaced by temporary female assistants, who were obliged to resign at the end of the war.[4] Similarly, Sheffield Public Museum and Art Gallery took on female assistants, although this is recorded in the minutes but not in the reports for this period. In March 1917 the Curator was authorized to find a discharged soldier to act as an attendant.[5]

Most of the women who came into museum work during the war appear to have left in 1919 or 1920. There is little if any record of their contribution. The exception is Gladys Barnard (c.1887–1972) who had joined the Castle Museum, Norwich in 1904 as a typist to catalogue the library. She was promoted to the curatorial staff during the war where she remained, eventually becoming Curator from 1937 until 1951 (Norfolk Museum Service 1984: 26). Thus, at least one woman was able to break into the male preserve of curatorship by virtue of assuming curatorial responsibilities during the war.

After the war the position of women as part of the workforce altered. By 1920 two-thirds of the women who had entered employment during the war had left it. The war industries were scaled down and work became scarce. Promises that men could return to work once released from war service were kept. But for every two women who returned to the home, one remained in employment. A significant proportion remained in traditional areas of women's work, for example textiles, but advances had nevertheless been made. Many women began building careers in Government or commercial work. The position of such women was enhanced by the Sex Discrimination (Removal) Act of 1919, which in theory at least allowed them to 'assume or carry on any civil profession or vocation' (Holdsworth 1988: 69). The National Insurance Acts of 1918, 1920 and 1921 further secured their position by making women eligible for national insurance benefits (Bourne 1989: 197). From this point on, the museums profession was more evidently open to both male and female labour. By 1928, Miers was referring to 14 per cent of museums being run by well selected and efficient men and women (Miers 1928: 19).

Women also assisted museums in the war by contributing various forms of voluntary work. For example, from late 1915, Birmingham Museum and Art Gallery benefited from the services of the Women's Volunteer Reserve. Each day, six or seven members of the local corps were on duty from 11.50 a.m. to 2.10 p.m. so that the galleries could remain open in the lunch hour.[6] The museum's committee was prompted to make a ten-guinea contribution to their funds for services rendered.[7] In 1918, the museum's committee chose to replace the women with special constables, although this was found subsequently not to be a satisfactory arrangement. The constables proved unreliable and in the light of the dwindling lunchtime attendances, in July 1918 the museum began to close from 1.00–2.00 p.m.[8]

Volunteers were used as temporary labour. The Annual Report for the Victoria and Albert Museum for 1916 (published after the war) records appreciation for the services of volunteers who had helped supplement the reduced staff. Their assistance had been 'of the greatest value and has made it possible to carry on several activities which would otherwise have had to

11. Gladys Barnard, promoted to the curatorial staff of the Castle
Museum, Norwich, during the war. She was the museum's Director
between 1937 and 1951.
Source: Norfolk County Museums Service

be suspended'. The activities included cataloguing, labelling, research and the
preparation of publications.[9] This was by no means an isolated instance of the
use of volunteers and certainly the position of the volunteer in museum service
was enhanced, even guaranteed, as a result of the war experience.

It came as some surprise, in the summer of 1918 when extreme hardship
was being felt everywhere, that Edward Rimbault Dibdin, Curator of the
Walker Art Gallery, Liverpool and past President of the Museums Association was retired by Liverpool Corporation (*Museums Journal* 18: 53–4). The
Editor of the *Museums Journal* commented: 'frankly we are amazed … every
man who can do a day's work is summoned to serve, and none thinks of
returning while strength endures'. He declared 'we have vanquished Apollyon,
and now, in April 1918, there springs up in our path – the Liverpool Corporation'. The Museums Association sent a strong letter of protest to the
Mayor of Liverpool, the result of which was a small increase in Dibdin's
pension. The Walker Art Gallery closed and was taken over by the Local
Food Control Committee. Dibdin invested his talents elsewhere.

The re-orientation of staff payments during the war (particularly the war bonus) and the dislocation this might cause after the war when low museum budgets were expected was the subject of a discussion led by E.E. Lowe,[10] curator of Leicester Museum, at the annual conference of the Museums Association held in Manchester in 1918. Lowe admitted that in the 1917–18 financial year, making ends meet was a 'practical impossibility'. He speculated that matters would have been much worse 'were it not for the fact that the majority of members of staff are away on war service and our expenditure in the way of salary on their behalf is much less than it would otherwise have been'. He considered that when they returned the position would be 'very serious' (Lowe 1918: 112).

The return of men from war service

Staff invalided out of the services were returning to their museum work while the war continued and with the on-set of peace those who had survived gradually returned to their duties. Little mention is made of this return in museum committee minutes. Birmingham Museum and Art Gallery committee on 16 December 1918 acknowledged the return of five attendants, as this facilitated the washing and cleaning of the whole of the lower lighting in the picture galleries.

In contrast, Howarth at Sheffield listed in the museum and art gallery report for this period the names and positions of all those who had joined up for service, and the dates of their enlistment and return. In February 1917, the museum's committee had repeated an assurance to the men who entered national service that it would 'keep open the places of those who go'. This was a promise that was kept. In 1919, Howarth recorded with an air of gratitude that 'all of them returned safely from the war'.[11]

The return of men from active service to their work at the Victoria and Albert Museum was seen as an occasion worth celebrating, and they did so in style. One-hundred and fifty-eight men from the museum, 40 per cent of the staff, had served in the forces, 15 were killed. On 25 March 1919, a Dinner and Smoking Concert was held in their honour, attended by H.A.L. Fisher, President of the Board of Education, Sir L. Amherst Selby-Bigge, his Permanent Secretary, and Sir Cecil Harcourt Smith, Director of the museum. While the men had been away on war service, the remaining staff members had watched their progress, even setting-up a Comforts Committee which sent parcels to V&A men in the trenches. In his address, Fisher was warm in his praise of what the men had done:

> ... you have all been in one way or another engaged in this museum, and I suppose of all types of employment, there is none which is further removed from the idea of war than life in a museum. I cannot imagine a more peaceful occupation than

a life in a museum. Yet at the call of your country and your King you went out to fight in the greatest war in which this country has ever been engaged and in the greatest cause with which any human being can be identified. One-hundred and fifty-eight of you served, and 15 have fallen on the field, and we remember them here gratefully tonight. (*Museums Journal* 18: 201)

After the war, Kenyon commissioned Eric Gill, the sculptor and print-maker, to design the British Museum's monument. It was to bear the names of the Bloomsbury dead and be installed on the facade of the museum for 'perpetual memory', with lines from the famous poem 'For the fallen' written in September 1914 by Lawrence Binyon, himself a member of the Museum staff (Kenyon 1934: 11). A carved wreath was added later in 1923. The cost of the memorial was met by subscriptions paid by the museum's staff, the Trustees contributed to the cost of adding the carved wreath. The memorial, positioned near the museum's main doors was unveiled in December 1921 in the presence of the Trustees, members of staff and the relatives of the dead. A guard of honour was furnished by the Artists Rifles. A Roll of Honour was displayed inside the British Museum until the 1930s. A war memorial was also erected at the British Museum (Natural History) and, in 1922, a War Memorial Record was published.

Research for the 'defence of the realm'

There were other direct contributions made by museums to the 'defence of the realm' besides releasing their staff for military service. The great science museums based in London each found a definite and much valued role in the war effort. The talents and facilities of the Science Museum, the Geological Survey and the Museum of Practical Geology, and the British Museum (Natural History) were fostered and fully utilized during this period.

In this, they benefited from a renewed commitment and interest in science. Marwick has pointed out the degree to which a war will:

> ... provide a stimulus to the development and application of existing ideas, this is to technology and applied science; a war will release purse strings and encourage politicians to found institutions for the practical applications of science; a war, itself a great creator of necessity, will foster an atmosphere favourable to invention. (Marwick 1965: 227)

This war was no exception. Throughout its course, scientific and technical talents were both exploited and promoted. As a result, their importance in the post-war years was recognized generally. The war unequivocally made science 'a proper full-time occupation for a growing professional and white-collar class' (Marwick 1965: 236). The science museums were not excluded in this regard.

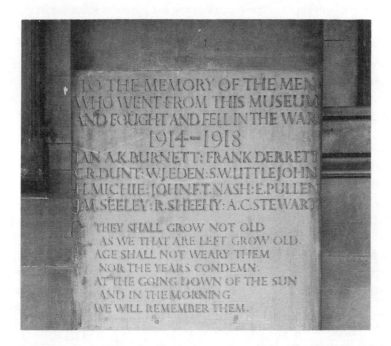

TO THE MEMORY OF THE MEN
WHO WENT FROM THIS MUSEUM
AND FOUGHT AND FELL IN THE WAR
1914–1918
IAN A.K.BURNETT: FRANK DERRETT
C.R.DUNT: W.J.EDEN: S.W.LITTLEJOHN
H.MICHIE: JOHN F.T.NASH: E.PULLEN
J.M.SEELEY: R.SHEEHY: A.C.STEWART

THEY SHALL GROW NOT OLD
AS WE THAT ARE LEFT GROW OLD.
AGE SHALL NOT WEARY THEM
NOR THE YEARS CONDEMN.
AT THE GOING DOWN OF THE SUN
AND IN THE MORNING
WE WILL REMEMBER THEM.

12. War memorial at the British Museum with lines from the poem
'For the fallen' by Lawrence Binyon, a member of the museum' staff.
The memorial was commissioned from Eric Gill.
Source: British Museum

Shortage of staff appears to have limited the war work carried out by the
Science Museum. By 1917, twenty-nine members of staff had joined the
forces (Follett 1978: 47). A number of others had left for civilian service with
the Ministry of Munitions and other Government departments, where their
specialist knowledge and experience would be of value.[12] Notably, in 1915
the Director, F.G. Ogilvie, left the museum for service with the Trench Warfare
Research Department. Some members of staff remained to carry out 'war
work', within the museum's workshops (Follett 1978: 48). Besides this un-
specified 'war work', the Science Museum's contribution to the war effort
lay in two areas: instruction using a special 'Warfare Collection' (see Chapter
5); and the availability of its collections and library to researchers and students.

The Science Museum found it had to pay 'special attention to things as
to which information was in demand'. The year 1915 was:

a period of pressing enquiry, and of change in industrial methods and processes –
a period of activity in the design and production of machines of all kinds. In such

relations the collections in the Museums and the books of reference in the Science Library have been of much use to those engaged in the development of the mechanical appliances and in new manufactures.[13]

Even after the closure of the Science Museum, access to objects and books was permitted. Many continued to use it for specialist investigation and research. There was a marked drop in the number of science teachers using the library, but a rise of over 50 per cent between 1914 and 1918 in the number of other readers (Follett 1978: 48).

Much use was also made of the Geological Survey and the Museum of Practical Geology even though, like the Science Museum, its staff was depleted by men leaving for military service. In 1914, the provision of water supplies to the numerous training camps in the south of England was one of the first matters upon which the museum's advice was sought. It involved the staff in 'a large number of interviews and much correspondence'.[14]

The Museum of Practical Geology was asked as well to provide instruction in 'obtaining supplies of drinking water at short notice'. This led to the museum publishing a guide to the geology of the south of England and the neighbouring part of the continent, which in non-technical language illustrated sites to be tried and those to be avoided. In 1914, advice was also given on sources of minerals, such as sands for glass-making and silica-ware, which had been obtained until that time from Germany. In the following year, the museum prepared reports and maps 'bearing on sanitary questions at the Front' for the War Office and consulted 'on subjects connected with military operations at a number of localities at home and abroad'.[15] By 1916, consultations with military establishments had become 'frequent'; enquiries continued throughout 1917.[16] One of the enquiries which 'occupied most of the curator's time' in 1918 came from the Imperial War Graves Commission.[17] As a result the Curator went to the headquarters of the Directorate of Graves Registration and Enquiries in France to advise upon the Marquise quarries and the stones to be employed in the cemeteries.

The record of war work at the British Museum (Natural History) is more readily available and detailed than that of the Science Museum and the Museum of Practical Geology. Details of some of it emerged in an anonymous letter to *The Times* on 4 February 1916, in defence of the museum under threat of closure, and in the papers published by Dr F.A. Bather in the *Museums Journal* (1914 and 1918) and the *Smithsonian Reports* for 1917 (1919: 619–33). Details were also included in the reports on the museum published after the war. With these precedents, it is not surprising that the Director of BMNH, Lazarus Fletcher, secured the Trustees' approval for

... a record of the work of the Museum during the war, including the war services of the staff, the protection of the collections and the extent to which the work of the Museum was affected by the War.[18]

This record, printed though never published, gives a detailed account of the war work undertaken.

Like the Science Museum and the Museum of Practical Geology, the British Museum (Natural History) operated through the war with a depleted establishment. Four members of staff left for work at the Ministry of Munitions, one worked as a bacteriologist at the Haslar Hospital for Admiralty and another as a protozoologist for the War Office in Salonika. However, sufficient staff remained to carry out research and respond to enquiries from Government departments. Examples of the 'sort of enquiries which were received and of the practical help which the museum was able to render during its progress'[19] illustrate the demands made on the museum and the effort on the museum's part to rise to the challenge.

This work ranged from setting-up special exhibitions to providing demonstrations and a wide range of topics was addressed. They included: protective colouration in nature; the structure of the horse; and insects as carriers of disease. The BMNH also provided information on numerous subjects including: whales; mosquitoes; and the food value of wild birds' eggs. Fifteen public departments (including Government ministries, the Armed Forces, and New Scotland Yard) made enquiries of the museum at this time.

The BMNH also undertook a variety of research tasks. The museum was brought in to identify: the larvae of moths and beetles which infested Army biscuits; the rocks used by the Germans in their concrete foundations in Flanders; the nature of an organism which was damaging the fabric of British ships; the fungus which destroyed army tents at Malta; and sources of sphagnum moss for dressings. It was believed that 'much of the important economic work carried out by the Entomological Department during the five war years had a direct bearing on the consequence of the war'.[20]

Dr F.A. Bather reflected on the war work undertaken by the BMNH and the role of museums in the advancement of learning in a paper published in America in 1919. He offered a defence of the museum naturalist, whose research he argued was not being given the recognition due, especially in the light of the British Museum (Natural History) war record. He pointed out that there were

> ... many distinguished biologists who appeared to be unaware of the research that is carried on in such an establishment as the Natural History Museum, and who seem to think that the work of museum naturalists can have little to do with their own studies in morphology genetics, experimental embryology and all those lines along which advance has of late been so rapid and brilliant.

Bather outlined the relationship of the museum to areas of academic study and argued the importance of opening the resources of the museum to the scientist. He concluded:

... if the true nature of museum work is not understood, even by men of science; if the advantages to be gained from a greater use of museums are not realized; if there is distrust rather than co-operation between those who are working for the same end by diverse methods – then it may be that the fault is in part our own. (Bather 1919: 633)

Bather's belief, which must have been much reinforced by his war experience, was that the most esoteric branches of museum work could and must be justified 'to ourselves, to our scientific colleagues, and to the public; and that it is our bounden duty to do so without delay'.

In spite of Bather's complaints, it is fair to say that the war work undertaken helped confirm the scientific integrity of the Science Museum, the Geology Museum and the BMNH. The value of well-curated collections was amply illustrated. In these museums at least, because of the relevance of their subject areas and the competence of their curators, relevant and purposeful war work was undertaken. Their reputations were enhanced as a result.

The British Museum (Natural History) also supported the war effort in an entirely different way: by late 1916 it was supplying propaganda to neutral and allied countries through its network of contacts, mainly to 'Professors at the Universities and scientific men generally'.[21] The propaganda material it distributed had originated at the Government's agency for propaganda based at Wellington House and which later became the Department of Information. The BMNH was not untypical of the type of institution used by Wellington House for the distribution of propaganda. Other national museums may have been involved although evidence for this has not been found.

In the post-war years, recognition of the value of these museums may be detected, at least in part, in a number of developments. The Science Museum found itself actively involved in the British Empire Exhibition and saw the main recommendations of the Bell Report 1911, come to fruition. In 1919, the Geological Survey and the Museum of Practical Geology passed from the Board of Education to the committee of the Council for Scientific and Industrial Research.[22] As for the BMNH, recognition came through the Royal Commission Report on National Museums and Galleries and the subsequent Act of Parliament in 1930, by which the Director of the British Museum (Natural History) became independent and no longer responsible to the Director of the British Museum (Stearn 1981: 132).

CHAPTER 5

ROLE AND PURPOSE
THROUGH EXHIBITIONS

As the war drew on, museums were put on their mettle, like every other institution and organization. The expectation was that, if museums were to remain open, they should provide a service which would contribute, in whatever way appropriate, to the war effort. It was obvious that war-related special exhibitions should be developed. For some museums, this became their role and purpose during the war years.

Inevitably, both the content and spirit of these exhibitions changed considerably as the years wore on, in ways that corresponded both to the need and mood of the moment. In addition to the traditional museum displays that continued throughout the war, three forms of special exhibition emerged, relating to: the war itself; health and hygiene; and the production of food. The exhibitions accommodated in museums were not always produced by them; many were touring exhibitions produced elsewhere. A number of organizations and later Government departments used the medium of exhibition to educate and inform. Museums were prime sites, especially after 1917, for domestic propaganda.

Honour and heroism

Between 1914 and 1920, the theme of the war itself reflected the changes in war mood. To begin with, the spirit was jingoistic, with an implicit belief in the justice of Britain's cause. In the first year of the war a number of museums picked up the cause of 'Little Belgium'. The plight of 100,000 Belgian refugees who had fled from the advancing German army and arrived in Britain in the early months of the war had been well covered by the press, often in lurid detail. A number of museums exhibited Belgian paintings, as a way of both keeping attention on the issue and raising money for the refugees. In the spring of 1915, the National Museum of Wales and Brighton Museum staged exhibitions of Belgian art (*Museums Journal* 14: 332–3; 392–3). Leicester Museum bought and exhibited a number of Belgian refugee artists' paintings[1] (*Museums Journal* 14: 368–9). Such exhibitions attracted much publicity and were well attended. But the welcome for the refugees wore thin and before the end of the war they were far from popular, being seen by many as a threat to their jobs in a competitive labour market. By 1918, museums had long ceased fêting them in exhibitions.

Public conviction regarding the honour and heroism of war held strongly throughout 1915. Certainly, in the first half of the year the state of enthusiasm had not as yet been fully overtaken by feelings of great anxiety. Hence in June a major exhibition intended to recall 'the heroic deeds of soldiers and sailors in the past, and in the war which is now engaging the forces of Europe', opened at the Guildhall Art Gallery in London. The *Museums Journal* commented that it showed what could be done by museums 'to stimulate an interest in the national cause'. Some of the paintings were later exhibited at the Mappin Art Gallery in Sheffield, where they were expected to be of interest to the munitions workers, and at the Walker Art Gallery, Liverpool (*Museums Journal* 15: 29–30).

At the beginning of the war, the public display of munitions and the technology of war in London, and later the provinces, fed a fascination with military hardware and modern warfare. The public had never before been so close to war and, until its terrible costs began to make themselves plain, its weaponry held an abstract interest. For the new troops preparing for war, the understanding of weaponry became a fundamental part of their training. Large guns particularly, the symbols of the war, were used in recruiting and fund-raising campaigns, especially in 1914 and 1915.

The Science Museum, in recognition of the mounting interest, both casual and military, established a 'Warfare Collection' which it exhibited from 1914 until the museum was closed in March 1916. The collection comprised models of British warships and submarines, British and foreign aircraft, including some of Germany's, and some full-sized aircraft engines. Also displayed were models of typical field bridges constructed by the Royal Engineers, photographs of bullets in flight, small arms and range-finding equipment. In 1915 a model of a Zeppelin was added. The range of the material included, particularly the aircraft engines given the relatively embryonic state of the Royal Flying Corps, suggests a considerable foresight on the part of the museum and an awareness of the changes taking place. The museum reported that the exhibition was attracting the interest of many soldiers either on leave or convalescing. Groups of material at the exhibition were used for the formal instruction of classes of soldiers.[2]

Exhibitions about the war were by no means discouraged. As long as the exhibitions followed what was almost an unwritten code of patriotism, neither the voluntary propaganda agencies nor the Government departments would do anything to prevent them. Where this code was threatened with infringement, firm action would be taken, as the proposal for an exhibition at Sheffield showed. Elijah Howarth, the museum's Curator, had seen the Warfare Collection at the Science Museum and, following advice from

Dr Ogilvie, Director of the Science Museum[3], set about making arrangements for a similar exhibition at Sheffield Museum. In this, he was conscious of the fact that the people of Sheffield were 'working day and night' making shells and munitions. He obtained the full co-operation of local munitions firms and manufacturers who were prepared to loan material. Howarth was advised by all of them that he would in the first instance have to secure the authority of the War Office. But what Howarth had in mind was a rather different affair from the exhibition at the Science Museum and this was made clear to the War Office, which as a result found itself unable to 'approve anything of the sort being done at the present time'. A disappointed Howarth later reflected, 'we could have given the public a much better appreciation of what is going on and of the horribly destructive power of munitions, and also the amount of science that is devoted to killing' (*Museums Journal* 15: 106). In sum, people could be educated in the technology of war at the Science Museum but at this stage in the war, early 1915, the effects of that technology on human life was not seen as a suitable subject for a museum exhibition.

Other exhibitions illustrating war equipment did go ahead, though not necessarily in museums and their point was somewhat different. A significant proportion of these were organized and presented by either national newspapers, voluntary agencies or commercial organizations. For example, in the summer of 1915 the London Chamber of Commerce organized a war exhibition to raise funds for the Belgian Red Cross Anglo-Belgian Committee. The exhibition, held at the Prince's Skating Club Knightsbridge, was designed to 'present an idea of the extent to which science and industry were being used in the war'. It had seven sections: trophies of war; armament and ammunition in the making; Red Cross work; science and industry in war; food and equipment; and naval and aerial warfare. The centre-piece was a large mural with a panoramic representation of Belgium. Museums were asked to contribute other material to it (*Museums Journal* 15: 86).

A similar exhibition, which also avoided concentration on the effects and costs of the war, was organized by the *Daily Mail* for the British Red Cross Society in March and April 1916. The 'Active Service' exhibition was a much larger affair and included a series of full-sized trenches, real dug-outs, and barbed-wire entanglements. The 'authenticity' of the landscaping was ensured through the involvement of Dudley Hardy, an artist who had witnessed conditions on the Western Front. Two halls were set aside so that they could be stocked with 'every possible requisite for our soldiers and sailors – bullet-proof waistcoats, British steel helmets, and various life-saving garments for use at sea'. An automatic range-finder was also being promoted. A collection of war trophies was part of the exhibition and an appeal went out for additional items which might be added to it (*Museums Journal* 15: 308).

Such exhibitions promoted the war as an adventure, an exciting and necessary experience. They fed public curiosity. Some advertised or sold the equipment and personal effects soldiers might need with them at the Front, a good deal of which was not provided by the War Office. The reality of war conditions was not on the agenda of such exhibtions at this time. Indeed a significant factor in the maintenance of public morale was civilian ignorance of the conditions many soldiers had to endure (Bourne 1989: 202).

In mid-1916, however, the mood shifted significantly. The war was no longer primarily about honour and heroism. It was about survival. The casualty figures, especially after the first few weeks of the Somme offensive, began to expose the true cost. All the news was bad. It was not going to be over soon, nor would it be concluded without further heavy losses. Conscription and food shortages took their toll on an increasingly weakened public morale. As the losses increased, so did war weariness, disaffection and dissent. In 1917, public tolerance of news of the war changed. People wanted to know much more about what was going on. The Government at last accepted the need to foster and cultivate both public opinion and support for the war. One of the ways that the public could be informed was through exhibitions, and in both their content and purpose these changed significantly from 1917 onwards.

Exhibitions in Birmingham 1917

The new mood of exhibitions is evident in some measure in the list of temporary exhibitions hosted by Birmingham Art Gallery and Museum during 1917.[4] Birmingham, England's second city, had industries crucial to the war effort. It was also a fertile recruitment ground and it mattered that the citizens maintained their support of the war. In June, the museum hosted two exhibitions. The first, an exhibition of military prints showing uniforms of the British Army 1797 to 1860 was put together by the museum itself and illustrated the homespun efforts to make exhibitions. It was accompanied by a collection of old uniforms, loaned by a number of local regiments and one of the members of the museum's committee, Alderman Gaunt. It remained open until March 1918.

The second exhibition was in direct contrast and was much more purposeful. It was a photographic exhibition dealing with all phases of the war on the various fronts and included sections on Great Britain and her colonies, France, Italy, Russia, Belgium, Romania, Serbia and Portugal. The exhibition was brought together by the art section of the Department of Information, part of the Foreign Office. The Department had been formed early in 1917, and was part of the efforts to galvanize a pro-war attitude. It subsumed the work of Wellington House, which had already established the importance of pictorial propaganda, leading to the publication of the all-picture publication *War Pictorial* in April 1916, and the commissioning of war artists and photographers, and later film-makers. It is likely that the photographs would have been carefully selected, with the aim of instilling a sense of moral outrage at the enemy and pride in the allied forces. It contained photographs which were to some degree explicit, although not representative of the worst excesses of combat. This exhibition toured to other venues.

The Department of Information (DoI) also supplied the next temporary exhibition to be held at Birmingham. This began in September and was a set of drawings from the Western Front by the first official war artist, Muirhead Bone. The DoI recognized that the muted images of Muirhead Bone were powerful propaganda to a certain section of society – the educated middle classes – and directed their use accordingly. Following its showing in Birmingham, the exhibition went on to other museums, including the Whitechapel Art Gallery in London, and Rochdale Museum. In general, public galleries were found by the DoI to be delighted to receive exhibitions such as this. Much could be made of the occasion especially if some form of social enhancement through art could be affected (Harries 1983: 74).

In October, a very different exhibition opened in Birmingham, this time on loan from the Labour Supply Department of the Ministry of Munitions. The exhibition was on women's work. It illustrated, through photographs and samples, the various types of engineering and munitions work in which women were engaged. It filled two large rooms and in its three weeks at the museum 'was visited by a large number of people interested in the subject'. The exhibition went on tour to other centres where the involvement of women in key industries was important: Nottingham, Liverpool, Swansea, Wolverhampton, Darlington, Glasgow and Dundee. Its success was later to influence the National War Museum in its choice of subject for touring exhibitions.

In December, the museum received another exhibition from the DoI. This was a collection of 66 lithographs brought together under the title 'Britain's Efforts and Ideals in the Great War'. This exhibition was initiated expressly for propaganda purposes. Using heavily allegorical material such as Rothenstein's *Triumph of Democracy*, it aimed to express both the ideals and efforts of the war. The series aimed to give 'artistic expression to themes which are of deep and widespread moment in our national life' (quoted in Harries 1983: 81). The series was significantly different in spirit and content from almost all the art work commissioned and exhibited up to this point by Wellington House and the DoI. The reasons why the DoI undertook this venture have been open to question. It has been proposed that the exhibition was put together at the behest of the National War Aims Committee who wanted an exhibition which would influence those becoming increasingly eloquent in advocating an end to the war. This was another touring exhibition which was seen in Britain and America. Its impact in America was significant. Its impact in Birmingham was not recorded by the museum, although clearly the City had been felt by the DoI to be an important venue for it (Harries 1983).

The year concluded with the opening of an exhibition of paintings loaned by Lady Horner whose home had recently been destroyed by fire. It contained works by Carlo Crivelli, Gabriel Rossetti and Benjamin West. In no other year of the war had there been so much going on at Birmingham Museum and Art Gallery and the visitor figures reflect this. For the year ending 31 December 1917 there were 409,817 visits, which compared with 321,641 in 1915, 325,532 in 1916, and 344,776 in 1918.[5] What these thousands of visitors felt or thought about the exhibitions is not mentioned in the museum's records.

War exhibitions from 1918

In the final, exhausted year of the war, there were yet more loan exhibitions touring the country. The DoI evolved into the Ministry of Information and issued further photographic exhibitions, seen in a number of museums including Swansea, Exeter, Brighton and the Whitechapel Art Gallery. The National War Museum, established in 1917, became the Imperial War Museum in 1918 and began creating exhibitions (see Chapter 9). These were seen in both London and the provinces and drew upon the museum's rapidly formed and still expanding collections of both objects and photographs. The exhibitions drew large crowds and excited much interest. A case in point was the exhibition of photographs of women's work shown at the Whitechapel Art Gallery in October 1918. The Women's Work Committee of the Imperial War Museum helped arrange the material and, with the Whitechapel, designed the exhibition to be a tribute and memorial to the large number of women who had lost their lives on war service. It was attended by 82,000 visitors (*Museums Journal* 17: 93; Griffiths 1991: 6).

Photographic exhibitions, which by the end of the war were able to give reasonably explicit images of the carnage created by the war, were only popular for a limited time. The end of the war brought a turning away from the realities of conditions on the battlefields and by 1921 such exhibitions were no longer popular. This was evident from the time of the Armistice and is perhaps best expressed in Vera Brittain's observations of the bitter contrast of the exhibitions of war photographs and the euphoria of the Armistice. She wrote, 'I could not remain blind to the hectic reactions of my generation, frantically dancing night after night in the Grafton Galleries while pictures

13. Opening of an exhibition of British war photographs at the People's Palace,
London, 1918.
Source: Imperial War Museum

14. Women's Work Exhibition at the Whitechapel Art Gallery, London, 1918.
Source: Imperial War Museum

of the Canadian soldiers' wartime agonies hung accusingly on the walls' (Brittain 1933: 468–9).

Exhibitions staged in museums, which ranged from the patriotic and jingoistic at the beginning to the starkly realistic at the end, were highly expressive of the changing war mood. However, other types of exhibition were developed by museum curators to aid the war effort in a rather different way. These were associated with the campaigns for better health and improved food production. In support of these causes a number of museums were able to find a wartime role and purpose, and were led into activities not experienced nor even dreamed of in peacetime.

Health, hygiene, motherhood and food

Since the years of the Boer War (1889–1902), attention had been focused on the ability of mothers to rear fit children. The Empire and the Army needed healthy recruits. Many of the working-class men who came forward were found to be puny, with weak hearts and lungs. Moreover, child mortality was unacceptably high. A campaign was begun to educate mothers so that they could build a healthy race. Although recognition was also given to the true underlying causes of the nation's poor health – poverty, sub-standard sanitation and atrocious living conditions – it was the mother who bore the brunt of the campaign.

Concern about the wastage of infant life increased in the immediate pre-war years. But with the war, alarms bells started ringing. In the Chief Medical Officer's Report for 1914–16, the argument was advanced that improved care of the young and their mothers was needed as 'the country needs both to mitigate the slaughter of war' (quoted in Marwick 1965:116). Fears about the quality of motherhood in Britain were compounded by the stark realization that the country needed able-bodied women to work in factories and munitions works. Many of the women who came forward were clearly undernourished. The Government was shaken into action (Holdsworth 1988).

Museums took part in the health and motherhood campaigns;though these had started before the war, particularly with exhibitions about vermin and the health dangers they posed. Museums with natural history collections were well placed to make a contribution here, although this was more scientific than social. For example, in 1913 the BMNH had published a pamphlet on *The House Fly as a Danger to Health* and had a display area dealing with this subject. In May 1915 it opened a small exhibition called 'War on House Flies', as did the Zoological Society. Museums in Norwich, Newcastle, Bristol, Salford and Belfast followed suit, as well as the National Museum of Wales and the Hancock Museum in Newcastle-upon-Tyne (*Museums Journal* 15: 156, 398). Later in the war, the chronic problems caused by vermin, especially lice, at the Front increased the scope of such exhibitions and publications (Stearn 1981:215; *Museums Journal* 15: 145–6).

Leicester Museum and Art Gallery was the first museum to tackle a subject well outside museum experience and collections, that of motherhood and infant welfare. Medical Officers of Health, health visitors and a range of voluntary groups and agencies had for some time been engaged in educating women on the 'art of mothering'. The first School for Mothers had been opened in 1907; others followed and were later taken over by the state and called Infant Welfare Centres.

In June 1915, the Curator of Leicester Museum, E.E. Lowe, attended a public meeting to establish a 'School for Mothers and Babies Welcome (*sic*)'. He felt prompted to have an exhibition on child care at the museum. In both its construction and provision, this exhibition was very much in line with the wider health campaign in the country. It was organized with the help and advice of Leicester Health Society, the Leicester Medical Officer for Health and local doctors and nurses. It contained specimens 'of a nature foreign to museums', by which Lowe meant explicit graphics, including diagrams, and equipment used to feed and clean children. The exhibition was designed largely by the School of Art and installed 'in a well finished and artistic manner'. Demonstrations and lectures were given in support of the exhibition (Lowe 1915: 254–64).

Other museums and institutions took up a similar theme. Sheffield Museum's exhibition on infant welfare opened in April 1916, attracting 192,300 people, 30,000 more than the average overall attendance at the museum and Mappin Art Gallery for a whole year. Howarth was moved to note that the exhibition demonstrated 'the value of a museum in affording opportunities to all citizens to obtain special information on any subject relating to the welfare of the whole community, whether in art, science, human economy, domestic life, commerce or industry.[6] Norwich Castle Museum followed suit (Durbin 1983). There were a number of other initiatives including, in February 1916, an exhibition at the Whitechapel Art Gallery on 'Mothercraft' (*Museums Journal* 15: 304) and one at the Institute of Hygiene called 'Childlife', which had the motto 'cherish our wartime babies' (*Museums Journal* 15: 402).

Parallel with this concern for health and hygiene was concern about food. Shortages were causing problems as early in the war as 1915. By 1916, there was a growing sense of urgency, especially as government initiatives were markedly absent. The press responded with a vigorous anti-waste campaign. This led to the organization of domestic economy exhibitions, including one on how to keep poultry (*Museums Journal* 15: 278) But, the most influential was the National Economy Exhibition organized at the Prince's Club Knightsbridge, in June and July 1916. It resulted in a committee being formed

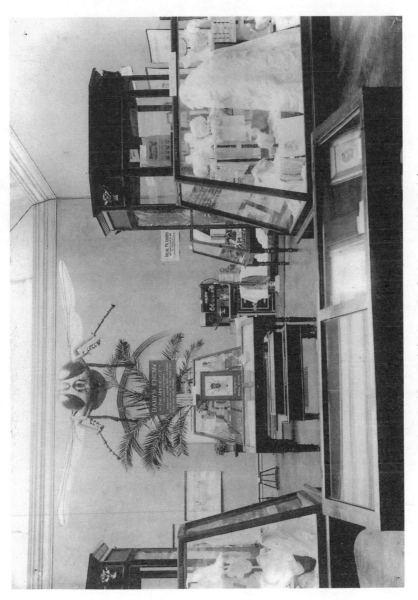

15 Infant Welfare Exhibition, Castle Museum, Norwich, 1916.
Source: Norfolk County Museums Service

16. Food Economy Exhibition, Castle Museum, Norwich, 1918.
Source: Norfolk County Museums Service

to prepare similar exhibitions elsewhere. The first exhibition planned was held at the People's Palace, Stepney Green, in London. It included war trophies, films to attract men to lectures and a weekly demonstration of Jewish methods of preparing food. Crèche facilities, with a trained nurse in attendance, were available to 'enable mothers to visit the exhibition without distraction'. The success and apparent comprehensiveness of the exhibition prompted the editor of the *Museums Journal* to ask 'why cannot museums arrange such exhibitions … work which can and should be done by museums is, by reason of their timidity in invading unaccustomed spheres, left to other agencies' (*Museums Journal* 16: 100).

Food shortages became even more severe as the war continued. C. S Peel wrote:

> 1917 dawned blackly, for now Germany had begun, by means of submarine attack, to endeavour to starve us into submission, which, had their blockade proved successful, would not have taken long. From that time onwards the question of food became of primary importance and the chief subject of conversation. (Peel 1929: 81)

In the same year, food control and rationing were introduced, and museums took up the challenge to provide exhibitions on food production. Yet again, it was Leicester and Norwich Museums that pioneered work in this field. In February 1917, the month in which Lord Davenport the new Food

Controller made his initial appeal for voluntary rationing, Leicester Museum's exhibition on food-growing opened. It demonstrated 'by means of models, the proper way of turning the ground … a plan of an allotment garden laid out to the best advantage', and provided examples of vegetable seeds that did well in Leicestershire. The exhibition was kept up to date in the hope it would form a conspectus of local horticulture. Books and pamphlets were available for reference and lectures complemented the exhibition (*Museums Journal* 16: 216–7). Such was the success of this work that the Curator was given leave of absence between November 1917 and January 1918 to advise the Ministry of Food on the production of similar exhibitions elsewhere. On his return, the museum opened its second food exhibition in March 1918. It also took up bee-keeping and gave public demonstrations and lectures on food topics.[7]

Frank Leney, Curator of Norwich Museum, had taken the initiative to put on a food exhibition at about the same time as Lowe, in February 1917. He was influenced by the National Economy Exhibition held in Manchester and, as a result, the exhibition at Norwich was not confined to food production but included trade exhibits. Through models, illustrations, symbols and food products, the Norwich exhibition explained food values, food economy, thrift garments and fuel economy. The expenses for it were met by the Norwich War Savings Committee. Between 10 February and 20 March 1917, 20,414 people visited the exhibition, as well as 3,647 children in organized school parties (Leney 1916: 221–4). A second food exhibition was staged between 19 January and 23 February 1918, for which Norwich Education Committee allowed the secondment of two cookery teachers to 'help with the practical side'. The exhibition attracted 17,185 people. Frank Leney, the Curator, observed of these exhibitions 'it certainly brings the museum into closer touch with the life of the people' (*Museums Journal* 17: 150–1; Durbin 1983).

Exhibitions on similar themes were held in other museums in the closing years of the war. One held in Hull on child welfare and food economy in September and October 1917 was particularly successful. It completely outgrew the museum and had to be held in the Guildhall. Unlike many of the other museum exhibitions, the Hull enterprise was commercial, with stands let and advertising sought. Film shows, lectures, and demonstrations were part of the attractions offered, as was an orchestra. The income amounted to £300, with £42 raised from advertising. Part of the exhibition was given over incongruously to a display of munitions (*Museums Journal* 17: 60–9). Sheppard reported that 90,000 people, equivalent to one-third of Hull's population, had attended the exhibition.

The British Museum (Natural History) took the food 'initiative' a stage further. It established a farm in its grounds, although it is not clear whether

17A. War Work Exhibition, St Andrews Hall, Norwich, 1919.
Source: Norfolk County Museums Service

17B. War Work Exhibition, St Andrews Hall, Norwich, 1919.
Source: Norfolk County Museums Service

17C. War Work Exhibition, St Andrews Hall, Norwich, 1919.
Source: Norfolk County Museums Service

this was for practical or demonstration purposes. Certainly, it benefited the large number of troops quartered at, or passing through, Cromwell Gardens who were able to take advantage of its

> ... excellent crops, specially priced eggs, rabbits and magnificent pigs. A profit of between £60 and £70 provided excellent dinners 'for the men for whom the usual Christmas dinner was not procurable'.[8]

These special wartime exhibitions provided museums with opportunities to explore the potential of the museum as a communicator; to test the relevance of the collections to a society in a state of crisis; to work alongside other specialists within the museum's area; and to become involved with and be responsive to the public. Theoretically, it was a test-bed for new ideas. However, the evidence would suggest that those involved saw these exhibitions purely as wartime expedients and not part of an evolving function of museums in society. In terms of museum practice, little seems to have been learned from them. When Miers came to write his report on provincial museums in 1928, he was dismayed at how limited were the exhibitions on offer and how poor was the understanding of the way in which an effective exhibition might be put together. Even the most fundamental of tasks, the writing of labels, appeared to be beyond the capabilities of many curators.

The wartime exhibitions on health, food and hygiene were new departures for museums and would perhaps today be described as 'community

18. Poster for the War Work Exhibition in Norwich, 1919.
Source: Norfolk County Museums Service

education'. The work obviously made an impression. When the British Association's Committee on Museums in Relation to Education published its report in 1920 it specifically recommended that 'the Public Health work of the district should be adequately illustrated in the museums'.[9] From both the Miers report (1928) and the Markham report (1938), it is clear this recommendation was not followed through.

More traditional forms of exhibitions

It should not be forgotten that these special exhibitions were in a number of museums, not all. Some museums continued their peacetime programmes of exhibitions throughout the war years. As the war began to reach its conclusion, exhibitions unconcerned with war or war-related themes provided the visual relief sought by many as an escape from the harsh realities of war. Everyone at some point desired to escape from present reality and exhibitions of paintings, particularly at the National Gallery once it had fully reopened, proved hugely popular (Marwick 1965 :140).

Particularly in the later stages of the war, the type of entertainment in highest demand was of the 'lowest quality'. Museums vied for visitors with cinemas, theatres, music halls, public houses and dance halls. Even so, the record of attendance was impressive. In 1919, Sheffield recorded an increase of 107,558 visits to the museum in the year ending March 1919 when compared with the year ending March 1915. Howarth was able to claim in a report written in February 1919, that the average number of visitors during the war was 'equal to three-quarters of the whole population of Sheffield, and greatly in excess of pre-war years'. Well-run museums had proved that they not only had a place but a part to play in contemporary life.

CHAPTER 6

EDUCATIONAL USES OF MUSEUMS

THROUGHOUT the country, children's education was fundamentally affected by the war. Many children had their education disrupted and a good number were forced or obliged to work. In August 1917, H.A.L. Fisher, President of the Board of Education, estimated that for the first year of the war 600,000 children had been put to work 'prematurely'. This figure does not include hundreds of other children set to work in total violation of the law (Marwick 1965: 116–7). Juvenile crime increased by 34 per cent in the early war years, and thefts by 50 per cent. The Howard League expressed its concern that the conditions in which children were growing up precluded healthy moral growth (Leeson 1917: 16).

Those children who could pursue their formal education often found that their school was appropriated for hospital or other war purposes, or that their teachers had been called up. Women and retired teachers were brought in to make up the shortfall. With severe limitations of space and a lack of qualified teachers, some authorities turned to the use of local museums and art galleries as a way of housing, occupying and educating their pupils.

Approaches to education

The extent to which museums were able to assist is open to question although there was definitely a spirit of co-operation in some quarters. Sheffield is again a good example. Such were Howarth's own convictions about the educational potential of museums, that in 1914 he persuaded his own museum authority, Sheffield City Council and Sheffield University to commission Dr F.G. Ogilvie, Director of the Science Museum, to prepare a report on the city's museums and their relationship with local educational institutions.[1] Ogilvie proposed a number of developments, none of which could be acted on because of the poor state of the post-war economy.

In the years before the war, as we have seen in Chapter 1, some museums were exploring the educational provision they could make. Given the success a number of them had met in this regard, the British Association felt moved to establish a committee 'to examine, inquire into and report on the character, work and maintenance of museums, with a view to their organisation and development of institutions for Education and Research; especially inquire into the requirements of schools' (British Association 1920:267).

The Committee's Chairman, Professor J.A. Green, considered that 'the organized visits of schoolchildren to museums is a twentieth-century contribution to the calls upon museum amenities ... neither teachers nor the museum officials have quite made up their minds what the museum can and should do for schoolchildren' (Green 1914: 344). The war was to give the committee a whole range of evidence about education in museums and this was to form the basis of its report when it emerged in 1920.

The Committee must have been aware from the outset of their enquiry that curators of public museums held very different views about what educational provision they should be making in museums. Three perhaps not untypical views emerged in 1914. The first of these was taken by E.E. Lowe, Curator of Leicester Museum, who held that 'it is not our function in museums to do the work of teachers. What we want to do is help them to do their work and to do ours at the same time'. He continued: '... museums are misunderstood, and if we show the rising generation that the museum is interesting and instructive, a place of delight, then they will have a different feeling for us and our delights' *(Museums Journal* 14: 288). Dr F.A. Bather, BMNH, a member of the British Association Committee went much further. He felt that museum staff 'should stick to our own business of curating and rendering those objects accessible' *(Museums Journal* 14: 284). Finally, a more liberal perspective was offered by Elijah Howarth. He acknowledged the growing professionalization of teaching and the enlargement of educational freedom, and believed in the possibility of using:

> ... all sources of knowledge for imparting instruction to youthful minds, not always too receptive ... in the more inspiring influence of the museum or outer air, where variety helps to inspire interest. (Howarth 1914: 282)

These views, ranging from the begrudging and unaccommodating through to the open-minded, were perhaps not untypical of curators at this time.

In 1915, Professor J.A. Green, chairman of the British Association Committee, laid before the Museums Association his own views of the educational potential of museums. He insisted that 'the mind that comes to the object is more important than the object itself'. He stressed the importance of working with and learning through real objects and saw the educational potential of the museum as facilitating the exploration of reality. This was a common feature of museum provision which everyone could experience in some way. His conclusion was that museums should actively teach people how to use them:

> ... otherwise it [the active museum] will not be fulfilling its purpose as it might, nor will it be occupying the place in men's minds that it should, for I can conceive

an actively worked museum as one of the greatest and most popular of institutions. (*Museums Journal* 15: 133)

The confidence he had in the educational worth of museums was shared by others. In a pamphlet written on the 'Child and the War', a case was made for much greater municipal provision for children as a means of engaging the interests and energies of children living in towns and cities. It held that 'after a little while, we should not wonder if the Museums and Libraries Committee discovered that it too could do something for the children – if only by introducing them to butterflies or Huck finn'. As an example, the pamphlet cited the work of the Manchester Education Committee and the education work then being provided by the museums (Leeson 1917: 61–2).

Manchester and the use of museums by local schools

The war gave plenty of scope for museums to teach people how to use them. The most well-known instance of schools use of museums was in Manchester, where twenty schools had their buildings appropriated for 'military purposes'. The education authority had to double-up on the use of remaining space and developed a 'half-time' system. Provision was made for the use of the museums on 'off half-days' when the children would be taught in the galleries by trained teachers using the collections. The teachers were paid by the education authority. Contemporary accounts differ as to the precise nature and philosophy of the scheme and to whom credit was due for the idea.

The Director of Education for the Manchester area, Spurley Hey, described how one teacher from each of the affected schools was selected by the education authority to receive instruction from the curatorial staff on the collections. A certain number of these remained at the museum to teach school parties. Hey believed that the use of the museum should be tackled from the 'education side' and commented that 'the staff of the museum have been a difficulty, willing as they were to help us' (*Museums Journal* 15: 138–40).

A different version of events came from one of the curators, Mr Bateman of the Whitworth Art Gallery, who was reported as claiming that it was he who had initially called together a meeting of 120 teachers whose schools had been affected by the closures. Talks with 80 selected teachers and instructions on the collections were given. The teachers were then allowed to give instruction in the galleries, 'though other teachers may and do bring their classes and personally instruct them'. Bateman also arranged Saturday morning talks for teachers 'voluntarily desiring to come'. In the account, Bateman made no mention of the other museums and galleries that were involved in the scheme or of any input from the Education Committee (Dibdin 1916: 36).

A more plausible and detailed account came from Lawrence Haward, Curator of the Corporation Art Galleries, Manchester. He described how the Museum and Art Gallery Committee worked with the Education Committee in the development of the scheme. A group of teachers volunteered to work at the Art Galleries and were given lectures on their contents. At the end of the course, they were examined and a prize awarded for the best essay. A few of the teachers were selected provisionally as the most suitable for the work. These teachers returned to the galleries for more detailed instruction, and were then allotted certain hours when they were on duty. The gallery teachers worked with the schools, advising on pre- and post-visit work, and took school parties for lessons in the galleries. They continued to receive instruction from the curatorial staff. According to Haward the same scheme was adopted at the Whitworth Institute, Ancoats Hall Museum and Manchester Museum (Haward in Howarth 1918: 36–7).

The effects of this contact with the museums and galleries on the children was, in Haward's view, 'more marked than anyone had anticipated'. He saw the educational work benefiting the children by sharpening their intelligence and improving their powers of observation. Haward believed it stimulated their creativity and made them 'think and feel for themselves'. The children also acquired the habit 'of coming by themselves to the Gallery'. Haward was in no doubt about the potential of an integrated relationship between the museum and the school. He believed it to be:

> ...imperative that these visits to art galleries should not be considered merely wartime measures, but should be regarded as only a beginning. When the idea of retaining and extending the present system has been accepted, I would wage that those who are most closely in touch with the children in school hours should be trained as far as possible to do the work themselves. (Haward in Howarth 1918: 16–7)

Schools, children and museum facilities
elsewhere

There were a number of other instances of school use of museum facilities. One of them was at nearby Salford, where an advisory committee,[2] including schools inspectors, union representatives and the Curator, Ben Mullen,[3] jointly drew up a scheme for the use of Salford Museum (Mullen 1918). Specific subjects were set each year for the children to explore. In 1915 it was birds, in 1916 pictures and in 1917 the history of Salford. An integrated pattern of school and museum activity was set to deal with each topic. The scheme was well received by the curator who appeared to have seen the scheme's potential in terms of the social and moral development it could affect upon children. He approvingly noticed boys:

... removing their caps upon entering the building, an action which I never observed until the establishment of the school system. It appeared to indicate a newly developed reverence for things belonging to a higher and more inspiring order than the drab and prosaic affairs of everyday life. (Mullen 1918: 21–5)

Other museums, such as Liverpool and Sheffield extended their schools' provision (*Museums Journal* 16: 143–4; Howarth 1918: 6–20). The success of the teaching carried out at Norwich Castle Museum, from the winter of 1915 when local schools began to close early because of the black-out, was such that a museum demonstrator was appointed after the war to continue the work (Norfolk Museums Service 1984: 23).

Educational provision in museums was not solely a provincial development. The Victoria and Albert Museum began making provision for children in August 1915, when it was anticipated that there would be 'more youthful visitors to the museum ... owing to the shortage of the ordinary country holiday funds.'[4] The Children's Room, established with the help of a volunteer, Miss E.M. Spiller, secretary of the Teachers Guild, was the first of the Victoria and Albert Museum's wartime initiatives to provide holiday activities for children. The exhibits in the Children's Room were chosen with a view to interesting both boys and girls, stereotypes unconsciously being used. For the boys, there were objects connected with war and fighting, such as rubbings of medieval brasses showing the armour of the period. For the girls, there were models of costume of different periods, three dollshouses and a display of Japanese dolls. Elementary instruction was provided and selected works of art discussed.

The Children's Room activities with accompanying exhibitions proved very popular and were held each year at Christmas and in August. The Christmas activities in December 1915 attracted 14,000 visitors, most of them children (*Museums Journal* 15: 345). The activities were highly dependent on the active co-operation of members of the curatorial and security staff, and volunteer participation. This dependence on volunteers, experienced in other aspects of the museum's work, led to the enhanced status of the volunteer at the Victoria and Albert Museum (Spiller 1918).

Official interest and curatorial resistance

The continuing role of the British Association Committee kept the issue of education in museums alive, as did the occasional debate attended by curators. Much of the discussion was concerned with the purpose and future of educational provision in museums. In October 1917, at a two-day conference held in Sheffield on the themes of the educational value of museums, and the formation of local war museums, delegates reviewed in detail several aspects of schools use of museums, including schools' use of the Manchester museums.[5] These were the two themes most in the museum profession's mind at this time. In the absence not only of effective debate, such as in the pages of the *Museums Journal*, but also adequate consultation on these subjects, Howarth took the initiative and organized this meeting.

H.A.L. Fisher, President of the Board of Education and vice-chancellor of Sheffield University, was invited to attend. Unable to do so, he instead asked for a copy of any report which 'you may issue as to the conclusions raised at the conference'. Five members of the Board of Education's staff attended the conference: a measure of it's interest. Fisher's request for further information at this point should not be underestimated. The role of museums was undergoing serious reconsideration by central government.

The first firm indication of a revised view of museums came in the Education Act of 1918, which made it possible for local education committees to seek the assistance of museums in the furtherance of local schemes for educational development. However, the Ministry of Reconstruction's Committee on Adult Education went much further in the scope of its recommendations. Having taken soundings, including the opinions of Elijah Howarth,[6] the committee was prepared to argue that museums should be included in any scheme of education for a local area developed after the war. This should be taken into account in the allocation of state grants to the local authorities. A further suggestion was that libraries and museums should be transferred to the Board of Education and that powers and duties should be exercised by the local government board.[7]

There was considerable resistance to this move and not a little hostility from museum curators, the Museums Association and the Library Association. In October 1919, a meeting was arranged between representatives of the Board of Education and the Museums Association to discuss the Ministry of Reconstruction's proposals (*Museums Journal* 19:123–9). The technical point of the arguments hinged on the term 'local education authority' used in the Ministry's report. It was not clear to the Museums Association whether this meant authorities with education responsibilities or an authority's education committee.

There was, however, a far more fundamental concern – the proximity of museums to education and to educational control. Sir Martin Conway MP, Director of the Imperial War Museum and president of the Museums Association, insisted that 'museums are not fundamentally educational institutions'. The apparent fear was that acquisition, research and exhibition would be prejudiced by too strong an educational requirement. E.E. Lowe, of Leicester Museum, exemplified this myopic attitude when he tried to argue: 'when we long for a rare or beautiful or typical object, we are desiring it for its own sake primarily, and not chiefly because it will educate person or persons unknown'.

Sir Amherst Selby-Bigge, Permanent Secretary at the Board of Education, fruitlessly tried to persuade the Museums Association that it was taking too narrow a view of education: 'the whole concept of education has widened very greatly recently'. He insisted that museums 'were a necessary part of any live system of education', but his was a lone voice.

The final arguments rested on finance: the Museums Association's representatives pleaded the case for more funds. The exasperated reply was that if assistance was to be forthcoming from local public funds, it was necessary that the museum be linked to a public authority able and willing to look after their interests. The only possible authority for this purpose was the local education authority. The meeting ended; there was no common ground on which the parties could meet.

The British Association's Committee published its report in 1920. Its principal contribution to the museums and education debate was to advise that 'the transference of museums by Order in Council to the control of the Board of Education may, if pressed too far, seriously prejudice the functions of museums as conservators of material and centres of research'. The committee appeared to have taken the line strongly advocated elsewhere by one of its members, Dr F.A. Bather of the BMNH (who was possibly the report's author), that museums should be centres of research, parallel to universities. Any deviation from that role and function was seen as likely to weaken dangerously the structure of the museum as an institution.

Although the committee was pleased to acknowledge the ways specific museums had worked with teachers and schools, and to point to experimental education work being carried out in the United States, it had nothing new to offer and was cautious in the extreme regarding the development of educational provision in museums. It was prepared to acknowledge the services museums could render to 'schools, advanced students, to classical education and the humanities', but went no further than this.

The creative and original exhibition and education work carried out by museums during the war period must have led, in part at least, to the proposals from the Ministry of Reconstruction. It is ironic, therefore, that leading curators appear not to have recognized the significance of their achievements and experiences, nor the opportunities offered to them in the immediate post-war years, and that the very committee established to consider the development of museums as institutions for education and research should advise rejection of this positive move. Ironically too, the leading spokesmen against the education proposals, F.A. Bather, E.E. Lowe and Sir Martin Conway, were all men who had made tremendous efforts to ensure that museums found a positive role and purpose during the war.

Post-war educational work in museums

After the war, limited legislation did come into effect. The Library Act of
1919 enabled both town and county authorities to run museums should they
so choose, and removed the rate limit for museum support. It also allowed
for the transfer of museums to county education committees. In the face of
resistance from curators and the economic reversals of the 1920s, the latter
provision was rarely used. However, the other provisions made in the Act
made were greeted with enthusiasm. Lowe expressed the opinion that by the
1919 Act 'museums and galleries had received their charter. The removal of
the rate limit should lead to great developments in museums throughout the
country' *(Museums Journal* 20: 53). Nothing could have been further from the
truth.

In the post-war years, the economy was in chaos. Many of the proposals
for reconstruction were lost. With the depression that followed, both national and local government had to work to a set of priorities; and even then
there was no favoured activity or sector. If there was a choice between funding education and funding museums, however, then education would win
every time. As museum curators had made obvious their wish to remain
distant from the educational needs of children, their museums would in consequence be substantially under-funded.

The Miers report in 1928 revealed that half the museums in the country
were rate-supported, but in no case was a museum granted more than 3/4d
rate for its total upkeep, and that below 1/2d rate per annum was not untypical. Only three museums, Aylesbury, Leeds and Salford received grant-
aid from an education committee. Essentially the lack of adequate funds
affected all that museums did or could do. The under-funding was particularly evident in the payment of salaries, which were extremely low (see
Chapters 7 and 13). Miers had little hope that the situation would change:
'it is not to be expected, in the present state of public finance, that public
authorities will for some time be able to spend large sums on museum
development' (Miers 1928: 80).

Three years later, the Board of Education published its report on museums
and schools and it was very direct in its criticism of museums. It made reference to a number of recent reports and summarized from them that:

> Resources equal in richness and variety of any country in the world, upon which
> large sums of public money are annually expended, were not being used as they could
> and should be used in the service of education. (Board of Education 1931: 5).

The report pointed out that many of the museums were not originally set
up with a directly educational intent and that education had been an after-
thought. Disappointingly, many museums had not been able to rise above

their original condition. It was considered that collections were neither housed nor organized according to modern educational needs.

It has to be remembered, however, that even before the war a small number of museums had started to make progress on developing their educational functions, and this continued into the 1920s. Their example showed the way ahead. The work at Aylesbury, Batley, Haslemere, Huddersfield, Norwich, Leeds, Sunderland and Salford museums, much of which had flourished during the war, set ample precedent. The Miers Report and that of the Board of Education freely acknowledged this. As a result of the war, the potential of museums in both the education of the child and in what is now termed 'community' education had been, at the very least, more fully revealed. It was sufficient evidence that museums had a potential which could not be dismissed out of hand, even if some curators thought it could.

CHAPTER 7

MAKING DO

WITH or without a war, there are three prerequisites of museum provision: sufficient funds for salaries and wages, purchases, and running costs; the ability to develop the collections; and a willingness on behalf of the public to visit. Between 1914 and 1918, most museums struggled as best they could to work within their budgets, take whatever opportunities were presented to expand their collections, and keep their doors open to the public. The nature of the times was such that, in each of these areas, many difficulties (and some occasional opportunities) were experienced.

Funding, salaries, and wages

In spite of all the pre-war rhetoric about the social worth of museums, and the value (particularly financial) of the collections they contained, most were very poorly funded and existed within tight spending limits. The war simply underlined this problem. This is illustrated in the calculations, made in February 1916, by Whitworth Wallis at Birmingham City Art Gallery on being asked by his committee to consider savings and the possibility of closure. His report spoke for itself:

> Your Chairman and Keeper have gone very closely into the question of expenditure and probable saving. The collections are valued at £250,000 and require constant care and attention.
>
> <u>Probable saving, if closed</u>

Under Salaries, Wages etc., £101 per annum might be saved by having only one Police Constable on duty, day and night (three in all). Considering the very large area of the building and the valuable contents, the latter requiring constant attention, I do not think it would be possible to keep the building, etc., in proper order without a staff of six or seven attendants, viz., Foreman, Deputy Foreman, Chief Attendant (all well over 50 years of age), and say four others. The roofs (53,000 square feet of glass) must be kept clean – this is very heavy and dangerous work – and formerly two to four attendants were on this work for one or two days a week. The cleaning of the Museum of Casts, not yet open, is also a serious matter. The casts themselves always require attention, and the staircase, metal-work, marble, etc., must be kept clean – all this apart from the big floor area of the whole buildings (72,000 square feet).

The wages of the umbrella attendant, £50 per annum, would be saved. The services of the women cleaners could in a great measure be dispensed with – they could, in rotation, be given occasional employment scrubbing and washing. Their dismissal would be a serious hardship for them, many being more or less dependent on their weekly wage of 11/-, a possible saving, though, of £200 or £250 might be effected. A post might have to be found for Mr Bristoll, the clerk and secretary, though he was attested under Lord Derby's Scheme and expects before long to be called up. The attendants are also liable to be called on very shortly, one in fact, will probably go at the end of the present month.

We are using very little gas and electric light – only for office and cleaning purposes. The fixed charge for heating and water, £120 and £45 respectively, would continue. The dead charges of Ground Rent, Loan Charges, etc., on the new buildings and Natural History Department, would continue, viz., £2,500 per annum. Similar charges on the Second Extension, Museum of Casts, etc., may be made at any time.

General repairs might possibly be reduced by £50, from £150 to £100, but the roof of the old building is in a bad state, and increased expenditure may at any time be incurred. The amount taken under this heading was very low.

Insurance is now over £600, due to bomb insurance – this amount is not likely to be reduced, but may be increased.

Miscellaneous Expenses – £230 – could hardly be reduced as it included annual charges such as telephones, cleaning materials, postage, stationery, fire inspection, window-cleaning. There might possibly be a saving of £30. Superannuation and Optional allowances, National Insurance, Loan Charges, would remain the same, about £300.

The probable savings and expenditure would be on the lines of the statement sent to members of the Committee.

Considering that the Galleries are only open from 10 till 4, I hope [from] the middle of next month to keep open until 5 o'clock, the attendance of visitors is a large one.[1]

Rimbault Dibdin, as President of the Museums Association observed that 'the Municipalities have been so severely schooled by the Government on the subject of economy that their councils scarcely dare to sanction any avoidable expenditure' (*Museums Journal* 16: 37). Few if any curators would have disagreed with him. Expenditure at Sheffield Museum, certainly one of the better run provincial museums at this time, was no exception. Its record of annual expenditure illustrates the limited scope its Curator, Elijah Howarth, had for the development of the museum and how strictly everything was budgeted.

There was no grant-aid system to support museum expenses, such as now exists through area museum councils and the Museums and Galleries Commission; and of course at this time there was no experience of fund-raising or the use of sponsorship. Although taken for granted today, such possibilities did not exist then. Indeed, how museums could or should be funded was a constant source of concern. Towards the end of the war, at the annual conference of the Museums Association, E. E. Lowe of Leicester Museum claimed

Table 1 Expenditure on Sheffield City Museum, Weston Park, Sheffield 1914–1920.

	1914–15	1915–16	1916–17	1917–18[e]	1918–19	1919–20
Salaries, wages and uniforms	1205[a]	1252[d]	–	–	–	–
Salaries, war allowance, HI	–	–	661	686	686	865
Wages, war allowance, HI	–	–	614	670	994	1033
Uniforms	–	–	13	22	21	40
Electric current, gas, water	45	30	30	30	33	60
Coal, coke	35	40	50	55	48	50
Cleaning materials, chemicals	17	15	15	15	15	15
Printing, stationery	19	20	20	20	20	30
Telephone, insurance, Compensation fund	34	34	65	65	49	58
Travelling expenses, petty disbursements	49[b]	60	39	40	40	47
Subscriptions to societies	20	21	21	21	19	16
Carriage of specimens, cartage	24	20	24	25	20	25
Painting, ironmongery, fittings, repairs	70	37	60	60	60	184
Fee for sunshine records	4	4	3	3	3	3
Contingencies	40	–	40	30	60	–
Specimens, taxidermy, mounting	450	100	100	80	100	331
Furniture, showcases and fittings	100	94	–	50	50	40
Books and binding	28	20	20	20	20	21
Total annual expenditure	2,140[c]	1,722	1,775	1,892	2,238	2,818

Notes: a. includes health insurance; b. treated separately, but added here for convenience; c. in 1914–15, the combined expenditure of Weston Park Museum and High Hazels Museum was £2, 691, which was off-set by a grant of £141 from the Board of Education; d. includes War Allowances; e. estimate only; HI Health Insurance.

that 'the working expenses of museums and art galleries have gone up generally from 50 to 100 per cent' (*Museums Journal* 18: 114). Little did he realise at this time that this level of expense would not only continue to exist, but also the low funding of museums was to drop even further in the years after the war (see Chapter 13).

The restricted spending on museum services was reflected in payments made to members of staff. The evidence of the levels of salaries and wages and the conditions of employment offered to museum workers at this time is rather limited. However, there is sufficient to suggest that in some of the larger museums, where the staff were more able to organize and speak through staff associations, pay levels had become a matter of concern. The war did little to redress the problem. Many staff members benefited from bonuses under the war bonus scheme, yet still found themselves in a very disadvantaged position compared with other workers. This was as true for the curatorial staff as it was for the attendants.

Birmingham Museum and Art Gallery was a case in point. In the months before the war, Birmingham City Council had been in negotiation with the Birmingham and District Municipal Employees Association over rates of pay for museum attendants. Although these negotiations pre-date the war and were abandoned with its advent , they provide a picture of pay, staffing levels, hours and conditions in a number of provincial museums.

In February 1914, Birmingham Museum and Art Gallery had 20 attendants. Through their association they were petitioning the Council to increase the commencing salary to 26 shillings and raise the maximum to 36 shillings, to be attained in increments over a 12 year period. At the time of their petition, the maximum wage was 32 shillings and 6 pence, attained after 11 years of service. The attendants worked a 48 hour week. In defence of their claim, they pointed out that their level of pay had remained stable for 17 years, in spite of the cost of living having increased by 17 per cent. The finance sub-committee considered the petition and reported back to the Museum and Art Gallery Committee.

In their deliberations on this issue, the sub-committee had reviewed conditions at 15 other museums. In eight of them, attendants worked 51 to 58 hours per week. In the remaining seven, attendants worked 42 to 49 hours per week. At Manchester and Leicester museums, the attendants worked 58 and 54 hours per week respectively. In addition, each attendant was required to undertake night duty every third or fourth week. Of the museums surveyed, Sheffield City Council was paying its museum attendants the highest wage at 34 shillings per week for between 48 and 56 hours duty. At other museums and galleries the maximum wages varied from 30 shillings to 32 shillings and 6 pence. Twenty-five shillings to 32 shillings per week was the average. At Manchester, Nottingham and Newcastle the attendants started at a wage of 28 shillings. At the other museums surveyed, the starting wage was either 24 or 25 shillings a week. On the strength of these figures, Birmingham's Museum and Art Gallery Committee saw no justification for raising the pay of the attendants it employed.

Ironically, for many workers, including the staff of museums, the war brought increases in wages and salaries – constant employment, longer hours and war bonuses meant an upward movement in earnings for most employees. By the early autumn of 1918, the Birmingham attendants were in receipt of a war bonus of 5 shillings per week, which brought the maximum wage to 41 shillings per week.

How do these wages compare with those of other workers? In the years before the war, there were major differences in the wages paid to skilled and unskilled labour, to men as opposed to women, and between different trades and regions. A significant number of skilled men in 1913 could earn over 40 shillings a week. Unskilled men would be fortunate if they earned over 25 shillings a week (Stevenson 1984: 38–9). The wages of attendants in provincial museums, therefore, were slightly below those for skilled workers, such as decorators and fitters, and in some cases only just above those for unskilled workers, such as labourers. Even though the work of museum attendants may have appeared 'unskilled', requiring little more than passive invigilation, they had, among other duties, responsibility for the safety of the collections during opening hours – a considerable role in the custodianship of public property.

During the war, wage levels for both skilled and unskilled workers rose dramatically. The enlistment, then conscription, of able-bodied men resulted in a shortage of labour, especially skilled labour. Those who were ineligible for war service, either because of their age or because of some form of impairment, found that their bargaining power had increased considerably, especially if they worked in heavy industry. A steep rise in the cost of living during these years eroded some of the advantages of the higher wages but not all. Many sectors of the working classes became better off. Women working in munitions and other industries enjoyed a level of financial independence most had not experienced before. For the war period at least, this brought with it improvements in health, through the purchase of healthier, fresher foods, and a greater consumption of luxury goods. For example, it was in these boom years that many families found they had sufficient surplus funds to buy a piano or a sewing machine for the first time. However, it appears that this good fortune did not necessarily extend to museum attendants nor indeed to most provincial museum curators.

The Keeper of Birmingham Museum and Art Gallery, Sir Whitworth Wallis, did not have to negotiate in the same manner as the attendants. On 18 March 1918 his museum committee resolved to increase his salary from £800 to

£900 per annum. He was higher paid than most provincial museum directors, who were lucky if they succeeded in any form of re-negotiation of salaries. When Miers conducted his survey of provincial museums for the Carnegie Trustees in 1928, he discovered that only 14 per cent of the museums in the British Isles had fully-paid curatorial staff. On average, a curator received a salary 50 cent below the minimum which the Museums Association recommended and in some cases the curator was paid less than the caretaker (Miers: 1928 20–1). There is little to suggest that the levels of salary cited in the table Miers drew up, had altered at all during the previous 20 years.

Table 2 The Miers report of 1928 drew a comparison between the range of salaries paid to curators and the Museums Association's recommended levels.

Towns with population over:	Museums Associations recommended minimum for Head Officer (£)	Actual salaries paid (£)	
		Minimum	Maximum
600,000	1,200	500	1,061
400,000	1,000	350	900
300,000	900	198	800
200,000	800	120	650
150,000	700		
100,000	600	15	500
50,000	500	50	445
under 50,000	350–25 to 350	45	600[a]

Note: a. this was quite an exception to the norm.

How do these salaries compare with other professional workers? Before the war, a non-resident public-school teacher might earn £200 per annum after four year's service, reaching a maximum of £300 after ten years. Elementary-school teachers earned less than £100 per annum. A bank manager might earn £600 a year. After the war, salaried staff received a rather smaller increase in income than wage earners. Their salaries rose by an average of 71 per cent between 1911–13 and 1938, compared with 103 per cent for wage earners. The advantages for most salaried staff came in continuous employment and benefits such as pensions.

After the war, curators' salaries were more aligned with clerical workers, such as railway and bank clerks, than with those of professional groups such as the clergy and managers. In 1924, the annual salary of a civil service clerical officer was £284, that of a general practioner £756. In comparison, in 1928 the salary of the curator of the museum in Gloucester was set at £250.

Salaries paid to staff in private businesses grew faster than those paid to Government employees; and in the 1930s the wages of local government staff (including, of course, provincial museum curators) and of teachers, were cut because of the economic crisis (Stevenson 1984: 120–21).

Acquisitions

The restrictions the war brought on the already insufficient funding of museums was, for many curators, most evident in the amount of money they had available for acquisitions. Even in pre-war years the level of purchase grants, especially for the national collections was seen as inadequate. A Committee of Trustees from the National Gallery concluded a parliamentary report on art collections in 1913 with a set of recommendations including one that the purchase grant to the Trustees of the National Gallery be increased five fold, from £5,000 per year to £25,000.[2] This may have struck a hopeful note for some, but the optimism did not last long. Purchase grants for the majority of national museums were suspended from April 1915. The British Museum was the exception; it continued to receive a sum each year for the purchase of books not secured under the Copyright Act.[3] The purchase of material for museum collections was by no means seen as a priority. Referring to further cuts for the financial year 1915–16, a spokesman for the Government said:

> ... these grants are mainly expended on the acquisition of pictures and objects of artistic or antiquarian interest, and in the present crisis I think it reasonable to forego expenditure of public money for such purpose. (*Museums Journal* 14: 332)

The effects of curtailment of funds on provincial museums and art galleries were partially revealed in a survey of galleries, undertaken by Rimbault Dibdin, President of the Museums Association, for his presidential address in 1916. Institutions which had access to endowments or enjoyed patronage or bequests were able to continue collecting. Worcester, Brighton and Birmingham Museums and Art Gallery and the National Museum of Wales were cited by Dibdin as institutions still able to make acquisitions. On Birmingham, he commented:

> Sir Whitworth Wallis has made me envious by his list of valuable acquisitions. He has never had any grant or endowment, and his achievements remind me of the Conjurer who need never be short of a cab-fare because, at will, he can snatch half crowns from the surrounding air. (*Museums Journal* 16: 37)

Few institutions were able to find alternative funds and most were existing without any acquisition funds at all. Dibdin's solution came in the recommendation that wealthier citizens should be schooled in giving 'more and oftener' in terms of works of art and money.

The national museums also had to depend on alternative funding sources, such as reserves acquired before the war. Even so, the acquisition record of many of the national museums and galleries is notable, given the difficulties they faced. The National Gallery continued to acquire paintings during the war, through purchase, bequest and donations. A number of trust funds were used in order to make purchases, including the Temple West Fund, the National Art Collections Fund, the Lewis Fund and the Mackerell Fund.[4]

The National Portrait Gallery was by no means so fortunate. In the Annual Report for the 1915–16 financial year, the Director commented:

> The grant-in-aid purchase of portraits has been suspended for the duration of the war and the Trustees are dependent either upon gifts or upon such small savings as have been effected in the past.[5]

Although donations continued to be made to the National Portrait Gallery, the loss of purchase funds obviously had a severe effect. At the end of 1917, owing to the lack of any endowment and:

> … the exhaustion of the savings effected in the former years, the Trustees, reluctantly disposed of a duplicate portrait in order to make some provision towards the acquisition of such important historical portraits as may be offered for purchase or thrown on the market in the immediate future.[6]

Even in such straightened times, however, the National Portrait Gallery did not lose sight of its purpose. It set about expanding its photographic collection of 'eminent living persons'. The aim was to build a record of all persons 'naval, military or aviation' who held important rank or who served their country and the Empire with valour.

For the majority of museums, material acquired through gift or fieldwork accounted for most of the accessions made during the war period. Perhaps the most poignant gift was that made by Rodin to the Victoria and Albert Museum, in the form of a personal selection of his sculptures. The gift was made 'in honour of the British troops fighting in France beside M. Rodin's countrymen'.[7] However, the ability to rely on donations varied from museum to museum, according to the type of objects that were of interest. Art galleries, with their long histories of receiving generous bequests and endowments from the wealthy, were better placed than science museums, which had to rely on the goodwill of industry and inventors. The Science Museum in London was especially hard hit. It could no longer expect the active cooperation of engineers, manufacturers, inventors and Government departments – who were fully employed elsewhere – in the identification and gift of important material. Acquisition of science objects therefore was much reduced during these years.[8]

The British Museum took advantage of the peculiar circumstances of the war and became particularly astute at making acquisitions. For example, it made important acquisitions for the Department of Prints and Drawings through application to various Government departments. The presence of the Keeper of that department, Campbell Dodgson, as advisor to Wellington House and later the Ministry of Information was helpful here. A fully representative series of German War Medals was acquired by the Department of Coins and Medals, mainly by donation. Moreover, the deployment in the war effort of academics and British Museum curators resulted in unforeseen opportunities for excavation and survey. Thus, material from Salonika, Carchemish and Ephesus, Turkey, Northern Syria and Mesopotamia found its way back to the British Museum. The work carried out in Mesopotamia, particularly by H.R. Hall on Tell el-Mukyyar (Ur of the Chaldees), was of considerable importance and yielded 'the richest harvest of antiquities to the Museum' (Kenyon 1934: 38).

Visitors

The figures available appear to suggest that during the war the number of visits to museums did not decline substantially. It was to be expected that

Table 3 British Museum visitor figures, 1914–1919

	1914	1915	1916	1917	1918	1919
January	75,401	64,988	60,622			50,346
February	66,528	56,194	42,111			39,239
March	69,495	63,293				54,314
April	75,639	77,086				74,698
May	80,526	59,415				56,143
June	71,388	52,956				50,635
July	84,743	62,836				55,990
August	62,245	69,919			33,995	75,735
September	53,522	53,835			28,408	63,930
October	65,151	60,131			27,417	54,227
November	52,891	53,413			24,590	57,732
December	53,988	59,025			36,032	58,661
Total	814,517	733,091	102,733		150,442	691,650

Note: In 1914, because of suffragette activity, the British Museum placed restrictions on the access of women to its galleries, although this appears not to have affected visitor figures greatly. There was a noticeable drop in attendances in the early months of the war. Between March 1916 and July 1918, the galleries were closed. From July 1918, the public were allowed in to see temporary exhibitions. Access was on a week-day basis only until 1920.

there would be some drop in the number of visits overall. In London, the absence of tourists, especially Americans, was very noticeable at the national museums in the early months of the war and as the war dragged on restricted access to most museums in Britain was experienced. This ranged from full-scale closure to limited opening hours. Few potential visitors would have found a museum open in the evenings or on Sundays in the capital cities; and the situation became much the same in the provinces.

Table 4 Number of visits made to Birmingham City Museum and Art Gallery and Aston Hall, 1913–1919

	City Museum and Art Gallery	Aston Hall
1913	627,117	90,843
1914	141,247	101,171
1915	321,641	71,841
1916	325,532	44,636
1917	409,817	16,924
1918	344,766	22,369
1919	405,378	46,511

Notes: In 1914, the City Museum and Art Gallery were closed for six weeks because of suffragette action. It closed on Sundays and in the evenings throughout the war. Aston Hall was open only two days a week between 1916 and 1919.

Before the war, the rhetoric about the moral value, especially for the lower classes, of visiting museums was still to be heard. In 1913 John Burns, President of the Board of Trade, expressed the view that 'museums were absolutely essential if they [the authorities] were to provide for the greater mass of the people a nobler method of spending their leisure time than the public house' (*Museums Journal* 12: 260–61). But what proportion of museum visitors during the war were from 'the greater mass of the people' and whether the experience was actually worthy of the investment of their leisure time is impossible to gauge. Certainly leisure patterns changed during the war period. The presence of soldiers on leave or convalescence and the brief breaks of those engaged in munitions and other industries created a demand for distracting and engaging entertainment such as light plays, reviews and musicals, one of the most popular being *Chu Chin Chow*. Cinema-going increased significantly. It was estimated that in 1917, half the population went to the cinema once a week.

Museums maintained their attraction. The number of people in uniform using museums was frequently noted in the annual reports of the national museums. The National Gallery and the Tate Gallery let men and women in uniform into the galleries free on student days until they were closed in 1916. Marwick suggests that before the closure of the national museums there was a growth in the appeal of the Tate and the National Gallery because of aesthetic interest, a need for beautiful things in time of war. There are no means available to test or support this view; the available information is very limited indeed. Other than tables of statistics published in museum reports and the protests raised in the press over the closure of the national museums, there is little if any evidence relating to the interests and opinions of museum visitors. Why people visited museums and the benefits they derived from their visits remain matters of speculation. Curators, who were best placed to understand museum visitors, rarely wrote or commented on such matters. In the years before the war, museum visitors had had an able champion in Lord Sudeley who valiantly supported the cause of adult education in museums and prompted the national museums to appoint gallery teachers (see Chapter 1). After his death, a committee, under the chairmanship of Lord Northbourne, continued in his name, advocating such developments as the evening opening of the National Gallery and the installation of a lift in the British Museum. Thus 'audience advocacy', making clear the needs and interests of the visitors, appears to have come largely from outside museums and the museums profession before the war and after it.

Curators, in the main, seem to have been content with their distance from the people who visited museums. In November 1919, the *Museums Journal* published a humorous paper on the 'Modern principles of Museums Administration by A. Sinnick'. Reprinted from an American journal, it parodied 'Principles of Museum Administration' written by the secretary of the Smithsonian Institute in Washington, which had received considerable attention, not least in Britain in 1905. Clearly intended as a spoof, a grain of truth about contemporary attitudes to museum work, museums and visitors might be present. The final paragraph reads:

SUGGESTIONS TO VISITORS – No visitor should harbor the delusion that the Director, or for that matter, any member of staff has anything special to do.

Visitors wishing to see the Director on unimportant matters should preferably call about lunch-time or just before he wishes to leave the building. Visitors really desiring information should be treated with silent contempt.

Any visitor not finding on exhibition any object he may wish to see, displayed and labelled as he thinks should be done, is requested to file a complaint with the Trustees.

In most occupations people are supposed to know something about the work in which they are engaged, but with museum work it is different and the less acquaintance one has with museum administration, and the fewer facts he has to interfere with his theories, the better.

Hence the visitor should not hesitate to offer Museum Officers advice – it is stimulating to the visitor and enlightening to the Curator. (*Museums Journal* 19: 80–1)

The paper has to be taken for what it was, a spoof on museum work, written for curators in the United States, willingly published by the *Museums Journal* in Britain. In sum it was deemed suitable, if not acceptable, for a British readership. If from nothing more than what the author chose to ridicule and what he left out, it indicates something about the attitudes at the time: the visitor who took the trouble to seek out a member of staff and ask questions was worthy of the satirist's attention. The visitors who came to museums in their hundreds and thousands and who tried to make sense not only of what was on display, but also of what the museum was for, and who would not have dreamed of 'bothering' the staff, did not get as much as a mention – even in fun. Wartime or not, in jest or not, visitors were largely invisible to the people who ran museums. That people continued to visit museums in significant numbers says a great deal about the attraction of museums and quality of museum collections, regardless of the standard of facilities offered and the relative warmth of the welcome.

CHAPTER 8

LOCAL WAR MUSEUMS

MUSEUM curators, as much as soldiers and statesmen, were slow to appreciate the demands of 'total war'. For the first year of the war, a number of papers published in the *Museums Journal* rang with jingoistic patriotism. Strong on rhetoric, but short of practical ideas, such papers, especially those written by Dr F.A. Bather, established a climate of anxiety about the roles museums might play in the war.

In October 1914, in his paper on 'Museums and National Service', Bather pleaded the cause of museums, arguing that the services they provided, as a matter of course were patriotic. Three months later, Bather passionately defended curators whom he believed 'may be just as good patriots within the walls of our museum as if we had gone on military service' (Bather 1915: 249–53). In these early months of the war, when the expectation was that it would all be over soon, neatly and definitely, such grand but empty prose passed unnoticed. But by the summer of 1915, it would no longer do. It was more than evident that no institution would survive the war solely on the credentials it had built for itself in peacetime. Museums would need to be seen to be contributing to the war effort.

Finding a propaganda role

The direct contributions museums could make were not immediately apparent. Therefore, the Museums Association devoted a morning of its conference in July 1915, to a series of papers examining the museum and the war. The Association invited G.W. Prothero, Vice-President of the Central Committee for National Patriotic Organisation (CCNPO), to speak on its work and advise the Association. At this stage in war, propaganda initiatives were voluntary. The CCNPO had been set up to co-ordinate the various voluntary organizations and its work was not without controversy. It had to be watched closely and at times restrained by the Foreign Office because of the form of its propagandist activities (Sanders and Taylor 1982: 42–3). Nevertheless, it was the most obvious, and maybe the only national patriotic body to which the Museums Association could refer for advice at this time.

Prothero certainly gave the Museums Association conference food for thought. A range of suggestions emerged from the papers and the subsequent discussion: in particular that museums should exhibit war material, and especially 'trophies'. Bather identified four purposes the exhibition of war material could serve: the exemplification of warfare contrary to the laws of nations; an explanation of trench warfare; an illustration and witness to the Germans' cruelty, hate or determination; and an appreciation of the dangers threatening shipping (Bather 1915a: 6).

At the conference, Bather expressed the over-optimistic view that material brought back from the war could be loaned or given to museums. However, it would appear that museum collecting of war material had hitherto been very passive, and the level of donations low. It was to remain so. There were, nevertheless, isolated instances of donations to museums with romantic or heroic connotations, such as the German banner donated to Oldham Museum by the two Oldham soldiers who had captured it (*Museums Journal* 15: 181).

In the main, the collection of war material was random. Leicester Museum is a typical case in point. The first war object accessioned at Leicester Museum was a piece of German shell fired at Scarborough 'between 8 and 8.30 am on the morning of the bombardment'. This was presented by a former Leicester resident and recorded in the accessions register in January 1915. Not until 1918 and 1919 were any significant (albeit few) accessions made to the museum and these came from the War Trophies Committee and the 7th Battalion Leicestershire Regiment.[1]

The exception was London Museum. Sir Guy Laking,[2] who had done so much to establish a viable pattern of collecting for the museum in pre-war years, was prevented from taking an active part in the war because of his failing health. The London Museum was closed, along with the other national museums, in March 1916. Neither his failing health nor a closed museum prevented him acquiring material illustrative of London during the war. This included two bombs, a set of war posters, an air-raid siren, menus from the Savoy Hotel, women's uniforms and a map of London found in a German plane shot down after a raid on the capital (Sheppard 1991: 87).

Several museums managed to put displays together of whatever war material they could muster. Hull Museum in 1915 staged an exhibition of war relics 'of unusual interest at the present time' (*Museums Journal* 15: 150). It included badges, war medals, helmets, fragments of bombs from the east coast Zeppelin raids and one of the first two forgings made in Hull, on 7 August 1915, for a 4.5 high explosive howitzer shell, Mark 5. In the planning of the exhibition, it was hoped that one of the shells in its finished state could also be included.

The subjects of war exhibitions, war memorials and museums as war memorials had been raised in the press and in parliament at various times in the early years of the war. The *Museums Journal* published a number of reports about war collections and war museums in Britain and elsewhere. In its February 1916 edition, it republished a report from *The Times* on how the Admiralty Museum, Petrograd, through the initiative of the Imperial Historical Society, was exhibiting war trophies. In May 1916, it published a report from *Museumskunde* that as early as 1915 special museums for trophies and other objects commemorative of the war had been established in 16 provincial German towns.[3]

The art magazine *Connoisseur*, under the editorship of C. Reginald Grundy (1869–1945), began concerning itself with these and other issues. In the early months of 1915, Grundy had had contact with Charles ffoulkes, Curator of the Royal Armouries. Later in the war, ffoulkes was to be a prime mover on the initiative to found a national war museum and was to become its first secretary. He contributed a paper on Belgian art and culture to *Connoisseur*. Even though this had no bearing whatsoever on the war or museums, it was sufficient to bring him into contact with Grundy and possibly they exchanged ideas. Not long after ffoulkes' paper was published, Grundy wrote and published an article for *Connoisseur* on war memorials, which dealt with their aesthetics (Grundy 1915: 235). A further response on this subject was given in the following edition (Gardner 1915) and several months later Ronald Clewes contributed an article on 'Military curios' (Clewes 1915).

Local war museums: a proposal

The time was ripe for a positive proposal on war museums. This came in an article by Grundy entitled 'Local War Museums', published in the *Connoisseur* in November 1916. It was republished as a pamphlet, *Local War Museums: a Suggestion,* which was widely circulated in the early months of 1917. By this means, Grundy articulated his war museum philosophy and made recommendations on how such museums could be established.

Grundy's proposals centred on the local museum as a memorial to the 'rank and file'. He envisaged a scheme which would keep the events of the Great War fresh in public memory and seize the 'imaginations of posterity'. The material that would be provided should 'enable future generations to visualize the experiences, hopes, fears, disappointments and triumphs of the conflict'. One way of doing this was to establish a war museum in every centre of population. It would contain rolls of honour, records of local regiments and archives of press cuttings and photographs.

Grundy was concerned that a wide variety of material should be collected: uniforms, weapons, medals, decorations, swords 'and other interesting mementoes of the local officers and men who distinguished themselves during the war'. Trophies from the enemy, mementoes of local life during the war, and general relics from previous wars would also have a place. He warned 'nothing should be overlooked' because he saw that even 'illiterate letters from privates at the front giving an insight into their experiences, in 50 years time may be rated as more interesting than official despatches' (Grundy 1917: 11).

It is important to put Grundy's proposals into context. By November 1916, when the article was published, the full impact of the war had bitten deeply into all forms of normal life. Civilian morale was shaken. By the end of 1916, British forces had suffered over one million casualties. On the first day of the Battle of the Somme 20,000 British soldiers had been killed and as many as 40,000 injured. There was a general demand for records of the unprecedented sacrifice and efforts being made, in all their aspects (see Chapter 8). In this atmosphere, proposals for memorials to the 'rank and file' were readily and respectfully received.

Grundy established a committee, mainly of museum curators from the provinces, to promote the formation of local war museums.[4] There is no evidence that the committee ever met. Indeed, there is much to suggest that Grundy was the driving force and sole operator throughout, using both the notion of a formal 'committee' (and the obvious goodwill for his ideas) as a means of putting his plans into action. The press covered his ideas well, and on 20 February 1917, a question about local war museums was raised at the House of Commons by Sir C. Kinlock-Cooke, MP. Bonar-Law replied for the Government, pointing out that the local war museum scheme had not been adopted officially and was a matter for local negotiation: a seemingly indifferent response.

Less than two weeks later, however, on 5 March 1917, the formation of a National War Museum (NWM) was approved by the War Cabinet. One of the five groups of items on a list of reasons for the museum's formation in 'these strenuous times', given later in a confidential note from Commander Walcott, the representative of the Admiralty on the National War Museum Committee, was that 'local museums and local bodies are collecting and the necessity for a central organization to retrieve and decide on articles of national importance'.[5]

The first National War Museum Committee meeting took place on 29 March 1917. One of its considerations was the relationship with Grundy and his 'organization'. The movement for local war museums was perceived as a difficulty, even a possible threat to the newly formed National War Museum. It would have to be handled with care. The chairman of the NWM Committee, Sir Alfred Mond, MP (First Commissioner of Works), suggested that Sir Guy Laking, the King's Armourer and highly regarded Curator of the London Museum should be co-opted to act on behalf of the local museums.

However, Ian Malcolm MP successfully argued that 'difficulties on this score might arise'[6] if such a co-option was made. What these difficulties were is not made clear in the minutes. Laking was very ill at this time. But even so, he was very able and influential. These may not have been the qualities the NWM Committee wanted in a representative of the local war museums. Another approach was adopted.

In the following week, Sir Alfred Mond met Grundy at the House of Commons.[7] They discussed how the National War Museum and local museums might help each other by collecting and interchanging exhibits. Mond suggested that Grundy's committee should ask the Lord Mayor of London to call a meeting at the Mansion House to discuss a proposal that local museums should only act with the National War Museum as their intermediary. Grundy may well have construed this as a positive suggestion. It was, however, also a means through which the NWM could ensure always having the upper-hand in the formation of collections.

The Lord Mayor was persuaded and a meeting of the Metropolitan Boroughs was called on 22 May 1917 (*Museums Journal* 17: 272–3). By this time, the plans for the National War Museum were well advanced and it had been agreed by its committee that Sir Alfred Mond address this meeting and formally put to it the claims of the National War Museum.[8] In his address, he gave broad support to the local museum project, but made it quite clear that the National War Museum would have every priority with regard to relics and trophies from the war.

Local War Museums Association

Not to be put off, the meeting approved the formation of a new organization, the Local War Museums Association (LWMA), with a confusing hierarchy and power structure – sufficient to ensure that Grundy could keep control of the project. An executive committee was established, with power to add to its number and authority to appoint a general council and a museums committee. A list of adherents was drawn up from the local authority representatives and curators.[9] It is not clear if they ever met. The executive committee superseded Grundy's committee of curators and consisted of the Earl of Plymouth, Chairman; Sir Clement Kinlock-Cooke, MP, Hon. Treasurer; Field Marshal Viscount French; Admiral Lord Beresford; Lord Burnham; E. Rimbault Dibdin, Walker Art Gallery, Liverpool and President of the Museums Association; Sir Cecil Harcourt-Smith, Director of the Victoria and Albert Museum; and Sir Whitworth Wallis, Director of Birmingham City Museum and Art Gallery (*Museums Journal* 17: 272). The Association was to be funded by subscription. One of the executive committee's first acts was to publish and circulate a prospectus of the LWMA's aims and objectives.[10] The wildly over-optimistic nature of the enterprise and the uncertain nature of the association's funding were quite evident from this publication.

In May, the National War Museum Committee, on Grundy's prompting, co-opted Sir Whitworth Wallis as a representative of the Local War Museums Association.[11] However, the Committee agreed he was to be informed only of the meetings where subjects dealing with local museums were to be discussed. He was asked to give notice of any proposals he had to submit. Moreover, the Chairman ruled that his expenses 'should be borne by the Local Museums Committee as he was their representative'. The National War Museum thus ensured the LWMA could be kept at arms' length. Whitworth Wallis, perhaps insufficiently briefed, found himself in a very difficult position. He wrote several times to Charles ffoulkes to ask for committee papers, wondering whether he might not have been sent them because of a 'paper shortage'. In all, those involved with the National War Museum were not interested in the local war museums. Sir Martin Conway, the NWM's Director, in September 1917 made it clear in a letter to Colonel F.S.W. Cornwallis, that he viewed war museums, such as those in Italy, as being deadly dull, of interest to nobody and a burden on the institutions they encumbered.[12]

In this penultimate phase of the war, the strain of total war, rationing and firmer restrictions on travel led to a grim resignation and tired determination. There was little truck with wild ideas; all effort was needed in terms of what was practical and immediate. By now, people just wanted the war over with. The development of the LWMA's grand plans was stifled. At the Museums Association's annual business meeting in July 1917, the chairman of LWMA, the Earl of Plymouth, announced that the proposed Museums Committee would not be formed, because of the problems of calling together such a meeting (*Museums Journal* 17: 17–27). A difficult and, in places, acrimonious discussion followed in which many museum curators, perhaps more disillusioned than disappointed, participated.[13] There was agreement that people were 'too busily engaged trying to win the war to spend time in recording it' and that there were 'difficulties of travelling and inabilities of bodies to send representatives'. But serious concern about the absence of curatorial expertise in the development of the scheme was expressed.

Nine days later, the question of local war museums was raised again at a meeting of the National War Museum Committee. French and Beresford (members of the LWMA Executive Committee) had separately canvassed the Admiralty and the War Office for relics and trophies for the local war museums. Their representations were sent on to the National War Museum Committee, who in turn refused to deal with them on the grounds that the appropriate channels had not been used.[14]

In October, Whitworth Wallis wrote to ffoulkes with the observation that the LWMA did not seem to be making much headway and there had not been a meeting for some time. Perhaps with the aim of bringing the matter to a head, a conference on the subjects of local war museums and the educational value of museums was organized by E. Howarth, Curator of Sheffield Museum and Graves Art Gallery, and took place in Sheffield on 16 and 17 October 1917.[15] The conference was important because it gave curators and institutional representatives an opportunity to examine and consider the subjects in detail. It was neither addressed, nor attended, by a representative of the executive committee of the Local War Museums Association, although Sir Whitworth Wallis did send a letter.

The discussion touched on a range of matters including: the use of huts for housing museums; war museums on every village green; the organization of the museums, whether to vest this in a local club or society; current war collections being amassed at Salford and Wednesbury museums; problems of already congested collections; and funding.

The proposed philosophy of local war museums was considered by H. Bolton,[16] Director of Bristol Museum and Art Gallery, who argued that a war museum should aim to show 'what were the greatest stresses and dangers ever experienced by the British Empire', and to illustrate 'the way in which they were met and overcome'. Bolton also warned that

> since the present is itself the product of the evils of a deliberate glorification of military and naval aims and lust for power, war museums must not seek to exalt war, but rather show what war means in natural and personal loss, in devastation, and in reversion to barbaric standards.

Furthermore, Bolton cautioned against glorying over the enemy as 'for some day passion will die, and what we bring together must be viewed in the cold light of reason' (in Howarth 1918: 77).

How the conference report was received by the LWMA or the Museums Association is not recorded in either the *Museums Journal* or *Connoisseur*. The only mention the conference proceedings received in the *Museums Journal* was a short and rather disdainful review (*Museums Journal* 18: 85). Some measure of the interest in the proceedings is given in the number of copies of the proceedings sold: 1,300.

Plans for local war museums did, however, progress. In January 1918, Grundy placed a new set of proposals for the administration of a local war museum scheme before the Museums Association (*Museums Journal* 17: 99–100). The basis of these was that the country should be divided into 14 or 15 administrative areas, each with its own subcommittee. Grundy hoped to get all towns interested in the scheme, whether they already had a museum or not. Grundy announced that he already had a suggested list of representatives based on his correspondence with museums. He submitted that in this he was better able to judge than the Museums Association.

In 1918, the last year of the war, large collections had been amassed by, or earmarked for, the now 'Imperial' War Museum. The apparent support of the Government and the IWM channels of operation had ensured that their collecting proceeded efficiently and comprehensively. At the Imperial War Museum Committee's meeting on 14 February 1918, the question of collecting trophies was discussed. Apart from trophies collected for the museum by its designated officers 'all trophies would be collected by the Naval and Military Authorities and the first choice would be given to the Imperial War Museum'. After this, they would be distributed to local war museums as required, 'provided they were not needed for service purposes'.[17] The local war museums would therefore be at the end of the queue.

The LWMA had to find some means of securing relics and trophies from the war. In the summer of 1918, it was able to announce that Lieut-Colonel Sir Arthur Leetham, Director of the Royal United Services Institution (RUSI), had consented to act as chairman of the new Museums Committee. Not only did Sir Arthur have the experience of directing the RUSI museum, but also had a barely concealed grudge against the IWM proposals which had not enabled him to secure a prominent place for his own institution (ffoulkes 1939: 96–7). Most significantly, he was a member of the War Trophies Committee of the War Office (and, in time, a member of the IWM committee). Published along with the announcement of his appointment were yet more complicated and confusing details about the LWMA's proposals for the new museum committee, its structure and network. Regardless of the position being held by the IWM, the LWMA was anticipating that a great deal of material would be available for redistribution by its new museum committee.

Sir Arthur put together notes to be used as a guide to curators and others in forming collections of 'War Trophies, Relics etc.' These formed the basis of his address to the Museum Committee of the LWMA on 14 November 1918, three days after Armistice, and were subsequently published (Leetham 1918). He advised that there were many claims on the War Trophies Committee and the issue of 'relics and trophies' to the local war museums would not be straightforward. Delays were inevitable. Therefore, Sir Arthur recommended that local museums should contact the Commanding Officers of their county and local units to help substantiate claims. The LWMA's Museum Committee was given the assurance that, in spite of delays, there would be 'plenty of trophies to satisfy everyone'. Sir Arthur went on to give a list of 30 enemy trophies suitable for a local war museum, with instructions as to the applications procedure.

He laid great stress on every museum having a specimen of a Minenwerfer, it is a murderous weapon and utterly regardless of the Geneva Convention, being a wooden cylinder some 5 feet in length and 10 inch calibre, bound with stout wire; it was used in trench warfare, filled by a small charge of explosive and discharged a varied collection of old pieces of iron, nuts, bolts, nails, stones, flint and otherwise, and a variety of other missiles.

Table 5 The list of 'enemy trophies' Sir Arthur Leetham believed would be suitable for a local war museum.

1	Field Gun 77mm or
2	88mm
3	Finenwerfer
4	Granatenwerfer
5	Trench morter, 75mm
6	Trench morter, 90mm
7	Trench morter 170mm
8	Machine gun, Sledge Mt
9	Machine gun, Parallelum
10	Machine gun, Marsden
11	Machine gun, Austrian
12	Rifle and bayonet, German
13	Rifle and bayonet, Austrian
14	Rifle and bayonet, Turkish
15	Rifle and bayonet, Bulgarian
16	Rifle grenade stand
17	Sniper's shield
18	French clubs (various)
19	Body armour
20	Packs, skin
21	Packs, canvas
22	Set of equipment
23	Set of entrenching tools
24	Very light pistols
25	Revolver
26	Trench knives
27	Trench helmets
28	Swords
29	Leather helmets
30	Badges (regimental)

Note: He advised that museums requiring items 1–24 should apply to the War Office Trophies Committee. If the item required was captured by a local unit, the museum should also get in touch with them and ask that the museum's interest be communicated to the War Trophies Committee. Leetham believed museums could obtain items 25–29 from returned Expeditionary Force men, 'and would be of more interest if connected with an action in which a local unit took part'. For badges (item 30) museums should approach the Royal Army Clothing Department Pimlico. Leetham was conscious of at least one aspect of museum collecting, on items 1,2 and 3 he advised that 'if the museum is small, only one should be asked for, on account of space'.

Sir Arthur also suggested that every local museum should have models of trenches, tanks, guns, aircraft and anti-aircraft guns. As for navy exhibits, the advice was to take the matter up with the Admiralty, as there was no naval relic committee. The Ministry of Munitions should be approached for 'shells, bombs, grenades, etc.' No mention was made of the Royal Flying Corps, by 1918, the Royal Air Force. The 'most interesting war relics', Sir Arthur believed, were those of personal interest. He also urged museums to collect the personal property of officers and soldiers,

> after a little interval numbers of these will be easily obtained, and the men will look with pride at their names being recorded as the donor in their local museum, a part which should be carefully seen to, as also in cataloguing and describing such exhibits, especially in obtaining the correct account of where and how they were obtained and the date recorded. (Leetham 1918: 96)

The discussion which followed the address had considerable importance (*Museums Journal* 18: 114–20). The majority of speakers were directors or curators of national or provincial museums whose views had not been fully heard or articulated in earlier debates.[18] Caution was sounded for the selection of objects on proper principles: the ephemeral features of war should not be exaggerated. A warning was given against involving museums in intolerable expenditure, thus paralysing existing services. Moreover, it was felt that the roles of science and art museums should not be duplicated. The idea of a museum as a memorial was also explored. It was felt that the standards achieved in these war museums should not discredit the dead. Charles Madeley, Curator of Warrington Museum, whose only son Benton had been killed the previous year, expressed the opinion, 'A "Memorial Museum" would be judged as a museum. If it were a good museum, that would justify its existence and the memorial aspect of it would be soon forgotten'.

The Museum Committee, on the evidence of the report of this meeting, had at last brought to the Local War Museums Association the experience it so badly needed. Largely prevented from meeting hitherto, it had much that it needed to convey. The message the museum curators had to give the LWMA, at this meeting at least, was that war museums should only be tackled if they could be done thoroughly and well, and not at the expense of other types of museum activity. The report of the meeting was the last occasion the *Museums Journal* published any matter referring to local war museums. No mention of the LWMA was made in the minutes of the Imperial War Museum's Committee minutes after 11 July 1918.

Local initiatives and alternative approaches

In spite of all the difficulties involved, a number of towns were willing to make plans for a war museum. Charles ffoulkes at the Imperial War Museum received a number of letters of enquiry in 1918 including ones from the town councils in Hammersmith, Scarborough, Guildford, Dundee and Lowestoft. He advised them to contact the Local War Museums Association.

With the end of hostilities, the whole notion of war museums, especially war museums as memorials, was drastically revised at local level. The sheer cost alone of providing and equipping new buildings for them was more than the local authorities could bear. For example, Howarth estimated that Sheffield's War Museum would require a building with five galleries of 90ft x 30ft each and a vacant space 30ft wide round the whole building for outside exhibits. His detailed proposals for the museum were submitted to his committee on 13 February 1919. By May of the same year, it was obvious that not only would there be no money for such proposals, but also that a requested supplementary grant of £300 for existing services might not be forthcoming. By July, the Museums Committee agreed to make no further contributions to the Local War Museums Association and the proposals for a war museum in Sheffield were quietly dropped.[19]

Museums that memorialized the war through its own destructive hardware could not find public support. Instead, cities, towns and villages commemorated their dead either through dignified war memorials erected in prominent positions, so that all would see and remember, or through community facilities such as parks, halls and recreation grounds. Many felt that life itself should be celebrated and enjoyed, in the memory of those who gave their own.

The War Office's War Trophies Committee distributed relics of the war to those museums still interested. However, the relics and trophies it offered frequently had little, if anything, to do with local regiments or the part an area had played in the war. Small collections of war relics were amassed by a number of museums, only to be gradually disposed of in subsequent years. For example, at Leicester Museum, a large proportion of the war collection was surrendered to the police in 1939, the rest was found to be missing during a check held in 1951.[20] The War Trophies Committee managed to off-load some of their rusting guns and tanks to public parks, where they remained during the inter-war years until either being scrapped or 're-enlisted' in 1939. As for the Local War Museums Association, the most it appeared to offer museums was a distribution of brass 'Christmas boxes'.[21] Museums gradually disassociated themselves from the idea of war museums and from the LWMA. The latter eventually folded, a predictable end to an organization that had been weighed down by grandiose ideas, unstable committee structures and lack of funds.

The lack of war museums in the provinces, in spite of the genuinely felt though short-lived interest in war exhibitions and war collections, was redressed by a series of travelling exhibitions of material from the IWM collections. In 1918, the Treasury borrowed paintings and war trophies from the museum and organized a number of successful exhibitions. These raised money for war charities or publicized the War Savings Campaign. No statistics were kept of attendances as demonstrations and meetings usually accompanied the exhibitions.

The IWM formed an exhibition of 600 objects from its collections, 'War Trophies, Relics, Posters and Photographs', which toured nine provincial centres,[22] between June 1918 and April 1919, stopping at each for one month. Some of the attendances were recorded.[23] At Manchester 60,000 visits were made to the exhibition in the month of August 1918 and at Nottingham, in February 1919, the figure was 42,000. At the opening of an exhibition from the Imperial War Museum at Nottingham Castle Museum in February 1919, Alderman J.E. Pendleton advised the public not to spoil the Exhibition on a Sunday by hopelessly congesting the galleries (*Nottingham Daily Journal and Express*, 26 February 1919). The IWM estimated that the exhibitions loaned to the provincial centres were visited by over 300,000 people. Twelve smaller exhibitions were issued to 75 towns and villages.[24]

Birmingham's war museum

The fate of local war museums is evident in the study of the Birmingham War Museum. Birmingham Museum and Art Gallery was the largest and most prestigious museum to involve itself actively with the prospect of a local war museum. Sir Whitworth Wallis as a member of the executive committee of the LWMA and its representative on the National War Museum Committee must have felt some obligation to put the Local War Museums Association's ideas into practice in Birmingham.

On 11 October 1917, Birmingham City Council 'warmly' approved the proposal to form a war memorial museum. The Lord Mayor, Alderman A.D. Brooks, presided over the meeting which was attended by the Earl of Plymouth, Chairman of the Local War Museums Association and Lord Beresford (*Birmingham Daily Post* 12 October 1917). The Lord Mayor, in a speech supporting the proposal, outlined the reasons for the museum and the types of material it would seek to collect. He felt it would be particularly appropriate that Birmingham should establish a war museum 'because they were very proud of the part the city had played in regard to recruiting for the Army and Navy'.

Objects which illustrated the part Birmingham had played in the war, particularly objects associated with local units, voluntary and charity work, war manufactures, and work done by women would be collected. A Roll of Honour would be preserved in perpetuity. The Lord Mayor urged that the collecting should begin immediately. As for funding, he clearly hoped for donations as he believed 'they would be able to carry on with a small sum of money'. The possibility of a special building for the collection was not ruled out, but this was only by means of suggestion 'because the future character and scope of the collection must wait until a more favourable time arrived for considering it'. The proposal was supported by the Earl of Plymouth, Lord Beresford, the Bishop of Birmingham and Alderman Gaunt. A general committee was established.

Just over a month later, on 17 November, three days after attending the meeting of the Local War Museums Association at which Sir Arthur Leetham had given his 'Notes for Curators' address, Sir Whitworth Wallis, now Honorary Director of the Birmingham War Museum, published an article in the *Birmingham Gazette*. He explained in it the work of the Local War Museums Association and described how he envisaged Birmingham's War Museum. He concluded '... such a collection suitably arranged would become a local Valhalla and there is no memorial to our honoured dead which would be more popular, more instructive, or more appreciated'. He produced proposals for a committee structure not dissimilar from that of the Imperial War Museum, with sub-committees responsible for collecting in areas such as hospitals and ambulances, women's work, and munitions.

Enthusiasm for the War Museum was such that it appeared in a detailed set of plans for the re-development of the centre of Birmingham, published with the support of Neville Chamberlain in 1918. However, the architect concerned, William Haywood, was far more enthusiastic about building a People's Hall and pleasure gardens, and improving New Street Station, than he was about a war museum and memorial. He was cautious in the extreme about the idea, claiming: 'it will be remarkable if we escape from the confusion of thought which has brought so many of our attempts in this direction to nothing' (Haywood, 1918: 23).

By January 1919, the vision had faded. In a report to the Birmingham War Museum Committee, Sir Whitworth gave a résumé of work to date on the war museum scheme. Using guarded tones, carefully avoiding a totally negative approach, Sir Whitworth explained that progress had been slow. The museum building would cost at least £40,000–£50,000; the minimum budget for initial equipment would be £7,000, possibly £10,000. Costs were also given for models, photographs and glass cases. He went on: 'from the meagre response to the appeal which was issued last year, though only for preliminary expenses, the idea of a Local War Museum has not the support it deserves'.[25] He concluded by pointing out that there were other ways of honouring the dead and that if the museum idea could not be done adequately and properly 'we had better abandon the idea and gather together such fragments as can be occasionally exhibited as circumstances permit, in the Art Gallery and in one of the parks'.

Eight years later, the material collected by Sir Whitworth Wallis for the museum was the subject of an article in the *Birmingham Gazette*. Appearing on 11 November 1927, the article had the title 'City's dusty war relics: what will be done with them: Grim reminders'. Giving the background to the proposed war museum, the article explained that as a consequence of a campaign initiated by the *Birmingham Gazette*, the City had decided that its war memorial should take another form and thus had abandoned the museum idea. Since that time the collections had been held in a store room. The reporter described them thus:

> About this little room in a corner of Birmingham's Art Gallery there is a strange, depressing air of unreality. Around it, in the galleries, are massed the treasures of the creative artists of many lands and many centuries. But in this little three-cornered den there is nothing but the rusting dusty relics of destruction and poor pathetic reminders in cloth and metal and bloodstains of a host of broken lives.

He went on to analyse the purpose of a war museum as an 'attempt to confine the drama, the tragedy, the self-sacrifice, the agony and the gigantic folly to a glass case, with exhibits that rend the heart, coldly labelled in precise official English'. He concluded with the hope that the collection would not be used to establish a war museum.

CHAPTER 9

PROPOSALS FOR A
NATIONAL WAR MUSEUM

On 5 March 1917, the War Cabinet gave formal approval for the foundation of a Museum of the War. Initially called the National War Museum and known after January 1918 as the Imperial War Museum, it came to house an extraordinary archive of objects, documents, paintings and oral testimony. Its collections are, without doubt, the most telling record of the war. In Western Europe, the museum is without parallel. Its foundation has to be considered principally in two contexts: first, a willingness shared across class boundaries for the conflict to be chronicled and remembered; and secondly, the particular circumstances in which the War Cabinet decision of 5 March 1917 was taken.

Records, mementoes, memories and propaganda

A preparedness, even a predisposition, to keep some form of record of the war was evident from its early stages. The war was presented to the British public in such a way that its prosecution was fundamentally bound up with the protection of the essential values of nation and nationhood. Civilian morale hinged on the justice of the cause. With everyone disconnecting their peacetime lives and playing their wartime part, a sense of common purpose and joint endeavour developed. Whether at the Front, factory or farm, there was a very strong awareness of the magnitude of the event. People were prepared to sacrifice and endure but there was an expectation that the sacrifice and endurance would not be in vain and that they would be remembered.

The collective memory was proudly kept. Rolls of Honour were established in streets, homes and workplaces. As the years progressed, these took the form of shrines (Grundy 1917: 8). Not only did they record the names of enlisted or conscripted men but also the names of the dead. The lists of names were sometimes decorated with regimental insignia, candles, flowers, press-cuttings and mementoes.

The chronicle of the war was built up as the years wore on. The newspapers, especially those which orientated themselves to pictorial features, increased their circulation significantly (Marwick 1965: 146–7). The news

19. Rolls of Honour were erected in many offices, factories and streets. They listed
the names of men serving in the forces and in time took the form of shrines.
Source: The First World War, A Photographic History, Daily Express Publications, 1933

the papers contained was, if not heavily censored, then at least 'managed', a fact known at the time (Knightley 1982: 83). Daily newspapers produced maps, diaries of the war and accounts of first-hand experiences. Local papers printed the casualty lists of both officers and men. After the initial period, the national press, such as *The Times*, found space only for lists of officer casualties. People kept the editions that held interest for them: cuttings of campaigns, casualty lists containing the names of loved ones and friends. They formed part of their own chronicle of the war.

War books became hugely popular at this time. The obvious example was the work of John Buchan. In 1915, Buchan's novel *The Thirty-Nine Steps* was published, followed in the next year by *Greenmantle* (Harries 1983: 21). This was all stirring stuff and set the tone for a whole genre of war literature. Buchan was also involved with Nelson's *History of the War,* which he initiated and substantially wrote. Both the adventure stories and the history found a ready and increasing market. People wanted both.

The Government's agency, Wellington House, contributed to the wealth of material available - especially pictorial. Established to influence opinion abroad, a proportion of its material became available for home consumption. Wellington House was under the astute leadership of C.F. Masterman, until February 1917 when it became part of the new Department of Information under John Buchan. Believing in the need for quality work, Masterman had assembled a youthful team of journalists, writers, academics and civil servants. Reproductions of official documents and speeches, pamphlets, books, news sheets and periodicals were published (without a Government imprint) by Wellington House, the annual output 'totalled between ten and twenty million items' (Harries 1983: 6).

By 1915, Masterman was ready to recognize the importance of visual images. *Britain Prepared*, the first propaganda film, was issued to electric cinemas and picture houses throughout Britain in the autumn. Pictures, maps and photographs were more frequently seen in the popular press. In April 1916, Wellington House was sufficiently confident of the value of pictorial propaganda to establish a pictorial section, which published the periodical *War Pictorial*, dependent on photographs from the Front. The results were staggering. Masterman commented 'the enormous circulation of pictorial papers reveals, as much as the crowds at the cinematographs, that there are millions of voters who will not read the letterpress but from whom the demand for war pictures is unlimited' (quoted in Harries 1983: 7).

However, since there were too few photographers at the front and their range of subjects was limited by both the censor and the circumstances of war, there was a case for supplementing the photographs available with line drawings. Masterman took the bold decision to use cartoonists and artists rather than illustrators. He knew that the relatively new range of printing techniques would make the reproduction of art work a much more viable proposition than it had ever been and he was also aware that art could have a potentially stronger impact than photography.

Masterman had working with him at Wellington House a number of eminent figures from the art world, who gave him every encouragement. His colleagues at the time included: Eric Maclagan, later Director of the Victoria and Albert Museum; Campbell Dodgson, Keeper of Prints and Drawings at the British Museum; Thomas Derrick, an artist and teacher from the Royal College of Art; and Arthur Yockney, previous Editor of the *Art Journal* (Harries 1983: 7).

There had been growing agitation in artistic and society circles for artists to be sent to record the experience of being at the Front. The popular success of paintings, particularly Eric Kennington's *The Kensington at Laventie* appeared to justify their arguments. The first war artist, Muirhead Bone, accepted his appointment on 15 July 1916. He was to be followed by many others, including C.R.W. Nevinson, Paul Nash and William Orpen. The idea of recording the war through art gathered momentum. When Wellington House was subsumed into the Department of Information, the commitment to the art collection was renewed. And when the Department was itself upgraded to a Ministry, it established the British War Memorials Committee which continued to commission works. Much use was made of the paintings and drawings produced, in publications and exhibitions. The collection, now held by the Imperial War Museum, formed a vivid and powerful record of the war.

Other forms of propaganda and information-gathering further stimulated the need to record and remember. In 1915, John Buchan, who was being employed by the Foreign Office at the time, suggested that every regiment should have its own official historian. Literary figures of the calibre of George Bernard Shaw and John Masefield were sent to prepare eye-witness accounts of the Front. In addition there were other initiatives: for example, the Royal Army Medical Corps established a Committee for the Medical History of the War.

In a similar spirit, the Canadian War Records Office had been founded in 1916 by Sir Max Aitken (later Lord Beaverbrook and, from February 1918, Minister of Information). Aitken had been records officer since 1915 and had made tremendous progress. He was able to convince the authorities that the amount of material available warranted a more formal organization. Once established, the Canadian War Records Office, based in London, collected regimental unit war diaries and whatever British material related to Canadian actions. It also collected a wide range of other material including film, paintings, photographs and memorabilia, maps and private accounts. Aitken believed that the non-written material would give 'a more, truthful, and lasting impression than can be done by the written word' (McKernan 1991:37).

The Canadian efforts to make a war record did not stand alone. Charles Bean, Australia's Official War Correspondent, had witnessed some of the worst of the action at Gallipoli and Pozières. He had developed a great affection and high regard for the Australian troops, and was conscious of the individual efforts of the Australian soldiers to keep mementoes of their experiences. He began to canvass opinion at home and at the Australian High Commission in London for some form of war museum and war records office. In May 1917, the Australian War Records Section was established 'in the interests of national history of Australia and in order that Australia may have control of her own historical records' (quoted in McKernan 1991: 37). The officer-in-charge was Lieutenant John Treloar. He came to London to work closely with Bean and in time would be the first Director of the Australian War Memorial, which was to have collections twice the size of the Imperial War Museum. In 1918, the spur to the formation of a collection for such a museum was the refusal of the British to give adequate recognition to Australian achievements in France. There was every possibility that, unless formal action was taken by the Australians, their war record would exist only in the national war museum in London, where 'a less prominent role than justice deserved' would be given to Australian efforts (McKernan 1991: 40).

The political moment

A review of the political events of the period leading up to the decision to found a British war museum suggests that in Cabinet circles the support for the museum was given not necessarily because such a record would be right and just, although there were those who felt that this was true, but because a museum was a means of promoting the war and strengthening the war mood. The formal decision was taken by the War Cabinet. However, the generation of the original idea came not from those who were either witnessing or experiencing the fighting first-hand, as was the case with the Australian initiative, but from politicians and enthusiasts at home.

On 5 March 1917, the War Cabinet agreed to an outline proposal from Sir Alfred Mond MP, First Commissioner of Works, for the formation of a committee to establish a national war museum. The date and timing of this decision is significant. In the final months of 1916, a carefully co-ordinated campaign resulted in the political coup which toppled Asquith as Prime Minister and replaced him with a very willing David Lloyd George. The new Prime Minister wasted no time in trimming and redefining Cabinet structure, establishing new departments and re-organizing old ones.

Lloyd George sought and effected the re-direction and re-organization of

the war effort. He was in no doubt about the importance of opinion forming. He recognized that morale was low especially as a result of the high
number of casualties at the Somme. Furthermore, submarine warfare was
affecting food supplies. Enthusiasm in recruiting campaigns had waned and
there were popular fears of yet another year of war. Something had to be
done to re-focus the nation on the war effort and convince people that the
war was worthwhile. Propaganda, therefore, became an integral part of the
Prime Minister's 'total war' policy (Sanders and Taylor 1982: 66).

Only ten days after his appointment, Lloyd George received from the War
Office a summary of criticisms of the propaganda effort, in particular the
work of Wellington House.[1] As a result, on 19 February 1917, two weeks
before the National War Museum decision was taken, Wellington House was
superseded by a Department of Information. The Department's functions
were to include propaganda at home, a responsibility its predecessor did not
have.

It has been questioned whether the National War Museum was part of a
much larger initiative on propaganda, aimed at combating war weariness
(Harries 1983: 118). It coincided not only with the formation of the new
Department of Information, but also, ten weeks later, the National War Aims
Committee. A war museum could after all be used as a focus for patriotism.
If this argument is accepted and it seems very plausible, then the formation
of a National War Museum was dictated by immediate 'operational factors',
not long-term altruism. After all, Mond was suggesting a relatively inexpen-
sive enterprise, requiring only £3,000 to fund it. In political circles, therefore, the war museum may well have been born not out of any anxiety to
record and remember, but of an anxiety to maintain the war mood at all
costs.

A far more pragmatic version of the reasons for founding a war museum
in 'these strenuous times' appears in a note written by Commander Walcott,
the Admiralty's representative on the National War Museum Committee, on
6 May 1917, to the Assistant Secretary of the Admiralty Board, D. Murray.
This was a response to the Admiralty Board's criticism that the whole scheme
was premature. Walcott's list of reasons were:

1. Relics and exhibits etc. were being overlooked and in some cases irretrievably
   lost.
2. Other relics etc. were being bought, stolen or obtained by local units and private
   persons and some have been sent to USA.
3. Local museums and local bodies are collecting and [there is a] necessity for a
   control organization to retain and decide on articles of national importance.
4. Whilst the country is organized, the difficulties of obtaining exhibits, relics etc.
   are more easily overcome.
5. If postponed until the end of the war the difficulties of collecting articles of
   national worth would be very difficult.

6. There is reason to suppose that if the Government had not taken the matter up, a certain paper would have commenced subscriptions and much complicated matters.[2]

These reasons for initiating the museum were expressed two months after its inception and have to be viewed in the light of Walcott's having to justify the museum to a rather unsympathetic Admiralty Board: hence the pragmatism.

Forming the idea and the museum

At the outbreak of war, the only institution in existence which had a policy of collecting and preserving the relics, records and trophies of previous wars was the Royal United Services Institute. Curiously, it took no initiative in making a record of the war. Instead, the idea of a national war museum seems to have come about through a combination of individual initiatives, one of which came from Charles ffoulkes, Curator of the Tower Armouries. In his autobiography, published in 1939 after his retirement, ffoulkes claimed to have considered at this time that the Armouries should deal with 'the war material of the present, as it had dealt with the war equipment of the past' (ffoulkes 1939: 85–6). To this end, in 1915 he had made a few, very minor acquisitions of war material.

As Curator of the Tower Armouries, ffoulkes was employed by the Ministry of Works, which in the December 'coup' had passed from Lord Harcourt to the highly competent but controversial figure of Sir Alfred Mond. As ffoulkes claimed some acquaintance with Harcourt, it was to him he made his approach. A meeting took place at Harcourt's home on 7 February 1917, when ffoulkes attempted to stake a claim for his institution receiving war material. Harcourt was receptive to the idea and advised ffoulkes on some of the political and administrative difficulties that could be expected.[3] Harcourt particularly advised ffoulkes to encourage the press to take up the subject. Having informed Sir Lionel Earle, his superior at the Ministry of Works, of his meeting with Harcourt and given an outline of his suggestion, ffoulkes arranged to see Walters of *The Times* on 12 February.

Walters was willing to publish a short article which had been written in the previous year by ffoulkes on the reorganization of Tower Armouries, much of which had taken place in the immediate pre-war years. The article was very vague in its intent. It contained no explicit suggestion that a National War Museum should be formed, although it did comment on the few war items on display at the Tower (*The Times*, 15 February 1917). On 20 February 1917, *The Times* published another article, presumably from Ian Malcolm MP, on the war museum established privately by M. LeBlanc in Paris. This concluded with a suggestion that objects and memorabilia from the war should be collected and preserved, but for what purpose was not made clear. The next day *The Times* published an article by ffoulkes, with the agreement of Sir Lionel Earle, which suggested that a war museum should be formed in the precinct of the Tower.

In the meantime, Ian Malcolm, later to be on the National War Museum Committee, was building support for his suggestion. On the day of publication, 20 February, he wrote to Harcourt asking for his backing, and to Lord Curzon asking for both backing and a luncheon appointment to discuss the matter further.[4] He also wrote to Lord Stamfordham, the Queen's Private Secretary asking whether specimens of the Christmas gifts given by the Queen and Princess Mary to the troops in 1914, 1915 and 1916 could be made available to a National War Collection.[5]

However, it was the approach made by Harcourt to Sir Alfred Mond MP, First Commissioner of Works, that yielded the most effective results. Mond had both the power and position to take the idea further. On 27 February, Mond addressed a memorandum to the Prime Minister on the subject of a National War Museum.[6] He saw the immediate task as the collection of material 'which can be stored, if necessary until the end of the war'. He suggested a small grant of £3,000 from the Treasury 'to cover purchases, where gifts are not available, and any running expenses for secretarial and record work'. The War Cabinet approved this proposal on 5 March 1917 and authorized:

> The First Commission of Works, subject to the concurrence of the Admiralty, War Office, and Ministry of Munitions, to proceed with the formation of the following Committee proposed by him:

> First Commissioner of Works (Chairman, ex officio)
> A Director-General
> A representative of the Admiralty
> A representative of the War Office
> A representative of Minister of Munitions
> A representative of the Literary and Art side of the question
> An Honorary Secretary

> The Secretary of the War Cabinet to put himself in communication with the Admiralty, War Office and Ministry of Munitions in reference to this subject.[7]

Confusion over the management and control of the museum followed (Evans 1966; ffoulkes 1939). When ffoulkes called on Harcourt on 12 March, the latter clearly was hoping that the museum would be under the Office of Works with himself as Director General and Sir Guy Laking, King's Armourer and Curator of London Museum, as Assistant Director. The next day ffoulkes called again on Harcourt and was offered the post of Secretary to the museum, with offices at Lancaster House. He accepted in writing. However, on 14 March, he was stopped from making any further arrangements. Harcourt informed him that he could not take the appointment of Director General as it would involve him serving under his successor at the Ministry of Works, Sir Alfred Mond, who would now be Chairman of the Committee.

ffoulkes was again offered the post of Secretary on 15 March at a salary of £200, in addition to his salary at the Armouries. He accepted, but was later advised by Harcourt that the present arrangement had not been passed by the War Cabinet. However, ffoulkes did take up his appointment, on 17 March 1917. He may have been confused by all of this, but was perhaps not unaware that there had been a power struggle between Mond and Harcourt for the appointment of director general. Although Harcourt, since Asquith's resignation, was serving on the back benches he still wielded power and influence. His successor, Mond, was keen to see Sir Martin Conway (mountaineer, explorer, Slade Professor of Art at Cambridge, and author) in the position of Director General. Conway had seen Mond on a totally different matter on 23 January 1917 (Evans 1966: 227). This may have kept him fresh in Mond's mind when the appointment was under consideration. On 21 March, Conway noted in his diary: 'called on Alfred Mond. He says unless Lord Harcourt insists on having the post he will invite me to be director general of the proposed Museum of the War'[8] Harcourt appears to have been able to get the influential Curzon on his side. The matter ended when Mond secured the crucial support of Lloyd George, who approved of Sir Martin Conway's appointment: 'It seems to me an admirable appointment. But I suggest you give him a free hand in the matter'.[9]

On 26 March, *The Times* announced the decision to form a national war museum and listed the appointments to its committee. It was to consist of Sir Alfred Mond, MP (Chairman), Sir Martin Conway (Director General), Cmdr C.C. Walcott (Admiralty), Col. J.R. Stansfield, CB (Munitions), B.B. Cubitt, CB (War Office), and Ian Malcolm, MP. Professor C.W.C. Oman, Chichele Professor of Modern History, Oxford, a distinguished military historian was entrusted with special responsibility for the library. The first formal steps had been taken, and the strength of the museum's first committee would guarantee its success.

CHAPTER 10

ESTABLISHMENT OF THE NATIONAL WAR MUSEUM

THE National War Museum Committee, with the authority of a War Cabinet minute, set about its work in late March 1917. The records of the weekly committee meetings are evidence of the will and considerable enthusiasm the members brought to their task. Between March and August 1917, the committee was full of ideas and initiatives.

The pattern for these first few months, and for much of the subsequent development of the museum, can be determined from the very first meeting on 29 March 1917. The immediate priority was to form extensive and representative collections, before the opportunity was lost. To do this, a specialist sub-committee structure was devised. Each sub-committee was headed by a member of the museum committee and was charged with the responsibility of collecting in designated specialist areas. Thus Admiralty, munitions, War Office, Red Cross, records and literature, and women's work sub-committees were agreed upon. Later in the year, the Red Cross committee was dropped and air services, dominions, and loan exhibitions sub-committees established. Members of the sub-committees were carefully selected by the chairmen and as a result a range of skills and influence were attracted to each.

For example, the Admiralty sub-committee was announced on 5 April 1917, and consisted of: Commander Walcott (chairman), a representative of the Anti-Submarine Department, the director of Naval Construction, the Director of Naval Ordnance, the Director of Torpedoes and Mines, a representative of RNAS, the Engineer in Chief and the Director of Stores. The sub-committee had power to add to its number as the occasion arose.[1] The women's work sub-committee was influential and prestigious. It was chaired by Lady Norman, CBE, and included Lady Haig and Lady Askwith, CBE. Sir Martin Conway's daughter, Agnes, became its secretary. The War Office sub-committee never formed as such. Instead, the War Office transferred the War Trophies Committee to service the museum. Mr Cubbitt served as chairman and Sir Arthur Leetham of the Royal United Services Institution Museum (a critic of the war museum) was later co-opted as a member. There were acknowledged areas where the committees' collecting interests overlapped; for example, in the representation of the medical services, munitions, and 'womens work'. However, the sub-committee structure gave the mu-

20. The Committee of the National War Museum set up in March 1917. From left to right: Ian Malcolm MP, Sir Martin Conway (Director), Sir Alfred Mond (Chairman), Col J.R. Stansfield, Capt. C.C. Walcott RN, B.B. Cubitt, C.W. Oman MP, Charles ffoulkes (Secretary).
Source: Imperial War Museum

seum the opportunities to resolve such difficulties and to collect reasonably comprehensively, using the best possible advice.

Forming the collections

Even before the sub-committees were set up, the National War Museum Committee approved the use of a field collector in France, a Canadian Officer, Major Beckles Willson, who had been responsible for the Ypres exhibition held in October 1916 in aid of the Belgian Relief Fund and the Canadian Relief Fund. They agreed to approach GHQ and request authority for him to 'inspect and earmark trophies etc. in France and elsewhere on behalf of the museum'.[2] This would obviously assist the museum in the acquisition of relevant material at the earliest possible moment. In some respects, they had a headstart. For instance, there was already a large store of captured enemy material held at Croydon by the Ordnance Branch.

In these early weeks, the committee envisaged that their work of collecting and recording would be active and should be carried out with the co-operation of the Forces. It was also decided, on 29 March 1917, that opinion

21A and B. Material gathered on the Western Front and stored at a location in
Hesdin set aside for the museum's purposes, July 1917.
Source: Imperial War Museum

22. Clubs collected on the Western Front and made available to the National War
Museum, July 1917.
Source: Imperial War Museum

on the museum should be canvassed from the Fleet and some of the Expeditionary Forces, and an explanation of the museum be provided to them. Attention was to be drawn to matters of:

a. regimental importance
b. localities and different war areas
c. the Esprit de Corps of Colonial troops.

Thus, the first public statements of the aims and purposes of the National War Museum and the philosophy and intent in its collecting came in circulars to the Forces, which received the King's 'cordial approval of this method of interesting the Services on behalf of the museum'.[3] The first of these, written by Sir Martin Conway, was approved by the committee on 12 April 1917. In this, Conway argued that without a national museum future historians would have to use German museums for their research. This was an exaggerated claim but one intended to lean heavily on the patriotic feelings of the reader. He identified the purpose of the museum in this way:

When peace returns and men are back at home the years will pass and memory of the great days and adventures through which they lived will grow dim. It is the purpose of the Museum to be a place which they can visit with their comrades, their friends, or their children, and there revive the past and behold again the great guns and other weapons with which they fought, the uniforms they wore, pictures and models of the ships and trenches and dug-outs in which weary hours were spent, or of positions which they carried and ground every yard of it memorable to them. They will then be glad to recall also the occupations of their hours of leisure. They will be able to look up the likenesses of the men they knew, some of whom, it may be, fell fighting beside them. The best possible result will be desired by all. Let all co-operate heartily and it will be attained.[4]

Conway outlined the collecting interest of the National War Museum: the Admiralty, the War Office, and the Ministry of Munitions would be depositing the 'large mass of official exhibits, but such an assemblage will be a dead accumulation unless it is vitalized by contributions expressive of the action, the experiences, the valour and the endurance of individuals'. To accomplish this, the museum would collect personal documents and publications reflecting leisure; souvenirs and models would be collected; also photographic records of 'persons and places' would be made and 'must be as complete as possible'.

This pamphlet is the first indication that the museum would aim at creating collections which would be a total record of the war. The records of the first months of collecting confirm this. Moreover, in this they had the support of at least one member of the museums profession. W.R. Butterfield, writing in the *Museums Journal* in May 1917, urged systematic and comprehensive field collecting and pointed to the example of Hazelius and the methods of recording and collecting he employed in the creation of the collections for Nordiska Museet and Skansen, in Stockholm.

In June 1917, Conway presented a memorandum on the 'Scope of the National War Museum' to Mond. In this he summarized, for the information of the Cabinet, how the National War Museum Committee perceived its responsibilities:

> The Committee charged with the duty of organizing the National War Museum, understands that the end to be achieved is the provision of a record and memorial of the war by sea and land in all parts of the world, of the raising, equipment, and transportation of armies, of munition manufacture at home and elsewhere, of the medical and other subsidiary services of the work of women both directly for the war purposes and indirectly by substitution, and generally of all activities called forth by the war at home, in the Dominions, and in India, at all the fronts and on the sea.
>
> Such a museum if wisely collected and arranged, will be unique in this respect that, alone among museums, it will make a direct appeal to the millions of individuals who have taken part in the war or in war-work of any kind ... when they visit the museum in years to come, they should be able by its aid to revive the memory of their work for the war, and, pointing to some exhibit, to say 'This thing I did'.[5]

23. Corporal Biffen (HAC) with captured gun, outside the National Museum's
store in Hesdin, July 1917.
Source: Imperial War Museum

Years later, Conway referred to the disappointing and slow responses to their
call for material in this early period of the museum, and how although it was
first imagined that the exhibits would be largely captured trophies it was
decided that the museum should instead be able to show 'every nation what
their own effort had been'.[6]

While the sub-committees explored the extent and requirements of their
specialist areas, without any parameters, conditions or guidelines being laid
down centrally, Beckles Willson was collecting material in France, visiting
the Blanc Museum in Paris and acquiring storage space in Hesdin. He la-
boured under considerable difficulties, not least the fact that the National
War Museum Committee did not fully appreciate the nature of his task and
possibly even the conditions at the Front. When Mond and Conway visited
France in July 1917 they were initially 'not much impressed by what he had
done'. However, later they were to revise this opinion: 'We concluded that
he well understood the nature of his work, possesses a fund of energy, is
deeply interested in what he has undertaken to do'.[7] Mond and Conway had
to admit that one of the problems was that Beckles Willson's position was not
regularized. He lacked the rank and position with GHQ to carry out his role
effectively. It is also evident that his financial position was also somewhat

precarious; the source of his pay and his expenses became a matter of dispute, the National War Museum claiming it did not have the funds to support him.[8]

The backing of the armed services was expected, and networks were established through the sub-committees for the acquisition or earmarking of suitable material. However as 1917 wore on, the year in which Britain came closest to defeat, surplus equipment and material was not readily yielded. Goodwill for the museum started to run out. Commander Walcott, the Admiralty representative on the National War Museum Committee found himself in an 'invidious position' when his board severely criticized the 'premature nature' of the scheme.[9]

The National War Museum Committee carried on with great enthusiasm and as best it could given the circumstances. It had under consideration in these early months the use of war artists, the amassing of photographic collections, and the acquisition of medical collections.[10] They also considered recording railway work, and the inland waterways.[11] A separate section dealing with children's exhibits was undertaken.[12] Discussions were also held on the possibilities of acquiring the Public Records from the war, and receiving and housing the British Museum Library acquisitions for the war period.[13] Specialists were invited to advise in areas such as medals and folklore.[14]

Through the Foreign Office, the museum committee opened up relations with 'British Embassies, Legations and Consulates in all the allied and neutral countries' for the purpose of acquiring material.[15] Then an invitation was issued to the High Commissioners of the Dominions and the Secretary of State for India to appoint representatives to an India and Dominions sub-committee which would deal with Indian and Colonial matters.[16] As the National War Museum Committee had already agreed to limit the scope of the museum 'as far as possible to the British effort',[17] the sub-committee would appear to have had little more than a liaison role. In fact , they had a difficult task. Canada and Australia were both establishing their own war museums and there was the prospect of conflict arising from an 'Imperial' collecting policy. The first matters the sub-committee had to deal with arose from requests made to the Admiralty for exhibits by Col. Doughty of the National War Museum of Canada.[18]

Housing the museum

As early as 19 April 1917, at the Committee's third meeting, the type and size of premises needed to house the museum were under active consideration. ffoulkes had hoped the Tower would house the collections. However, the troops could not be moved and the Constable, Sir Evelyn Wood, refused to have any exhibits, except perhaps a few placed outside as a temporary

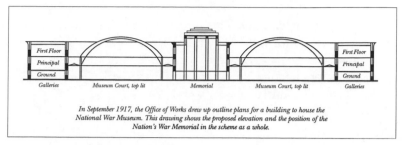

First Floor / Principal / Ground

Galleries   Museum Court, top lit   Memorial   Museum Court, top lit   Galleries

First Floor / Principal / Ground

In September 1917, the Office of Works drew up outline plans for a building to house the National War Museum. This drawing shows the proposed elevation and the position of the Nation's War Memorial in the scheme as a whole.

24. In September 1917, the Office of Works drew up outline plans for a building to house the National War Museum. The museum was to be arranged around a national war memorial. This drawing shows the proposed elevation.
Source: Imperial War Museum Archive, drawing by Jim Roberts

measure.[19] The Committee was aware it needed a very big site, one that could perhaps also accommodate naval and military tournaments in its precincts. C.R. Peers, Inspector of Ancient Monuments and Frank Baines, Principal Architect, both from Mond's Ministry of Works, were invited to advise on possible sites.

On 26 April, they presented a choice of nine locations for the Committee's consideration. The Earls Court Exhibition could provide a site of about 14 acres. The committee was concerned that the site was inconveniently divided by the railways, had no real fronting and had an established tradition of exhibitions. Moreover the site would be expensive to acquire. Then there was the White City, but as this comprised 130 acres it was considered too large. On the other hand, a three-acre site behind the British Museum was considered too small. The site of Charing Cross Railway Station, about five-and-a-half acres, was ruled out as being too small, far too costly and not likely to be obtainable for some years. The Tower of London, Burton Court, and the Duke of York's School could not be considered seriously. The Chelsea Hospital could not be considered owing to difficulties 'being foreseen with the present occupiers (the Chelsea Hospital's Commissioners, Guards, etc.)'.

The most satisfactory suggestion was an 11-acre site in Hyde Park with a frontage onto Bayswater Road. All the important exhibits could be shown in buildings or in glazed courtyards. A temporary exhibition of material might be put up while building operations progressed:

> It was urged that the above site would provide a worthy and dignified memorial to those who have fallen and those who have fought in the Great War and that this fact should weigh with the public as against the encroachment of open space.[20]

The National War Museum Committee decided that a formal memorandum should go to the Cabinet expressing their desire for the site. Proposals were to be kept from the press until plans had been more fully formulated. The sub-committees were requested to provide details of the size of an area they required for their exhibits. This information was needed so that more detailed plans could be formulated by Frank Baines and thus a full submission made to Cabinet.

The floor area required for the various exhibits was calculated at the meeting on 17 May 1917. The initial figures were:

Navy	127,000 ft^2
Army	65,000 ft^2
Munitions	60,000 ft^2
Trophies	10,000 ft^2
Records	12,000 ft^2
Women's work	5,000 ft^2
Total	279,000 ft^2

Space for expansion, for greater quantities of material if the war was a prolonged effort and for egress and access, was also considered. Conway calculated the cost at £2 per square foot, giving an approximate total cost of £600,000. Comparable figures were found and used to support their case: the British Museum Reading Room was 42,000 square feet, the Victoria and Albert Museum 330,000 square feet.

With the plans for the building, the Committee arrived at the conclusion that the National War Museum should be the nation's Memorial to the War. This then became central to their submission to the War Cabinet and an abiding hope of the Director, Sir Martin Conway:

A War Museum that did not record and honour the brave who sacrificed their lives for their country would be constructed on a fundamentally wrong principle. It is therefore suggested that the very heart and focus of the building should be of a memorial character. This might take the form of a Hall of Honour as rich and beautiful in character as artists can devise, and adjacent to it a Gallery devoted to the separate memorials of the Navy and the Army by ships, regiments, and contingents. The Hall of Honour could be designed to bear on its walls painted portraits and on its floor pedestals carrying busts or sculptured figures of such eminent individuals as the people as a whole may delight to single out for special honour. In the Memorial Gallery the name of every individual who fell in battle or died of wounds should be legibly inscribed on bronze plates, suitably framed, with the arms, badges and honours of each regiment; here also the special mementos of particular units would find place in the neighbourhood of the regimental or other collective material.

It is evident that if the core of the Museum is thus designed and equipped, it will by the very nature of the case become the National War Memorial, for no pile of sculpture wherever set up could possible vie in public interest or truly memorial character with this Hall and Gallery of Honour in the heart of a great War Museum. It is therefore suggested that the proposed Museum be adopted as the War Memorial. If that step is taken, all difficulties connected with finance will fall away; neither will there be any impediment to selecting as central and costly a site as may seem desirable. The public might resent what could be represented as extravagance in connection with a Museum; but the same public would insist that the memorial to the countless dead who gave their lives for its salvation should be costly in sacrifice, splendid in character, and central in position.[21]

Preliminary estimates for the museum building now reached £750,000.

Reversals and disappointments

Mond placed before the Cabinet on 21 August 1917 two documents: a memorandum from Conway to himself as First Commissioner of Works, outlining the proposed scope of the museum; and his own memorandum requesting the Cabinet's approval for the 'following features':

1. the adoption of the National War Museum as the National War Memorial
2. the sanction of the estimated expenditure
3. the approval of the proposed site.[22]

The Cabinet, however was in no mood to accept this grandiose scheme. The carnage at Passchendaele was at its height: the war was going very badly indeed. Curzon expressed his objections in the strongest terms. Although an early supporter of the War Museum:

… he had never contemplated a plan that would involve the erection of a building or buildings covering 5 acres of ground, and probably costing over one million sterling, in Hyde Park, that would apparently attempt to commemorate almost every incident and feature of a war which we have not yet won and which it was quite conceivable in the future we might desire as far as possible to forget… .[23]

The feeling of the Cabinet was that a museum was quite unsuitable as an Imperial War Memorial: 'it would be an unjustifiable extravagance now and a white elephant in the future'. Their views on the collections were equally damning 'a vast and hetrogeneous collection of models or memorials even, as suggested, of munitions workers, boy scouts and girl guides, would in a few years time interest nobody and merely encumber space'. Furthermore, pledges had been given that no building work could begin during the war. It was inconceivable that public space could even be considered for this purpose. The idea was seen as premature and formal decisions were shelved. Instead a ministerial committee under Lord Crawford and Lord Balcarries was appointed to examine the proposals of the National War Museum Committee.

This was the conclusion of the first phase of the National War Museum. The Committee was faced with a reversal. Conway was very depressed by the rebuff and by the prospects for the future. He recorded in his diary on 21 August 1917: 'Attended the War Cabinet this morning and they practically turned down our scheme. Referred it to a Committee of Ministers. Am in an utterly helpless and destroyed state of mind'[24] Shortly after this, Sir Henry Maxwell Lyte, the Keeper of the Public Record Office, decided against giving the custody of the War Records to the Museum.

The National War Museum Committee changed its tack: a higher public profile was needed and to this end it became even more active. On 13 September, it was agreed that the British Red Cross should be invited to hold an exhibition of war material from the collection. In October, an illustrated booklet outlining the scope and aims of the museum was approved. The Dominions sub-committee proposed that the museum should be the 'Imperial War Museum'.[25] Artists were commissioned by a number of the sub-committees to undertake studies of different aspects of the war effort at home and on the battle fronts.[26] Beckles Willson was made Deputy Inspector of Trophies with, on General Butler's recommendation, Major-General Donald placed in charge.[27]

All of these developments, however, were conducted in the shadow of the Crawford Committee's deliberations. The War Museum's Committee were informed of some of the matters arising from the meetings and knew their proposals for space requirements were being drastically cut. The one comfort was that the Treasury through Parliament agreed £21,000 towards the museum's costs under a class IV vote, thereby making the museum responsible for its own accounting.[28] This was, at least, some recognition of the museum's status as a formal, national institution.

THE IMPERIAL WAR MUSEUM

THE Interim Report of the Crawford Committee, published in December 1917, brought little clarification to the National War Museum's overall position. It offered general approval to the proposals for the Scottish National War Museum (now housed in St Andrews Chapel, Edinburgh) which was seen as not being contrary to the interests of the National War Museum. It also recommended to the War Cabinet, on a resolution received from the India and Dominions Committee, that the museum's title should be the 'Imperial War Museum'. The recommendation was accepted and the museum began 1918 under this name.[1]

Throughout its deliberations, the Crawford Committee had sought to temper and restrain the National War Museum Committee's proposals.[2] The significant figure in the moderation of the museum plans was H.A.L. Fisher, President of the Board of Education and distinguished historian, who sought to make the museum 'selective, not exhaustive' and to see implemented 'a plan less ambitious and less costly than the project which is outlined to us in Sir Martin Conway's memorandum'.[3]

The Crawford Report came out on 14 March 1918. Its principal recommendation was that the Imperial War Museum should be built on a 3.5 acre site on the south bank of the Thames opposite Westminster.[4] The Crawford Committee had reduced the space required by 28 per cent from the original estimates. The cost of the museum would amount to £665,000. The memorial proposal was not acceded to, although it was recommended that the National War Memorial should be positioned near the museum. The recommendations were not unanimous. Dr Addison strongly dissented from the recommendation to purchase the river site for £486,000; but it was not the total rebuff that might have been expected after the Cabinet's criticisms in August 1917. This has been seen as evidence of a rearguard action to defend the museum (Harries 1983: 120). The Cabinet received the report on 11 April 1918 and deferred a decision,[5] angered by press leaks about the report before they had had an opportunity to discuss it.[6]

Developing the collections

The Imperial War Museum (IWM) carried on as best it could. Collections were still being amassed. The First Annual Report of the museum records the considerable progress made from March 1917 until late March 1918. The library, publicity, records and photographic sections had made substantial acquisitions. The service sections, that is the collections of weapons and equipment, were not developing so coherently, although in the circumstances this is understandable. The war, which was exacting heavy losses of life, was draining the country of resources. The prospects of victory had never looked bleaker and there were few 'ornaments' to spare. The museum's most successful period of collecting was from the spring of 1918 until the early 1920's. It was able to earmark material while still in use, and collect all that was deemed suitable at the end of the conflict, when it was given up gladly.

The women's work sub-committee worked particularly energetically. Between 1917 and 1920, it brought together paintings and models, documents and uniforms, badges, books and photographs. The main part of this is now held by the Department of Printed Books and amounts to 189 boxes of papers, 20 albums of press cuttings, and 100 books. It covers the record of 1,200 war charities and 6,000 home hospitals (Wilkinson 1991: 31). Further, the sub-committee attempted to put together a record of all the women who had lost their lives during the war, either on war service or on the Home Front in munitions work or on the land. They wrote to the nearest known relatives and asked for photographs; the letters written in reply, now held in the IWM archive, are a painful record of lives lost. In April 1920, the womens' work sub-committee had compiled a Roll of Honour of 800 names and the albums of photographs were ready to be mounted.

Particularly important acquisitions were made for the IWM's art section. In 1917, the National War Museum Committee had taken the decision to acquire only eye-witness, as opposed to studio work.[7] In August 1917, Sir Martin Conway had met John Buchan, Director of the Department of Information, and reported back to his Committee that 'an undertaking would be given that all works of artists working officially would eventually come to the National War Museum'.[8] When Lord Beaverbrook and the Ministry of Information superseded Buchan and the Department of Information, it was evident that this agreement might not prevail. There were hopes for a separate home for the paintings amassed by the information agencies and the British War Memorials Committee. The IWM Committee considered there was evidence of a state of declared opposition between Lord Beaverbrook and the war museum and in this atmosphere, it chose to go its own way. Robert Ross, a connoisseur and gallery-owner, became Honorary Art Adviser in December 1917.[9] On his suggestion and with his guidance, the IWM acquired some of its best pictures. An art committee was formed and concerned itself with purchases of pictures. Works were also commissioned by the service committees. Meirion and Susie Harries note that:

> ... until as late as March 1919 ... the story of official art at the IWM is broadly the story of the services sub-committees' pursuit of their individual objectives and the attempts of the administrators and art sub-committee in the background to cover the remaining ground through additional purchases and commissions. (Harries 1983: 121–2)

In the areas where the DoI/MoI collection were strongest, particularly the Western Front, the IWM made limited efforts to acquire pictures of its own. Instead, it concentrated on areas where the MoI collections were weak, particularly the Grand Fleet and RAF subjects. This may well have been in the hope that the MoI's position would alter in time.

The first artist to work for the IWM was 2nd Lieutenant Adrian Hill, who was transferred from the War Trophies Section to work for the IWM on army pay and allowances. ffoulkes requested 'more uninteresting technical drawings' such as the interior design of pill-boxes and dug-outs. Hill produced 187 pictures, 'a vivid journalistic record of life on the war zone'. Jacob Epstein was to have been the second artist serving with the War Troops Section, but he was prevented from taking up the appointment for reasons which remain unclear (Harries 1938:127).

The munitions sub-committee, in recognition of the part played by women in the wartime munitions industry, appointed one of Britain's most successful women artists, Anna Airey. She was commissioned to paint four canvasses representing typical scenes at munitions works: a shell forge, a shell filling department, a gun forge and an aircraft assembly shop. Airey was one of the first women to be appointed an official war artist. Her contract was more stringent than those imposed on other artists. She was paid £280 for each canvas but her employers had the right to reject her work without payment. Furthermore, there was a penalty clause whereby there would be a 5 per cent reduction in price for each month's delay (Harries 1983: 128).

The Admiralty sub-committee also built up an art collection, believed to be the most comprehensive and well-organized at the time. This has been ascribed to the Admiralty's representative, Walcott, having a genuine interest in art. The sub-committee was also prepared to take advice from the Tate, the Victoria and Albert Museum and the National Gallery on the choice of artists. They approached eight artists and offered them a free hand in dealing with their subjects.[10] They urged that the paintings should be 'in every way representative and worthy as sea pictures to hand down to posterity, both as regards subject and quality of art'.[11]

An air services sub-committee had been established in November 1917 under Lieutenant-Colonel A.C. MacLean. The air services' role was difficult for an artist to document and MacLean had no time for 'modern art'. The work of RAF artists Richard and Sydney Carline provided the most interesting pictures produced under the auspices of the IWM. Even so, the work acquired by the Air Services sub-committee gave the art committee cause for concern (Harries 1983: 136–41). The women's work sub-committee acquired and commissioned work only in the later stages of the war. This is thought to have been because this section only belatedly awoke to the usefulness of paintings as records. In December 1918, the Ministry of Information was dismantled. The IWM, as it had always hoped, took control of all the paintings and drawings amassed during the war. The museum thus came to hold an astonishingly rich and varied art collection.

By the end of 1918, the IWM had extended its committee structure to include a religious work committee and a medical section committee. Lady Norman (women's work section) and the now Brigadier-General MacLean (air services section) had been co-opted to the IWM Committee. The museum had a staff of around twenty accommodated in at least nine different premises.[12]

When the war ended the IWM was inundated with material (earmarked or otherwise) from the services and elsewhere. ffoulkes commented in his autobiography:

> … with the end of the war exhibits began to pour in. Departments were closed down, munitions works and women's organizations ceased to be and demobilization succeeded the RNVR unit at Crystal Palace. Every Government Department was only too pleased to unload examples of their war activities. (ffoulkes 1939: 123–6)

The IWM's Second Annual Report provides evidence of the extensive acquisitions made at this time.

Making the museum's case through exhibitions

In the absence of any firm commitment from the War Cabinet on the Crawford Report, the IWM Committee kept its options open by entering into a series of temporary exhibitions. War exhibitions in general were popular and were often used to raise money (see Chapters 5 and 7). An elaborate example, not associated with the IWM, was the use of Trafalgar Square in the early months of 1918. It was turned into 'a model battlefield to stir the imaginations of those at home in order to increase contributions to the War Loan' (Anon 1935: 178).

The first exhibition of war material from the museum's collections was held at Burlington House in January 1918, in aid of the Red Cross. The

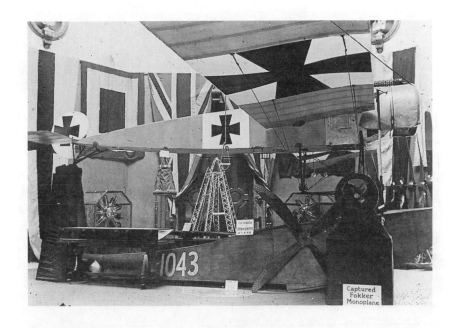

25 A and B. Air Section, which included a captured Fokker monoplane and other German exhibits at the Imperial War Museum exhibition at the Royal Academy, Burlington House in January 1918.
Source: Imperial War Museum

26. Women's Work Section at the Imperial War Museum exhibition at the Royal
Academy, Burlington House in January 1918.
Source: Imperial War Museum

exhibition was not a success and indeed raised controversy when one of the
exhibits, a parachute, was found to be wrongly labelled. The manufacturer
threatened to sue, but dropped the action when a correction was made. Instead
of raising money for the Red Cross, it made a loss.[13] The exhibition did,
however, show the Imperial War Museum Committee how temporary exhibitions could and should be organized. A loan exhibition sub-committee
was formed to deal with these problems and prepare temporary exhibitions.
One of the problems they faced was that exhibiting war material was a difficult
business: the objects had to be carefully selected and handled, both for security and safety reasons; and sketching and photography had to be explicitly
banned and notices of the relevant section of the Defence of the Realm Act
displayed at the exhibitions.[14]

In the spring of 1918, the Imperial War Museum organized the first of its
loan exhibitions for the provinces, an exhibition of British Official Photographs. This exhibition and all subsequent ones, toured to towns and cities
throught the United Kingdom. They kept the museum in the public eye and
generated much publicity and local comment. Moreover, the museum's
director, Sir Martin Conway, used the exhibitions to press home, yet again,
the museum's philosophies. The exhibitions' catalogues and the addresses given

at the official openings were occasions when the museum's purpose could be underlined. The forewords to the catalogues were little more than a slight rearrangement of his June 1917 memorandum on 'the Scope of the National War Museum', with emphasis laid on the potential of the museum as a National War Memorial.[15]

An exhibition of women's work was staged at the Whitechapel Art Gallery in October 1918. It proved a great success and was visited by 82,000 people, including Her Majesty, the Queen.[16] A 'Sea Power' exhibition was opened at the same time, also with material borrowed from the Imperial War Museum. This incurred the museum committee's wrath as they were neither invited nor mentioned in the exhibition's publicity.[17] One exhibition took place abroad; Beckles Willson organized in Alexandria an exhibition of the collections he had amassed there before he resigned at the time of the Armistice.[18]

Decisions and a future

With the conclusion of the war, the IWM Committee hoped for some official confirmation of their status and future provision. The War Cabinet met on 4 December 1918 and gave further consideration to the Crawford Report and a letter from Mond to the Prime Minister requesting action. It decided that the question of the museum should be postponed until after the general election. Even then, there was no progress.

By March 1919, Conway was entertaining real fears for the museum. In a letter to R.P.M. Gower of the Treasury he wrote:

> England is filled with botched institutions due to the fact that before they were set up their scope and purpose were not sufficiently examined by the responsible authorities. The Imperial Institute is a standing memorial of this kind of white elephant. I am terribly afraid that the War Museum may become another white elephant.[19]

He saw the central problem as one purely of finance, 'if a war museum is to be a living organism of continuing utility to future generations it will involve a large initial expense, certainly not less than one million sterling'. Conway still clung to the possibility that the IWM might become a war memorial. Clearly, he saw this as the principal means by which money for the museum could be raised. The success of the Kitchener Fund had much influenced Conway, and others, into this way of thinking. There was a belief that substantial sums could be raised for the IWM by subscription. This was never tested.

Drastic cuts were made in public spending in the immediate post-war period. The lack of Government response to the museum's needs has to be viewed against a background of an economy in crisis. Frustrated by the lack of any move on their position, the IWM Committee responded to an approach from the Trustees of the Crystal Palace to the lease of part of their building. Ironically, when they had viewed the Crystal Palace two years before in 1917 they had ruled it out as totally unsuitable.[20] In spite of the fact that the building was so inadequate for the display of the collections, particularly the paintings, negotiations progressed and agreement was reached, with the IWM due to take over the lease in April 1920.[21]

Mond set the wheels in motion for the transference of authority for the IWM, from a committee constituted under a Cabinet minute, to a more formal and authoritative body. On 14 May 1919, Mond wrote to Conway:

> ... it seems as though the first stage in the creation of the Museum may be regarded as past and that the time has come to consider whether the present organizing committee has not done its work and whether some more permanent body should not be set up in the form of a Board of Trustees to carry on the future organization and development of the museum.[22]

In a secret memorandum to the Cabinet on 16 March 1920, Mond raised the question of the permanent organization and administration of the Imperial War Museum. He considered that the task of collecting had almost reached its end and he argued that it was now necessary to create a corporate and legal body for the IWM. He submitted with his memo a draft bill, prepared in consultation with Conway and the Treasury, based 'on the lines of that dealing with the national collections'.[23] Mond had already persuaded the Prince of Wales to consent to being the first President of the Board of Trustees. As Mond was not asking for any money for the museum in the Bill 'its purpose being merely to regularize the existing position', he did not anticipate opposition in any of its stages. The Cabinet did just as Mond asked and placed the draft bill before the Home Affairs Committee. Mond steered the Bill through the Commons.

Hector Bolitho, Mond's biographer assesses this as one of his best achievements in office as First Commissioner of Works. He wrote:

> ... much of the work he did was temporary because of the war. But he secured Stonehenge for the nation, and he restored and preserved Westminster Hall, without destroying either its form or its spirit. The most interesting memorials to his control of the Department are the war graves and memorials he built in France, the War Museum, the War Memorial in Edinburgh and the Cenotaph: all memorials which are free from smallness, meanness or anger. The Cenotaph and the War Museum were designed in a time when mass passions were twisted and when human nature was suffering in the dark. Sir Alfred Mond wished what he eventually achieved: that the two great memorials should exalt the dignity of sacrifice without tears, the emotional battle without sentimentality, and the passion of patriotism without its insularity. (Bolitho 1933: 2–4)

The passage of the Bill was not trouble-free. The division on the second reading was passed by 110 to 14 votes. The museum was criticized by Commander Kenworthy MP (Liberal), for being likely to perpetuate the war spirit. Tom Myers MP (Labour), argued that there was no public demand for such an institution which would familiarize youth 'with all the barbarism of warfare'. Some sections of the popular press joined in the protest and Professor J.L. Myers had already offered his opinion to the museums profession that there was a case for a Peace Museum rather than a Museum of War. (*Museums Journal* 19: 73–6)

The Act received the Royal assent on 2 July 1920. It did not specify that the Imperial War Museum was to collect only First World War material. Specifically titled the Imperial War Museum Act, there would have appeared to be no need to define the museum's responsibility further. However, a controversy arose later when Charles ffoulkes attempted to expand his responsibilities. As is clear from ffoulkes' autobiography and his correspondence at the Imperial War Museum, he was an expert on arms and armour and was committed to the idea that collections of such material should be organized for serious students (ffoulkes 1939). He wanted the Imperial War Museum to expand so that it could cover the history of armoury, for the benefit of those who shared his interests. In 1926, Sir Lionel Earle was forced to point out to him that of the 300,000 visitors to the Tower in 1926 'very few of these can have been serious students of the subject of arms and armour: they were probably nearly all average sightseers mildly interested in the collection in its present setting'.

Nevertheless, ffoulkes persisted in his views and sought support for the merger of at least some of the collections of the Tower Armouries and Imperial War Museum. He used the fact that the Imperial War Museum Act did not specify the Great War as the defining boundary of collections, and canvassed a number of people to support him, including Major General J.E.B. Sealy and General Sir Charles Munro. He was also prepared to use his position on the Cottesloe Committee. This had been established by the War Office in 1921. Its terms of reference were to consider the distribution of military weapons and equipment between the major military and armoury collections. It has to be questioned what part ffoulkes had in the formation of the committee and its terms of reference: he certainly wrote a substantial part of the subsequent reports.

ffoulkes even went to the lengths of casting doubts on the legal definition of the Imperial War Museum in his evidence to the Royal Commission of National Museums and Galleries in December 1928. Documents at the Imperial War Museum suggest ffoulkes was putting forward the Cottesloe Committee's views (with their agreement) and not those of the Imperial War Museum. He found himself corrected during the course of giving his evidence by members of the Royal Commission, Sir Thomas Heath, Sir Lionel

Earle and Sir Martin Conway, each of whom had had intimate involvement with the development of the Imperial War Museum from its earliest stages.[24]

Sir Frederic Kenyon, Director of the British Museum and Trustee of the Imperial War Museum affirmed at a later date:

> The Imperial War Museum was founded to commemorate the war of 1914–18; and though the Act is so loosely drawn that the objects of the museum are nowhere defined, I am sure there was no suggestion at the time that it was to be a general museum of military history of the country. Nor has there hitherto been any suggestion to this effect. On the contrary, the policy of the Trustees has regularly been (for instance when gifts have been offered to them) to ask whether any proposed accession really illustrates the war of 1914–18. If the scope of the museum is to be changed, I think it should have been brought up as a question of policy to be deliberately discussed by the Trustees. I am sure the Trustees were surprised to find that the Cottesloe Committee had been assured that they (the Trustees) would be ready to accept a fundamental change in principle which had never been so much as hinted to them.[25]

The Imperial War Museum at Crystal Palace

On 9 June 1920 the King and Queen attended the opening of the IWM collections at the Crystal Palace. The collection on exhibition was much reduced. Arrangements for the disposal of some of the collections began as early as 27 November 1919, when the Treasury approved the sale of toys from the collection.[26] Professor Oman had refused to move the library there. The floor of the Crystal Palace had had to be under-propped so that it could carry heavy weights; screens had to be erected and platforms built. Some exhibits failed to arrive and others could not be taken until the floor was made ready. ffoulkes reported that the staff had 'worked assiduously and loyally, but were entirely unable to cope with the rush of exhibits which approximated four or five hundred tons in five weeks.'[27]

After the official opening of the collections, theft and interference with the exhibits became a problem. There was, moreover, dissatisfaction with the displays. Beckles Willson wrote to Mond, having failed to get an appointment to see him:

> I felt that you ought to be personally appealed to in order to save this great project from becoming what is bound to become, in its present hands, an inglorious fiasco. Every officer and man with whom I have spoken on the subject who has visited the exhibition is of the same opinion as myself concerning it.
>
> I may say nothing of the treatment accorded by Mr ffoulkes to the relics contributed officially by myself to the museum (only a tenth of these appear to be exhibited at all and those that are shown are undocumented): but the whole plan or want of plan of the show and its undignified and irrelevant surroundings and accessories, are truly deplorable.[28]

27. Moving a French tank into the Crystal Palace, the Imperial War Museum's first
'home', 1920.
Source: Imperial War Museum

ffoulkes himself admitted that he was 'very much dissatisfied with the present scheme', and thought that 'drastic alterations, compressions and rearrangements should be made as opportunity occurs'. He considered that he was capable of grouping the collections for serious study by the student and cited his work at the Tower Armouries as evidence of this.

At the opening of the museum at the Crystal Palace the disorganization of the collections displayed and the unsuitability of the building were not discussed. Years of inadequate funding and poor accommodation lay ahead, but these had only begun to suggest themselves to the IWM Committee, who still hoped for appropriate recognition. This was the moment to celebrate the achievements of forming the collection. Mond, in his speech, said:

> The museum was not conceived as a monument to military glory, but rather as a record of toil and sacrifice; as a place of study to the technician in studying the development of armaments; to the historian as an assembly of material and archives to instruct his work; and to the people of the Empire, as a record of their toil and sacrifice through these fateful years.[29]

28. War trophies outside the Imperial War Museum, Crystal Palace, 1920. Many of the larger exhibits had to remain outside without any cover. Over the years, the corrosion and general decay of these exhibits was such that many had to be scrapped.
Source: Imperial War Museum

29. The Army Section of the Imperial War Museum at the Crystal Palace, 1920.
Source: Imperial War Museum

The King, in his speech formally opening the museum, spoke of the museum as a memorial to the common sacrifice of men and women, soldiers and civilians, 'It was a democratic victory … the work of a nation in arms'.

Several weeks later Robert Cecil, Chairman of the Executive Committee of the League of Nations Union, wrote to Mond to suggest that there was an opportunity afforded by 'the Victory Exhibition at the Crystal Palace to bring the principles of the League of Nations into vivid contrast with the machinery of war'.[30] He asked for a space at the Crystal Palace to erect a League of Nations stall. Mond refused permission, although he was prepared to suggest that the Trustees of the Crystal Palace might be able to find space in some other part of the building.[31] In 1928, ffoulkes gave evidence to the Royal Commission on National Museums and Galleries, that the League of Nations used the museum a considerable amount:

> To go through a large collection of photographs is enough to show anyone what a terrible thing war is and how it should be avoided at all costs.[32]

Of the two-and-a-half million people who visited the IWM at the Crystal Palace in its first year, a 'considerable proportion' had served in the fighting and ancillary forces during the war.[33] For them at least, the meaning and significance of the amassed collections on view were not lost. What they

30. The Imperial War Museum at the Crystal Palace, 1920. The museum was criticised for the way the collections were shown. The juxtaposition of so many potted plants with material used in the mud and blood of Flanders was, to say the least, odd.
Source: Imperial War Museum

made of such brutally familiar things nestling amongst the potted plants at Crystal Palace has not been recorded.

Those who knew only the home front found memories and conversation of the four years of war uninteresting and unfashionable by this time. Those who had experienced the war first-hand could not suppress the nightmare, although they were expected to repress the memory. Ex-servicemen turned to each other for intelligent conversation and to whatever means were available to confirm the reality of what was for many an horrendously surreal experience (Graves and Hodge 1940: 22).

For many of the former soldiers who visited it, the museum may have been part of their own personal confrontation with the truth of their experience and survival. It could have given them a unique opportunity to describe it to others. In the post-war years such an outlet may have been helpful (Leed 1979: 210–3). This can be little more than speculation. Whether the museum truly met their needs and expectations is open to question.

CHAPTER 12
MEMORIES, MEMORIALS AND MEMENTOES

THE Armistice took effect at 11 a.m. on 11 November 1918. It was greeted with huge relief and much celebration. It was the end of the war, but not the end of it all. The transition of society from war to peace could not be achieved by the cessation of hostilities alone. Nothing would be easy, nor would anything happen overnight. As the war ended, an influenza epidemic, pan-European in scale, was reaching its peak. Over 220,000 people in Britain died from it. It cost the lives of many who were weak, infirm, elderly, or simply exhausted and dispirited. In June 1919, the Peace Treaty was formalized at Versailles. Germany was disarmed, in part demilitarized, stripped of its Empire in Africa and the Pacific, and made to pay financial indemnities or 'reparations'.

The machinery of war had to be dismantled and all those on war service had to be returned home. The slowness of demobilization led to serious unrest in army camps both in England and France. In the summer of 1919, demobbed and demoralized soldiers were involved in a series of disturbances, some of which – such as the burning down of Luton Town Hall, and 'the Battle of Wood Green' in London – caused alarm (Stevenson 1984: 98). Industrial and political unrest lasted into the early 1920s.

Means had to be found to return Britain's economy to peacetime conditions and to aid the re-employment of those previously engaged in some form of war work. An immediate post-war boom led to false expectations, but by the winter of 1920–21, the boom had ended. Unemployment then doubled and by the summer of 1921, had reached two million. Britain entered the years of depression.

The excesses and demands of the war bled both into attitudes and values in the immediate post-war years. The licence for boisterous, reckless enjoyment which home leave had given, led to a hedonistic approach to life which was to underpin the Roaring Twenties. The young, especially those who had served in the war, wanted to enjoy all the good things in life while they could. The anger and hate, so tolerated – even fostered – in the war years, became an embarrassment. To be socially acceptable, people were expected to put the war behind them and show neither their grief nor their disillusionment.

High hopes for a re-constructed world, a land fit for heroes, became mixed with bitterness over high prices, long working hours, poor housing, and unequal access to food, education and opportunity (Bourne 1989: 237). People struggled with an extreme and frequently contradictory range of emotions and tried in their own ways to make some sense of it all. Writing ten years after the end of the war, C.S. Peel observed how people measured their lives according to the three periods the war had cut: before, during and after (Peel 1929: 1). Certainly the war was an experience to which constant reference was made. It was a 'discontinuity out of which they [people] kept extrapolating explanations and justifications, an experiment in which they sought lessons and precepts and a catastrophe on which they could blame the misfortunes of themselves and the world' (Marwick 1974: 224).

The outward manifestation of renewal and reconstruction could never mask totally the sense of loss; and as the economy began to fall apart a commitment that war should never be allowed to happen again became more and more evident. In the immediate post-war years, people were simply numbed by the human cost of the war. Later, especially in the early 1930s, they were repulsed by the very notion of war. This was summed-up in many ways, not least by the Oxford Union debate of 1933 which declared in favour of the proposition that 'this House will not fight for King and Country'.

Memorials

Different ways were found to mourn the dead and to ensure that the names of those who were killed would not be lost for ever. War memorials were erected on village greens, in churchyards, in railway stations and in city parks. Many offices, factories and shops erected memorials to staff members killed during the war, as did a number of national museums. Memorial hospitals and public halls were built, and playing fields laid out. Remembrance became ritualized, and the state played its part. In 1919, the Shrine of the Unknown Warrior was set-up in Westminster Abbey.

The Imperial War Graves Commission began laying out war cemeteries in France and Belgium, Italy, Palestine, Gallipoli and elsewhere. The commission's architectural advisor, appointed in November 1917, was Sir Frederic Kenyon, Director of the British Museum. It was he who proposed that the design of the cemeteries be entrusted to young architects who had seen service in the war, but that their work should be supervised by principal architects of note. As a result the responsibility for designing war cemeteries in France and Belgium was passed to Sir Edwin Lutyens, Reginald Blomfield, Herbert Baker and Charles Holden. Similarly prestigious appointments were made for war cemeteries in what had been other theatres of the war (Gibson and

Ward 1989: 49). Advice on the choice of stone was given by the Director of the Museum of Practical Geology.

A temporary plaster and wood Cenotaph, designed by Lutyens, was erected in Whitehall in 1919, and replaced in 1920 by the one made of Portland stone which stands there today. The Cenotaph became the centre of Armistice Day observance, with its two-minutes' silence, wreath laying, the sounding of the Last Post and Reveille. Even into the 1930s, traffic in the centre of London would stop to observe the silence. Moreover, throughout the year and not just on Armistice Sunday, the Cenotaph's meaning was understood; men would remove their hats when passing it.

The temporary plaster and wood Cenotaph was acquired for the Imperial War Museum's collections by Charles ffoulkes. It was removed to the Crystal Palace and installed in one of the bays. In 1922, the museum held its own memorial service on Armistice Day at the replica Cenotaph, a custom it repeated throughout the inter-war years in the museum's two subsequent homes in South Kensington and Lambeth (ffoulkes 1939:128–130). It was destroyed by a bomb in the Second World War (Boorman 1988: 2).

Even before the war ended, discussions were taking place in many towns, cities and organizations, about the form memorials might take. A number had already been commissioned. The principal arts bodies were swift to recognize that the provision of war memorials would represent the greatest commissioning of public sculpture and monuments the country had seen. Advice and guidance would be needed. In the spring of 1919, the Royal Academy's War Memorials Committee, with the assistance of staff at the Victoria and Albert Museum and the British Institute of Industrial Art, began organizing an exhibition on 'War Memorials to the Fallen'. The exhibition was intended to provide both artists and commissioning institutions, such as local authorities, with inspiration in the creation of memorials for the war dead. It was hoped to include in the exhibition 'every category of decorative art and craft which might have bearing on the production of memorials', and, overall, to provide a guide to the possible forms a memorial might take. An appeal went out:

> In view of the great importance of the subject, the committee trusts that artists and craftsmen, and all those who have at heart the interests of British art, will lend their aid in making this exhibition fulfil its purposes, not only by the actual contribution of material but by communicating information and suggestions as to appropriate designs. (*Museums Journal* 18: 201)

The exhibition was opened at the Victoria and Albert Museum on 8 July 1919 and included objects, designs and photographs chosen from the museum's collections, as well as designs and memorials in progress at this time, or recently executed by living artists. Works by Edwin Lutyens and Reginald Blomfield were included. The museum's quadrangle was used to exhibit a model of the Great War Cross by Blomfield, which was to be erected by the Imperial War Graves Commission in the war cemeteries abroad (Boorman 1988: 2). The exhibition occupied both the East and the West Halls of the museum. A Bureau of Reference was established to deal with enquiries and a lecture and guided tour given daily (*Museums Journal* 19: 30). The museum also arranged for the publication of a collection of poems and extracts from literature suitable for use as inscriptions on war memorials, such as this one by F.D. Ellis, seen as apt for memorials to women who had died in the war: 'We pray you to remember before this altar these our sisters who went before us with the sign of faith'.

The exhibition opened in July and closed in October. The material from the Victoria and Albert Museum's collection was kept on view for several weeks longer and the modern material was moved to Piccadilly to be shown at Burlington House. Visitor figures for the memorials exhibition were not kept separately; but the increase of average weekly attendances at the Victoria and Albert Museum from 9,404 in 1918 to 12,001 in 1919 was ascribed to the re-awakening interest in the collections and to the attraction of the war memorials exhibition. The extent to which the exhibition influenced the forms that memorials took is open to question. It is very possible that it had some impact. Certainly the First World War memorials we know today, with their dignified, passive but frequently sorrowful figurative images, were commissioned in preference to a more modern style: Vorticism had few echoes in war memorials. As sculptures, they owed much to the past and to classical tradition. The form they took may have been encouraged through the Victoria and Albert Museum's exhibition, but were more likely to have been rooted in the need for memorials to embody sentiments which people could immediately understand (Borg 1991).

Museums as memorials

Many towns and cities had to decide whether they wanted a functional memorial to the war dead, such as a playing field, or a formal monument. Many were able to raise sufficient funds for both. In addition to public efforts, private subscriptions and individual initiatives led to a host of monuments and memorials. A number of museums were built or extended in commemoration of the war dead. A precedent existed from an earlier Imperial war. Middlesborough had acquired a museum, opened in 1904, as a memorial to Lieutenant George Lockwood Dorman and the men of his regiment killed in the Boer War[1]. Whether this influenced later memorial-museum initiatives is open to question.

Most of the initiatives which in some way combined museum and memorial were characterized by the involvement of both local government and private initiatives. In Stockport, Cheshire, a local man, Samuel Kay, had gifted a site for the provision of an art gallery. The town's War Memorial Committee elected to combine the two elements of memorial and art gallery and raised £24,000 to this end. Further fund-raising led to the successful completion of the project: a classical building, with a Hall of Remembrance containing the Roll of Honour and a sculpted group of figures entitled 'Sacrifice', with Britannia and a fallen figure sacrificed in her defence (Bell 1991: 40). It bears the name Stockport Memorial Art Gallery.

A similarly combined museum and memorial scheme was planned in Aberdeen. Here a war memorial court was initiated, along with an art gallery extension. Money previously bequeathed to the Corporation was used for the extension and £25,000 raised for the war memorial court. The Corporation recorded in its minutes for 1 September 1919 the belief that the project would be 'a happy one … associating the glorious dead [with] all that is beautiful in Art and Sculpture' (quoted in Bell 1991: 40). Some museums, such as Preston's Harris Museum and Kettering's Alfred East Art Gallery, became hosts to the Rolls of Honour. Such museums were centrally located and in close proximity to their town's formal monument.

A number of other developments were rather more personal. John Nairn, the linoleum manufacturer, had lost his only son in the war. He donated an art gallery as part of Kirkcaldy's war memorial, which was also to comprise a memorial garden and cenotaph. The building had a museum on the ground floor and an art gallery above; a library extension was added later. Similarly, Ravensnowle Hall was given to Huddersfield Town Council by Leigh Tolson in 1919 in memory of his two nephews who had died fighting in France. At its opening ceremony in May 1922, Tolson declared that it was hoped that those who visited the Hall would 'give some thought not only to his nephews, but also to the great crowd of brave men … who died' (quoted in Bell 1991: 41). The Brian Hatton Gallery at Hereford Museum is a memorial to one man. A talented artist, Hatton was killed in Egypt in 1916. His sister preserved his work and the erection of the gallery in 1973 was a fulfilment of her ambitions.

In contrast, Sir William Gray as a 'thanks offering for the safe return of my only son from the war', bought a large stone villa, the Willows, and presented it to the town of Hartlepool for an art gallery. He also gifted a number of paintings to form the basis of a collection and erected a bandstand in the grounds. The Hartlepool Book of Remembrance was displayed in the house.[2]

A number of war memorials were later used for museum purposes. For example, in Yorkshire in 1929 the top floor of Pickering's Memorial Hall was used for a short time to house Dr Kirk's collection, which later went on to found the Castle Museum, York (Brears and Davies 1989); and the ground floor of the Carillon in Loughborough was also later used for exhibits (Bray

1981). Such developments were simply the product of expediency and frequently had no direct memorial function.

Regimental museums

In the years between the two wars, a different form of museum began to develop: the regimental museum. In the immediate post-war years, a significant number of war histories, biographical accounts written by officers, and unit histories were published. It is possible that regimental museums were seen by at least some of their instigators as a three-dimensional form of regimental history. On the other hand, a regimental museum could simply have been a means of tidying up extra-ordinary assemblages of trophies and mementoes the scale of which, in some regiments, was close to getting out of hand. The formation of regimental collections, and later museums, was no doubt stimulated by the establishment of a national war museum, and by each regiment's deep knowledge of what the war had cost its men. But such museums may have had other underlying purposes. As the country became less tolerant of militarism and all that reminded it of war, the regiments had to work harder to remind people of their purposes and the part they had played. They also had to hold the regiments' histories and inculcate an *esprit de corps* in new recruits, whose reasons for joining the forces might have had more to do with economic necessity than dedication to service (Thwaites 1992: 8). Infrequently open to the public in the same way as municipal museums, these collections in the first instance were for the regiments' purposes alone.

Many of the regiments had long-established collections of silver, armour, weapons and trophies. In the years after 1918, much First World War material was added. At least 14 formal collections or museums had been established by the end of the 1920s, and in the 1930s there were somewhere in the region of 50 (Cowper 1935). There were three important pre-war precedents: the Royal Artillery had a collection which dated back to 1778; it and the Royal Engineers were the only regiments which had some form of museum before the First World War began[3]. The Royal Armouries, under the curatorship of Charles ffoulkes, maintained the nation's collection of armour and weaponry.

The post-war regimental museums established by the Royal Corps of Signals, and the Buffs (Royal East Kent Regiment) are cases in point, and demonstrate both the difficulties and the unplanned nature of some of these developments. In 1920, the Royal Signals was a new regiment, having been formed from the Royal Engineers Signal Service units and personnel. The new Corps inherited many old traditions, trophies of war and ceremonial material. Much of this was lodged with the HQ Mess in Catterick, the committee of which in 1927 took the initiative to add to the collection. This led to an exhibition of medals, which once established remained largely untouched for the next 30 years. It was not until the 1930s that attempts were made to establish a museum. By then, the purpose was seen, officially at least, as supporting the training of men of the regiment. A museums committee was established in May 1936, and further acquisitions were made to supplement those held in the Mess. But progress was slow and was interrupted by the Second World War. Although from 1938 the collection had a home – a hut – it was not to have premises for any form of display until 1952.

Like the Royal Signals, the Buffs (Royal East Kent Regiment) were effectively a new regiment. Created as the Special Reserve Battalion in 1919, it had responsibility for the inheritance of the Old East Kent Militia and the 3rd (Militia) Battalion which it had become in 1881. By 1925, besides the 'older relics', trophies and mementoes of the First World War were beginning to accumulate. This material, seen as having both historical and sentimental value, was to be found in the Officers' and Sergeants' messes, Corporals' rooms and institutes, cellars and stores. When interest in it lapsed and there was a need for redecoration, something had to be done. Major (later Lieutenant-Colonel) J. V. R. Jackson took the initiative and between 1925 and 1928 tried to put the collection into some form of order. A room was 'appropriated' and any object which could be termed a 'museum exhibit' was gathered there. The messes were asked for the material they could spare and people were encouraged to send things in. More of a store than a museum, it was at least a start. Not until the 1950s was the regimental collection to have proper housing, and even then it was found to be inadequate.

Regimental collections and museums established after 1918, were in the main the initiative of individual officers, seeking solutions to immediate problems, but in full awareness of the importance of the material they had to hand. Neither the mood nor the economy of the country was right for formal regimental museums, so they sprang up (or quietly developed) in a rather *ad hoc* fashion. With this came a legacy. They were not managed by curators, as such. In the main they were managed by service personnel with other duties which precluded them from learning about museum practice elsewhere. The regimental museums were distanced from other forms of museum activity and did not cultivate public support. Indeed, of the 49 listed in 1935, one-third were not open to the public and the opening of some others was much restricted. Desperately under-resourced, the regimental museums were reliant on the goodwill of serving officers and the generosity of retired men who contributed mementoes and medals and sometimes their time and money to the well-being of the collection.

The war turned working men and women into components of a war machine. Their regiments did their best to keep the records of their efforts,

but the task was too great, too complex and untimely. But more than anything, the museums were too expensive and could not get the official support they needed to succeed.

CHAPTER 13

MUSEUMS AND THE
INTER-WAR YEARS

In the immediate post-war years, there was a strong desire to return the country to 'normality', to what was remembered of pre-war conditions. There had been too much change and too many challenges; people wanted what they could trust and many thought they could trust their memories of what used to be. This retreat into the past in the nation's psyche, led to the abandonment of many of the ideas and hopes that had been fostered and explored in the war years. It also led to a slow and unrealistic approach to dealing with the social and economic issues which faced the country. The practices in which museums had engaged to serve the needs of the home front were excused as one-off initiatives, to which there was now no need to return. Reflecting on the exhibitions and educational work on health, hygiene and food production in which the Norwich Castle Museum had been engaged during the war, the Curator, Frank Leney, questioned whether such activities 'really came under the scope of museum work'. His concern must have been shared by many of his fellow curators, as little, if any, of this type of work continued after 1919.

While prepared to sponsor some reforming legislation, such as Fisher's Education Act of 1918, the Government was not ready to see ideas of reconstruction followed through to their natural conclusions. The Ministry of Reconstruction, whose Adult Education Committee had explored positive and adventurous ideas about museums, was dismantled in June 1919, just when it should have been at the peak of its activity.

New legislation and high hopes

On the face of it, museums did reasonably well out of some of the new legislation, although this is a relative judgement. Official interest in them was at best moderate, but certainly more than was offered to other forms of cultural provision, such as opera or the theatre. Under the Education Act of 1918, local education authorities were empowered to make grants to museums. In 1919, the Public Libraries Act removed the limit on funds that could be spent

from the rates on museums. Further, in 1921, an amendment to the Finance
Act allowed part exemption from death duties to those selling paintings and
art objects to public collections. The situation looked promising, in this area
as in others, until the early 1920s. Then it became clear that the country's
economy was falling apart at the seams.

Such was the promise of the moment, that the Museums Association's
Council decided in October 1920 that the time was right to advocate a scale
of salaries for museum curators. It set out an explanation of the problem as
a means of making its case. The Museums Association argued that the level
of salaries paid was fundamental to the future of museums. But the wide and
diverse nature of curatorial work was seen as problematic in the formulation
of generally applicable salary scales. The Museums Association ascribed the
current poor salaries to inadequate funding overall, with the greater number
of museums operating on less than £2000 per year. It hoped that the new
legislation would help, and that the educational role of museums would aid
their case. Finally, the Museums Association blamed the low salaries of curators on the members of museum committees:

> ... recruited from classes that have little knowledge of, nor active interest in, museum
> work ... This defect in the governing body can be put right only by the wider
> education of classes from which those who serve on Museum Committees are drawn,
> and by the co-operation of a larger number of members with special qualifications
> for the duty. (*Museums Journal* 20: 125)

If curators could not convince their own museums committee of the worth
and value of museums and hence their curators, who else could they convince?

A salary scale was duly published by the Museums Association, along with
a number of recommendations including one that it was 'eminently unde-
sirable' that the posts of curator and librarian should be combined. In spite
of the efforts to pursue a 'strong case' with firmness and moderation, it had
little effect as Miers was to point out in his report of 1928 (see Chapter 7).
The salaries of museum curators in provincial museums saw no significant
improvement and in real terms fell further when compared to other professions' salaries. When, in 1928, the members of the Royal Commission on
National Museums and Galleries questioned members of the Museums
Association about the state of museums in the provinces, the President, Sir
Martin Conway, was asked about the salary levels. He replied that salaries
were not sufficient 'in any case' and, moreover, career prospects were hardly
encouraging. Conway commented that a man could 'take a degree in an
ordinary university and get a salary at once for which he would have to wait
10 to 15 years in a museum, so we cannot get the men' (Royal Commission
on National Museums and Galleries 1929: 143).

Municipal museums

In many respects, the local authority or municipal museums became worse off than the national museums during the inter-war years. In 1928, the condition and quality of local authority museums were the subjects of a damning report, commissioned by the Carnegie Trustees. Its author, Sir Henry Miers, surveyed 267 provincial museums and observed:

> It may surely be claimed that their chief function is by means of exhibited objects to instruct, and to inspire with a desire for knowledge, children and adults alike; to stimulate not only a keener appreciation of past history and present activities, but also a clearer vision of the potentialities of the future. They should stir the interest, and excite the imagination of the ordinary visitor, and also be for the specialist and the student the fruitful field for research.
>
> If this definition is accepted, the next question is, Do the public museums in the United Kingdom fulfil these functions? The stronger one's belief in the great work they do, the stronger is the conviction that at present they fail and fail lamentably. There is no doubt that the country is not getting what it should from the public museums. (Miers 1928: 38)

The explanation for such a poor state of affairs is not straightforward. Many museums had shown themselves to have the potential for real and effective public service during the war years; they had rich and exciting collections, in many cases built up over more than a century; they had buildings that were well sited; but still they were moribund during this period. It has to be remembered that provincial museums had come into being largely because the industrial towns and cities were wealthy and confident enough to see them as valid statements of the new urban order. The rise of local government had ensured their successful establishment. In the 1920s, the same structure of local government, now with even more authority and greater responsibilities, began to see them as a low priority.

By the inter-war years, local government in Britain had a well developed democratic apparatus and an independent system of finance through revenue derived from rates, borrowing and the provision of services such as gas and electricity. Central government had passed on more and more responsibility to local councils and their spending increased significantly as a result. This was especially true of spending on education which, between 1921 and 1940, rose by 44 per cent, compared with only a 13 per cent increase in exchequer grants. Local government found itself without responsibility for the shape of education it had to provide, but with increasing responsibility for a substantial part of its funding. There was simply not enough money for the extra duties central government had heaped upon the local authorities, and inevitably the ratepayers found themselves paying more and more. Priorities in this and other areas of local authority service provision had to be set. Those which were not seen as an essential functioning part of local services tended to get little if any support or funding.

This state of affairs is borne out by the Miers Report. He found museums 'the least valued of the municipal services'. Even a fairly good museum was receiving less than a ½d rate (Miers 1928: 47). The Public Libraries Act, therefore, seems to have made little difference and was not the 'charter for museums' that Lowe of Leicester Museum had once hailed it to be (*Museums Journal* 20: 53). Indeed, in 1921 Lowe saw his own museum close for two days a week, because there were not sufficient funds to run it efficiently. The underfunding and lack of support led to: understaffing; very low pay levels; curators still working in their seventies and eighties, being unable to retire without a pension; cramped and dirty buildings; and out of date displays. It has to be questioned whether it was this era that gave the word 'museum' its association with dead, silent and dusty places. Miers summed up his feelings:

> The very word 'museum' excites the wrong impression in the minds of people who have never seen one of the few that are really good. This is not surprising when one considers how dull many of them have become and how low the worst of them have sunk. (Miers 1928: 80)

There were of course some exceptions and a number of important initiatives, which Miers was pleased to acknowledge, such as the schools service in Leeds, and the founding of the Lancashire and Cheshire Museum Federation, but, in the main the situation was unpromising. Even an art gallery as significant as that in Birmingham existed without a purchase fund.

It must be said that curators did not help their own case. Positive steps to establish appropriate salary scales had little if any impact, and tentative moves towards a formal system of curatorial training were slow and hesitant. The intolerance shown towards the proposals to develop the educational roles of museums and the failure to see the relevance of their wartime experiences to peacetime provision resulted in entrenched and reactionary positions, from which few if any developments were possible. Moreover, attempts to publicize and popularize museums were treated with poorly disguised scorn.[1] It was taken as quite natural that a director or curator would be 'keenly interested in the technical side of his work' and therefore 'hardly likely to be much intrigued by the prosaic business of advertising' (*Museums Journal* 22: 272).

Curators wanted to see the museum's role as totally centred on the 'specimen'. A letter from the Museums Association to the Ministry of Reconstruction in December 1918 had laid this out as clearly as possible: 'the primary function of a museum ... is to collect, preserve and utilize specimens' (*Museums Journal* 18: 110). All the rhetoric about how museums could educate, inspire and motivate people seemed to have gone. Curators wanted to curate. Many of them had been in the museum service for over 40 years; they had no truck with the new way of things, and certainly no will to adjust their thinking.

The case for provincial museums was further weakened by their inability to offer a service which could fit in with the changing patterns of cultural consumption and mass entertainment. More people than ever before had access to the cinema, the gramophone, the wireless and the popular press. Significant advances in the technology which underpinned these media forms ensured they not only captured but also retained the public's interest. The opportunities for disseminating information, ideas and attitudes were seemingly without limit and were eagerly grasped, not least by the British Broadcasting Company established in 1926.[2] Moreover, forms of recreation popular before the war, became even more so in the 1920s as people dedicated more of their scarce leisuretime and resources to them. There was a significant increase in the number of people engaged in such pursuits as cycling, walking, going to the theatre and the music halls, attending sporting fixtures, reading and taking up domestic craft work. Unchanging provincial museums, with little apparent concern for their visitors' interests, would be unlikely to find a constituency in such times.

National museums and galleries

The national museums fared comparatively better, but even so faced many difficulties. In part at least, this may have been due to their location, close to the decision-making apparatuses. But there was more to it than this. It has been pointed out that if the 19th century was the great age of the provincial cities, the 20th century belonged to London, and London's cultural dominance was cumulative (Stevenson 1984). London had so much to offer intellectually, culturally, spiritually; so much more than the increasingly impoverished provinces. The climate was stimulating and adventurous. The national museums, with their staff of high academic calibre and collections of world importance, secured an unassailable place.

These museums attracted patronage on a significant scale. For example, in 1923, Samuel Courtauld, chairman of Courtaulds Ltd gave £50,000 to the Tate Gallery trustees for the purchase of modern French paintings. The gift bought incomparable Impressionist and Post-Impressionist works to the Tate. Joseph Duveen the younger spent £250,000 on public museums between 1930–1938 (Minihan 1977: 182). The national museums and galleries were also not afraid to attract new audiences and to enhance educational provision. For example, the Science Museum experimented with means of making its collections more understandable (Follett 1978: 98). By the end of the 1920s it had over 300 working models. The declared policy was to draw the visitor's attention to all the things that 'are worth looking at, sometimes by illumination, sometimes by keeping them in movement, sometimes by making them workable' (Royal Commission on National Museums and Galleries 1928: 152–3). The Science Museum was also mounting exhibitions illustrating the results of recent research and discovery; and in 1931 it built its famous Children's Gallery.

Nevertheless, it would be false to suggest that the national museums somehow managed to avoid the effects of the Depression. Expenditure, other than for agreed capital developments, did not increase and did not rise above a total of £1 million for the inter-war years. For the financial year 1920–21, the cost of running the Victoria and Albert Museum was £211,285, for the Science Museum it was £57,015, and for the Natural History Museum it was £123,876. The Government's Committee on National Expenditure recommended in 1921 that entry charges be brought in at the national museums and art galleries on certain days of the week. It met some resistance. Pre-war, charges had been levied at the Tate, the Victoria and Albert Museum and the National Gallery. At the time the recommendation was made, charges were still in force at some of the national museums and galleries; the National Gallery, for example, was charging 6d on days other than Wednesdays, Saturdays and Sundays. The British Museum would resist charges at all costs. Sir Frederick Kenyon, the Director, pointed out that the museum had been free since it was opened in 1756 and that legislation would be needed to bring in charges at the BM and Natural History Museum. The *Museums Journal* joined in the argument by estimating that:

> ... the slight income raised will be counterbalanced by the decrease in the sale of publications. Over-head and establishment charges will, presumably, remain unaltered; but the educational work accomplished will be about halved. (*Museums Journal* 21: 238)

In 1927, a Royal Commission was established to look into the affairs of the national museums and galleries. One of the areas which the Commissioners were instructed to consider was 'in what way, if any, expenditure may be limited without crippling the educational and general usefulness of the Institutions'. The Commission took extensive evidence from all the national museum directors and many other interested parties. In their final report, they supported the museums and advocated that they should be adequately maintained by Government funding: 'in our view economy has already been pushed beyond the point of prudent administration' (Royal Commission 1929: 29).

Preparing for another war

Both the Miers Report and that of the Royal Commission contained recommendations which both in spirit and substance marked the way forward for museums. What was needed was: better exhibitions and services; better salaries and a formal system of training; a national body to represent museums and an enhanced role for the Museums Association; a greater awareness of the needs and interests of the visitor, and an expansion of museums to include a new type evident in Scandinavia – folk museums. Overall they asked for a greater openness and a preparedness to accept change. In the 1930s, some of these strands were being picked up and there was some evidence of growth, although this was mostly in the margins of museum provision (Markham 1938; Kavanagh 1990). But as promising as some of these developments were, they were interrupted by the prospect of another war.

The Government was alert to the dangers and as early as July 1933, Lord Harlech (Mr Ormsby Gore) called a meeting of representatives of the national galleries, museums and libraries at the Office of Works to discuss plans for the evacuation of national art treasures. The Government was particularly alert this time to the importance of the national museums and collections to popular morale. At the suggestion that the national art treasures be sent abroad for safe-keeping, Winston Churchill sent a note to Kenneth Clark, Director of the National Gallery: 'Bury them in the bowels of the earth, but not a picture shall leave this island' (Alberge 1991). In 1938, national museums were putting plans into effect for the removal of their collections and in 1939 the British Museum published a booklet advising all museums on the protection of collections from air raids.

With the outbreak of war in September 1939, the Museums Association published this advice and sent copies to all members:

MUSEUMS AND THE WAR

At the present time, when the energies of the Nation are necessarily directed to winning the war, there may be a tendency to overlook the fundamental importance of museums and art galleries as essential parts of that civilisation for which we are fighting. These institutions contain collections of great importance, not only to us, but to the whole civilised world, and whatever the stress of circumstances it is our duty to see that such collections are adequately safeguarded and preserved.

The museums movement therefore must carry on with the maximum possible efficiency, and if the work of conserving the Nation's treasures can be supplemented by ever extending educational and inspirational activities, the position of museums after this war will be far stronger than it was in 1918. There is in effect a great opportunity before us.

During the last war, some museums played a tremendous part and established themselves once and for ever in the estimation of local authorities. We most strongly urge that full advantage should be taken of the present opportunity for service.

S.F. MARKHAM, President
E.W. WIGNALL, Secretary
(*Museums Journal* 39: 317)

Clearly, echoes of what would soon be termed the First – as opposed to the Great – War were evident in this statement. Subsequent war circulars from the Museums Association and individual war policy statements from museums also lent heavily on this experience. For some museums, the most useful lesson that had emerged from the First World War was how to prepare for the Second.

CHAPTER 14

MUSEUMS AND THE FIRST WORLD WAR

THE experience of war affected people in different ways. In the armed forces, a person's rank, the theatre of war in which he or she had been placed and the moment of involvement dictated in significant part the kind of memories held in later life. For those at home, whether working in munitions, on the land, in clerical work or in museums, the memories were of a different cast. Yet what bound most together was the profound experience of loss. And the losses were extreme: opportunities, hopes and dreams, ways of believing, and, of course – more than anything else – the lives of those known and loved. Perversely, the war also provided some positive gains, although even now these are hard to see, obscured as they are by the trauma of it all.

Both museum curators and the trustees of museums had, in the main, attempted to do the right thing at the right time, within the context of the political climate. They were as much caught up in the train of events as were most people. The balance sheet in terms of losses and gains is not easy to lay out: partly because it is false to see the four years of war as being totally disconnected from pre- and post-war trends; and partly because there was no such thing as a united museum movement where what was true for one was true for all. However, some general and specific points can be made.

Positive outcomes

The first of these has to be the positioning of museums, but primarily the nationals, in the public's consciousness; arguably in a deep awareness of their place as part of the apparatus which underpinned a broad cultural identity. In the midst of the crisis, the Britishness of the '*British*' Museum and the '*National*' Gallery were keenly felt, especially by the middle classes – although significantly less so by politicians – the depth of this turned these museums into symbolic standards of beleagured nationhood. The regard for the museums stood the test of extreme circumstances. It was best expressed in the popular support given in 1916 when the nationals were on the brink of closure and again in 1917 when it was rumoured that the Air Ministry was about to take over the British Museum. The campaign to keep the national museums open was spontaneous and pursued with vigour. It perturbed even the press, itself not given to anything that might suggest even the mildest of criticisms of Governmental decisions and wary of anything that might 'rock the boat'. But in this instance, the matter seemed clear: the decision to close the national museums was made for the wrong reasons, and the strength of public feeling had been underestimated.

Yet, in spite of the national museums and galleries in London being closed or partially closed from 1916 and the restrictions on the facilities available at a number of provincial museums, people were still disposed to visit those that remained open when they could. Given that Britain was engaged in a total war, the visitor figures for this period are worthy of note. The relative consistency of these figures suggests that in the capital cities and in the provincial towns, museums must have been providing something that people needed: intellectually, socially or personally. Visiting patterns inevitably altered, but the levels remained of note. Admittedly, museums were not universally adored, and significant social sectors may well have been indifferent to them or alienated by them. But if anything, the war may have enhanced public attachment to them, at least for a time, by first threatening them with closure and worst still destruction, and second by giving them an opportunity to provide for the public in ways not considered before.

The second positive outcome centres on the exhibitions museums mounted during the war. These varied greatly in content. Some sought to meet the mood of the moment, others to press for a suitably positive attitude or simply impart what was seen as important information. Whether about fleas, rats, feeding infants, growing potatoes, the plight of Belgian refugees or the weaponry of war, all the exhibitions mounted had an underlying purpose: the war effort and its successful conclusion. In terms of museum practice, they provided ample evidence that museums could mount popular, instructive and socially useful exhibitions that would be well received and well attended. Such work involved curators in organizing a range of material in an instructive manner, working in co-operation with others and engaging in supporting educational activities.

In terms of the war effort, it is impossible to gauge the degree to which such exhibitions fulfilled the intentions of the authorities which funded and encouraged them. As has been seen, visitor figures for some of these exhibitions exceeded all expectations. But just because large numbers of people went to see the exhibitions, it does not necessarily follow that a uniform message was taken away by each and every single visitor, although the spirit of the thing may well have been consciously understood. Even today, when museums are equipped with a fairly sophisticated understanding of how visitors use the museum environment and can, to some degree, test whether the intentions behind an exhibition have been successful, it is impossible to gauge *precisely* its impact. We now recognize that people, within their given cultural and educational contexts, freely make up their own agendas when visiting exhibitions, and will pick and choose what they want to be interested in, and how much information they take away with them. There is nothing to suppose that in this regard visitors in 1918 were any different from visitors in 1993.

Suffice it to say that the confident belief that such exhibitions had been and were worthwhile, coupled with the educational work museums had developed with schools especially in Manchester, were enough to convince key figures in the civil service, Parliament and elsewhere that museums had a real educational purpose. The pre-war rhetoric about the educational and social potential of museums had been tested and found to have in it more than a grain of truth. The view evolved that after the war museums could be developed to engage more directly in educational work and public service, but these proposals lapsed in the face of curatorial indifference and a failing post-war economy. However, what had been achieved was an important indicator that not only could museums cope in wartime, but that if appropriately employed, they could be both useful and advantageous on the home front, whether as part of the country's internal propaganda or as part of a search for rest and stability. For all the faults, shortcomings and inherent dangers, museums between 1914 and 1918 – whether as sites for exhibitions or as homes for collections – had something to offer.

The third positive outcome, sprang unexpectedly from the risks of war. The problems of caring for major collections in such times, and especially the movement of collections to and from places of safety, sharply focused attention on the importance and condition of the material held. One of the places of safety, a section of London Underground, used by the British Museum, the National Gallery and the National Portrait Gallery, was climatically unsuited to the well-being of the collections stored there. On the return of the material, a thorough audit was instigated: a cuneiform tablet once thought to have been lost was found. But of greater significance, as a result of the movement of the collections, the British Museum and the National Gallery took steps to investigate the physical well-being of their holdings. This led ultimately to the founding of a scientific conservation department at the British Museum and leant considerable weight to the development of conservation facilities at the National Gallery and elsewhere. The new approaches to science in conservation successfully joined with high levels of craft skill which had been employed for some time in the restoration of materials. Better informed collection management at the nationals and, as the years progressed, elsewhere was a result. The conservation techniques developed in Britain, ongoing scientific research, and ever greater understanding of the importance of environmental conditions and handling procedures have resulted in Britain being a world leader in this field.

Science in particular was a beneficiary of war: it became popular and respectable in ways not experienced in the pre-war decades. As far as museums were concerned, the war gave ample opportunity for the science museums to prove their worth. The collections, research facilities and the expertise of curatorial staff came into use in unprecedented ways. Work conducted at the British Museum (Natural History), the Geological Museum and the Science Museum contributed directly to the war effort. The reputations of these museums were enhanced as a result. Not only that, but in the post-war years, the heightened interest in science, among the public as much as official departments of state, ensured that these museums held a secure position. They adopted a positive attitude to this and were prepared to build on their success by expanding their services and experimenting with their exhibitions. Compared to other museums, they weathered the difficult years of the 1920s and 1930s relatively well.

One of the outcomes of the war was the forming of a new national collection and museum: the Imperial War Museum. Regardless of the perspective taken of the war, as an evil mistake, an heroic adventure or complex conjoining of bitter circumstances, it was a profound human experience and deserved an adequate and full record. No museum has ever been established without some underlying political purpose. Sometimes if the subject is an easy one (such as water-colour paintings, costume or veteran cars), the purpose may be obscured and all those involved innocently, but falsely, claim their neutrality. But when the subject is complex (such as religion, industry or war), the political agenda can be more obvious. The founding of the Imperial War Museum was one of a range of initiatives taken to maintain a supportive attitude to the war at a moment when the country came near to defeat. The all-important immediate aim was balanced out by the long-term goals of those directly involved with the museum. The adventurous approach adopted in the formation of the collections, and the comprehensiveness of record aimed for, ensured that the museum would find a role once the war ended. Although beset by difficulties in the 1920s and 1930s, its collection became, and remains, a principal source of reference to those studying the war. The fortunes of the museum fluctuated over the decades with each shift in public tolerance to the idea of war. It has emerged in the 1990s as a museum of international status, with well defined academic and educational roles. The complexities of interpretation and the balance between portraying war as heroics and war as human experience nevertheless remains.

Some post-war changes were unexpectedly enabling for museum developments. The shifts in world power, the continued rise of stronger centres of industrial and economic powers, particularly America and Japan, and the growing inability to cope with the demands of the Empire, resulted in a rediscovery of a domestic past. A regard for the countryside grew, as did enthusiasm for images of pre-industrial times. This view was often highly generalized and nearly always totally romanticized. It is little wonder that in the 1920s and 1930s folk-life collections and folk museums developed. Substantial progress was made in Scotland, Wales and the Isle of Man, where collections were formed and records gathered. Such broad based museum archives are now of considerable importance in our study of the cultural configurations of these areas and the daily lives of the people who lived in them. In England, progress was far less assured and more sporadic. The strength of regionalism and, of greater importance, the lack of political necessity to define England as a cultural whole, did not provide the conditions necessary for an English Folk Museum. In the absence of a national initiative, and for reasons mostly of their own, important regional folk collections did develop in parts of England. However, not until after the Second World War, when the Empire was being dismantled, did the folk life collection and museum become a common feature of museum provision throughout Britain (Kavanagh 1990).

The war had an impact on most forms of employment, including that in museums. Women came into curatorial work on a salaried basis. Some had to leave in 1919, but others did not and by the end of the 1920s, the idea of female museum curators was being accepted, although their subsequent rise to positions of seniority in museums has been very slow. There were other labour issues. During the war, museums – especially the nationals and large provincial museums – became increasingly dependent on volunteers for tasks such as the packaging of collections for removal, with which the hard-pressed staff could not deal. The concept of volunteers in museums, either as helpers or as free curatorial labour, had been established in the late 18th century with the learned societies and was well developed in the 19th century in provinical museums. This did not change because of the war; indeed, if anything, it was reinforced by the war experience. Museums have always benefited from the talents and interests people elect to share with them. This form of participation undoubtedly has had its merits. But it has had many consequences for the development of professionalism and for the salary levels of museum posts, especially in the provinces. Museum authorities could and did pose the question: if able volunteers could carry out museum work, at least adequately and often very well, what need was there for the recruitment of young talented staff, or improved salaries in line with responsibilities?

Finally, the war taught some lessons which were remembered. When in the mid-1930s it became increasingly likely that there would be another war, regardless of the manifestly empty reassurances to the contrary, curators and museum trustees had the experience of the First War to which they could refer. They knew a great deal about the movement of collections to places of safety, the securing of buildings, the use of museum space for Government

and other departments, and the possible roles of museums in the maintenance of morale on the home front. The Second World War was different in
so many ways from the First, it called for a much stronger response and, if
anything, even greater endurance. In particular, the bomb damage was more
extreme and geographically widespread, and a number of museums were
either damaged or destroyed. The British Museum was badly hit, Liverpool
and Hull museums lost a substantial part of their buildings and also major
collections. The Victoria and Albert Museum, on the wall nearest the entrance to the Henry Cole Wing, still bears scars from the Blitz. It is impossible to calculate how much greater the losses would have been had not the
museums been aware of the risks and taken appropriate action. If the national
museum and gallery collections had remained on view in London, it is highly
likely they would have been either destroyed or damaged.

Negative outcomes

Of the three quarters of a million British men who lost their lives in the First
World War, a very small number were men who worked in museums and
who no doubt believed they would return to such work when the war was
over. It is impossible to calculate the loss of talent this represented, or the
losses which accrued from the deaths of younger men who, once their
university education was completed, might have come into curatorial work.
The Lost Generation could have made a world of difference had they survived to experience the bulk of the twentieth century, or so we tend to
think. Of those that did survive the war, the scars were often as much on
the personality and memory, as over the body. Healing was about much more
than the repair of bone and body tissue.

Even before the war ended, the proposal that every city, town and village
should have a war museum was no longer taken seriously. Other ways of
remembering were found: people needed the quiet dignity of the memorials
and memorial gardens, and the positive contributions such as memorial
hospitals. The broken bodies of ex-servicemen were everywhere to be seen,
and the broken lives of those who had lost someone very close escaped no
one. As time went on people became less inclined to look upon the facts and
material of war. The Imperial War Museum filled the need as far as it went,
but at the local level things were different. In these circumstances, it is as well
that local museums devoted to the war were not established. Not only would
they have been out of tune with a nation in grief but also, more practically,
the cost and the responsibility for their development might have resulted in
the over-burdening of local authority museum services to the point of collapse. For the inter-war years, the local authorities had difficulty enough
financing essential services such as education, let alone funding established

or new museums. Provincial museums managed to keep going somehow: the status quo was maintained, more or less. It would have been impossible to sustain local war museums in such circumstances.

In contrast, there was a very noticable increase in the number of service – especially regimental – museums and collections which were developed for very different reasons. The common factor, however, was that their purpose was not directed outwards to the general public, but inwards to the services' own needs. For some regiments, the exercise may well have been pragmatic; for others, much more deliberate and conscious. However, for the first time ever important material was brought together from a variety of 'lodging' places and identified as worthy of the type of care given in museums. The service museums, the majority embryonic, struggled on as best they could well into the 1950s. Some have managed well enough; others, perhaps the majority, have faced stagnation. This can be ascribed in part to the fact that in the critical period of their early development, that is in the inter-war years, there was not sufficient political or social purpose to facilitate their growth and hence funds were not made available for them.

With the economy in disarray and far-reaching social problems to cope with, the Government no longer had a place for museums – of any sort – on their political agenda. A great deal of museum work in the war had indicated the potential of both well-thought out collections and exhibitions timed to meet people's interests. Many people, including a number of politicians, were convinced but even this was not sufficient in such hard times. Established on the Victorian philosophy of self-help and the moral purposes of education, museums were left in the hands of underpaid, untrained and ageing curators. Certainly, there were people of calibre employed in museums; for example, from the war period itself Elijah Howarth and Frederic Kenyon stand out. But there were many, many others – weary men, in need of both rest and retirement. More than adequately conversant with the well-articulated philosophies of museum provision, a good part of which they had help develop, they had not the stamina, the resources or the attitudes necessary to produce the form of provision needed in the 1920s and 1930s. A good proportion of museums survived the inter-war period in the relative security of stagnation, which the curators did little to disturb.

The museums which prospered during this time were those where relevant scholarly work was conducted and where efforts were made to interpret collections in interesting ways. The Science Museum is a case in point. Here, much good, solid academic work was conducted and collections of importance were acquired. But the majority failed to shake off their reputation for being dusty places where dead objects rested. This did not go unnoticed. For example, a Board of Education Report in 1931, paid warm tribute to the richness and variety of museum collections, but pointed out that large sums of public money were being spent on them and that they were not being used 'as they could or should be in the service of education'.

Underlying this was the failure of curators, especially those who spoke on behalf of the majority, to grasp the importance of what had been achieved and to adapt the ideas and methods for use in peacetime. There was more than enough here to argue a convincing case for enhanced museum provision. But instead, temporary exhibitions addressing current interests and public education were abandoned, there was a reluctance to accept fully the educational roles of museums, and an inability to see how the precedent of contemporary collecting at the Imperial War Museum might be adapted and used elsewhere. This inability to learn from the war experience set back museum provision at a time when it could be ill-afforded. Several generations later, these ideas were discovered all over again and are in use today.

In so many respects, the case for museums in the 1990s would be all the stronger had not momentum been lost in the 1920s. Admittedly, curators knew there was a problem, hence the efforts throughout the 1920s to establish some system of professional training. But much more was needed; in particular, open minds, a willingness to learn and an ability to see the world as it was: in a state of rapid change. Museums had proven their usefulness in the war, but in times of peace their purposes became much less certain. It took another war and a new generation of curators before different ideas were allowed to prevail.

CHAPTER 15
MUSEUMS AND WAR

THE First World War was the key event of the past two centuries. The nineteenth century led to it: the twentieth century has been created out of it. Just as the events of the nineteenth century guaranteed there would be war, so in the twentieth century this particular war guaranteed there would be others. Moreover, in spite of the futility of it all, it did little to dissuade the powerful, at the time or in subsequent generations, that war provides few true victors. In every year since 1918, war has raged in some part of the world.

On the kinds of balance sheets that wars create – lives lost, territories gained, economies wrecked, fortunes made – museums and the cultural heritage are small beer. They may appear so insignificant as to be hardly worth thinking about. In such a view, bodies are more important than buildings, military objectives more important than preservation, lives saved more important than paintings or archaeological remains destroyed. The judgements are not easy ones and it is little wonder that museums have not made it even to the margins of the histories written about the First World War and later conflicts.

Nevertheless, the social and cultural dimensions of war are significant: they become as much part of the prosecution of war as the politics and the fighting. Modern wars, which began with the First World War, have been and are 'total' wars. No sector can remain untouched by them. Culture, in terms of the systems of being and believing that make one people in some way different from the next, has been the focus of much of this century's hatred and bloodshed. Museums aim to embody evidence of the cultural whole, through carefully gathered material things. In general terms, museums are an element of our humanity, and usually contain the most positive expressions of ourselves as worthwhile, creative and inventive people. War is the reverse; it exposes our inhumanity and makes evident our capacities for destructiveness and greed. The basis of museums is to preserve all that records and celebrates. The basis of war is to destroy all that is in the way of a desired outcome.

Museums, collections and the places and processes which constitute someone's heritage have been in the front line of most of the wars this century. Many museums, especially in Europe, have been literally in the front line, either because of random strategic military necessity, or more often because their power as symbols for the cultural whole is such that they become legitimate targets for belligerent forces. At the crudest level museums – like churches – have been rich sources of booty. The hatred that courses through all wars spills over in the wanton destruction of places and things of value to the other side. But this is more than mindless theft and vandalism. Time and again, military conquest has been exercised through the denial of a people's history, cultural expression and ideals. In this regard, to the belligerent, museums – like libraries, newspapers and churches – are dangerous places. They are often places where people can think, debate and question. Museums can tell us who we are, what we are and when we are: a fact which makes them a great inconvenience, and also a great weapon, to those trying to re-draw a political map and impose a new order.

The history of museums during the wars this century has still to be re-searched and written. If it were to deal with the histories of the wars in which Europe has been engaged, it would need to address many important topics, including: how museums and collections in the 1930s were developed to express revised political identities; the collections commissioned and amassed in Nazi Germany to promote the ideals of the fatherland and the master race; the preparations made for the Second World War and the lengths taken to store collections in places of safety; the uses museums were put to in the war and the extent of their contribution to the home front; the long-term consequences of the illegal movement of both private and public col-lections in Europe during the Second World War; and the aftermath of war, especially in terms of re-building a number of museums damaged by enemy action. Such a history would need to question the importance the Hague Convention of 1954 based on earlier, equally unsuccessful, agreements to protect cultural property, including museums, in time of war, which marks a dichotomy of views about responsibility to cultural heritage. The history would examine museum responses to later, geographically more distant, wars, for example Korea, Vietnam, the Falklands and the Gulf, and how these experiences were and are represented in museum collections and exhibition programmes. There would also be the issue of conflict nearer to home, specifically in Northern Ireland. Further, the work would have to encompass the foundation and development of peace museums this century. By the time the research was complete, no doubt, there would be other conflicts needing to be chronicled.

On 28 June 1914, the Archduke Franz Ferdinand of Austria and his wife were assassinated in Sarajevo, the capital city of Bosnia-Herzegovina. By the beginning of August, Europe was at war. The First World War had begun. That was 80 years ago, and as I complete this text, the bitterest of wars has been raging in Croatia and Bosnia. Genocide, masquerading under the euphemism of 'ethnic cleansing', has been relentlessly pursued, along with

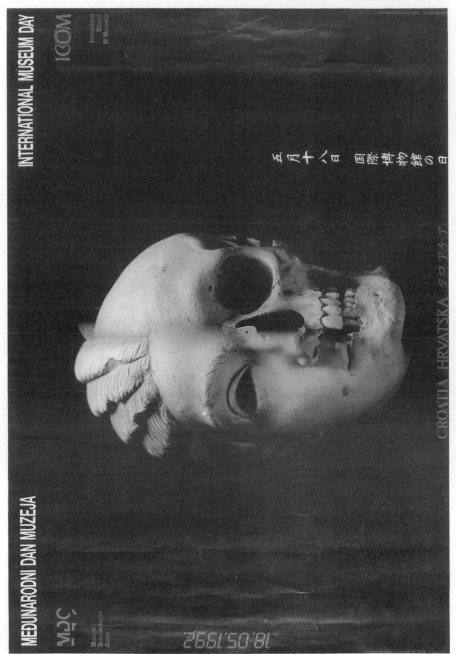

31. Poster published by the museums in Croatia to mark International Museums Day.
Source: Museum Documentation Centre, Zagreb, Republic of Croatia

the destruction of all those things and special places which give people their identity. Museums, religious and cultural sites are again in the front line and the destruction has been wholesale. This time, the shots ringing out from Sarajevo, a city of 380,000 people under siege, have had very little effect on Europe, which now deliberately chooses to stand to one side. Whatever the outcome of the war may be, in time it will involve the rescuing of those elements of the cultural heritage which suit best the new order, and the creation of new museums. That which has not been eradicated will be suppressed. That which fits the politics of the situation will be glorified. Depending on the prevailing circumstances, museums will become a weapon, a salve, or a rallying point. The history of museums, like the history of war, will repeat itself.

POSTSCRIPT

A MEMORIAL to the 16 men from the British Museum who 'fought and fell' was erected in the front entrance in 1921. Commissioned from the sculptor Eric Gill, it bears as part of the inscription four lines from the poem 'For the Fallen', written in September 1914 by the poet Laurence Binyon, who was also the Deputy Keeper in charge of Oriental Prints and Drawings 1909–32.

> They shall not grow old as we that are left grow old.
> Age shall not weary them, nor the years condemn.
> At the going down of the sun and in the morning,
>
> We will remember them.

CHAPTER NOTES

1. Museums and pre-war Britain

1. E. Howarth (d. 1938). Assistant at Liverpool Museum 1871–76, Curator of Public Museum and Mappin Art Gallery, Sheffield 1876–1928. One of the founders of the Museums Association; secretary of the Museums Association 1891–1909. Editor of the *Museums Journal* 1901–1909. President of the Museums Association 1912–1913.

2. Howarth was referring to statistics he compiled with H. M. Platnauer for the *Directory of Museums*, published in 1911. The figures he quoted included Irish Museums.

3. These were Sunderland (1846), Canterbury (1847), Warrington (1848), and Dover, Leicester and Salford (1849).

4. The British Museum was at far greater risk from the Chelsea pensioners than from the Chartists. The pensioners would not desist from smoking, even though they were very close to open barrels of ammunition.

5. Professional bodies established in the nineteenth century include: the Royal College of Surgeons 1800; Institute of Civil Engineers 1818; Law Society 1825; Royal Institute of British Architects 1834; Pharmaceutical Society of Great Britain 1841; Institute of Actuaries 1848; British Medical Association 1856; Library Association 1877; Civil and Public Services Association 1903.

2. Museums and collections at risk

1. *Report for the years 1914–1916 on the National Gallery*, P.P., 1916 116 xxix 303.

2. *Report for the years 1914–19 on the National Portrait Gallery*, P. P., 1916 Col. 7984 xxix 491.

3. British Museum Standing Committee Minutes, 12 April 1913.

4. Some time later, it transpired that 'Mary Stewart' had been released under the provisions of the 'Cat and Mouse' Act. She failed to appear for later hearings and the museum witnesses were therefore dismissed. British Museum Standing Committee Minutes, 9 May 1914.

5. British Museum Standing Committee Minutes, 13 June 1914.

6. E. Rimbault Dibdin (1853–1941). Trained in Scottish Law 1870–1877. Insurance Official 1877–1904. Art Critic Liverpool Courier 1887–1904. Curator Walker Art Gallery 1904–18. President of the Museums Association 1915–18. Organised and arranged Barroda Art Gallery 1919–21.

7. BM 4562. Letter to Kenyon from C.H. Read, 12 November 1914. British Museum Archives.

8. 'Notes on the British Museum (Natural History) and the War 1914–1918', (unpublished pamphlet) CP/746/1, British Museum (Natural History), Central Museum Archives.

9. *Agreements made between His Majesty's Government and the War Risks Insurance Associations: 1914–16* Cmd. 7838 iv 863.

10. Leicester Museum and Art Gallery Committee Minutes 12 July 1915. Leicester Record Office.

11. Sheffield Public Museum Minutes, 16 September 1915. Sheffield City Museums Archives.

12. Sir Whitworth Wallis (1855–1927). Younger son of George Wallis FSA, Senior Keeper South Kensington Museum. In charge of Bethnal Green Museum 1879–81. In charge of Indian Collections, South Kensington Museum 1881–84. Appointed Director of Birmingham Art Gallery 1885. Delivered special lectures to the troops in France 1917.

13. Birmingham Museum and Art Gallery Committee Minutes, 1 July 1918. Birmingham Records Office.

14. *Report for the year 1916 on the Science Museum and on Geological Survey and the Museum of Practical Geology*, P.P., 1917–18, Cmd. 8603 xi 595.

15. *Report for the year 1917 on the Science Museum*, P.P., 1918 Cmd. 9131 ix 891; and *Report for the year 1918 on the Science Museum*, P.P., 1919 Cmd. 121 xxi 439.

16. *Report for the year 1917 on the Victoria and Albert Museum*: P.P., 1920 Cmd. 561 xv.

17. 'Notes on the British Museum (Natural History) and the War 1914–1918', (unpublished pamphlet) CP/746/1, British Museum (Natural History), Central Museum Archives.

18. Sir F. G. Kenyon (1863–1952). Assistant, British Museum 1889–98. Assistant Keeper of Manuscripts 1898–1909. Director and Principal Librarian, British Museum 1909–30. Lt-Col in Territorial Forces (Inns of Court), served with Expeditionary Forces in France, August – September 1914 and with his regiment until 1919. Advisor to Imperial War Graves Commission. Trustee of the Imperial War Museum 1920–46.

19. BM 319. Letter to Kenyon from Lionel Earle, H. M. Office of Works, 11 February 1918.

20. 'Notes on the British Museum (Natural History) and the War 1914–18', (unpublished pamphlet) *op cit.*

3. Closures and take-overs

1. *First Report of the Committee on Retrenchment in Public Expenditure 1915*, P.P., 1914–16, Cmd. 8068, xxiii 369.

2. *Third Report of the Committee on Retrenchment in Public Expenditure 1916*, P.P., 1916, Cmd. 8180, xv, 177.

3. *Reports for the years 1914–16 for the National Portrait Gallery*: P.P., 1916 Cmd. 8290 xiv 7.

4. Ghost stories appear to have been associated with an Egyptian coffin, held by some people to be responsible for the sinking of the Titanic. A series of stories became associated with it over the years. The British Museum has issued a number of disclaimers about the myths surrounding the coffin, the last one in 1980 (Caygill 1981: 51).

5. Nottingham Castle and School of Art Committee Minutes, 10 May 1916: NCM.

6. Birmingham Museum and Art Gallery Committee Minutes, 1 July 1918: BRO.

7. Sir Alfred Mond was a talented and highly efficient Minister, who throughout his term of office was in receipt of much unwarranted vilification because of his German–Jewish origins and industrial as opposed to class background (Bolitho 1933: 165).

4. Due share and defence of the realm

1. The museum employee at South Kensington who was medically classified as C3 may have been B.F. Cummings (1889–1919) who wrote under the name of Wilhelm Nero Pilate

Barbellion. He wrote two autobiographical works *Journal of a Disappointed Man* (1919) and *A Last Diary* (1921). It is thought he died from multiple sclerosis.

2. 'Notes on the British Museum (Natural History) and the War 1914–18', (unpublished pamphlet) CP/746/1,BMNH, CMA.

3. The conscientious objector at the British Museum was H.C. Gregory, a Clerk of the Second Division. In 1916, he had been transferred from the British Museum's employ to take up duties with the War Risks Insurance Commission. In January 1917, he entered the army where, having refused an order, he was court martialled and given a six-month prison sentence. On learning this, the Trustees of the British Museum dismissed him from their service. However, in May his sentence was remitted when a Central Tribunal agreed he was a conscientious objector. He was allowed to do work of 'national importance' and his dismissal was commuted to suspension. He was re-instated at the museum in the spring of 1919 and returned to work in the summer. Kenyon was later willing to argue his case in respect of discriminatory employment conditions placed on all conscientious objectors in the post-war years. British Museum Standing Committee Minutes: 10 March 1917, 12 May 1917, 9 June 1917, 10 May 1919, 12 July 1919, 11 October 1919.

4. City of Leicester Museum and Art Gallery, *Twentieth Report of the Committee 1912–24*, 8.

5. Sheffield Public Museum Minutes, 20 March 1917.

6. Birmingham Museum and Art Gallery Committee Minutes, 2 December 1915, BRO.

7. Birmingham Museum and Art Gallery Committee Minutes, 7 March 1916, BRO.

8. Birmingham Museum and Art Gallery Committee Minutes, 7 May 1918, BRO.

9. *Report for the year 1916 on the Victoria and Albert Museum*, P.P., 1919, Cmd. 292 xxi 463.

10. E.E. Lowe (1877–1958). Assistant Warrington Museum 1891–1901. Curator Plymouth Museum and Art Gallery 1901–07. Curator Leicester Museum 1907–18. Director Leicester City Museum, Art Gallery and Library 1918–40. Hon. Secretary of Museums Association 1908–18. President of the Museums Association 1922. Prepared Report on American Museum Work for the Carnegie Trustees 1922.

11. City of Sheffield, Report of the Museums and Mappin Art Gallery, 1919.

12. *Reports for the year 1915 on the Science Museum and on Geological Survey and the Museum of Practical Geology*, P.P., 1916, Cmd. 8269 viii 525.
Reports for the year 1916 on the Science Museum and on Geological Survey and the Museum of Practical Geology, P.P., 1917–18, Cmd. 8603 xi 595.

13. Cmd. 8269.
Reports for the year 1917 on the Science Museum and on Geological Survey and the Museum of Practical Geology, P.P., 1918, Cmd. 9131 ix 891.

14. *Reports for the year 1915 on the Science Museum and on Geological Survey and the Museum of Practical Geology*, P.P., 1914–16, Cmd. 7948 xx 71.

15. Cmd. 8603.

16. Cmd. 9131.

17. *Report for the year 1918 on the Science Museum*, P.P., 1919 Cmd. 121 xxi 439.

18. 'Record of the museum in wartime', British Museum Committee Minutes, 7 December 1918. BMNH CMA.

19. 'Notes on the British Museum (Natural History) and the War 1914–18', (unpublished pamphlet) CP/746/1,BMNH, CMA.

20. *Ibid*.

21. Letter to Colonel Buchan from C.E. Fagan, Secretary of the British Museum (Natural History), 3 December 1918. BMNH CMA.

22. *Reports for the year 1919 on the Science Museum and on the Geological Survey and the Museum of Practical Geology*, P.P. 1920, Cmd. 740 xv 631.

5. Role and purpose through exhibition

1. Leicester Museum and Art Gallery Committee Minutes, 29 March 1915: LRO.

2. *Report for the year 1915 on the Science Museum*, P.P., 1916, Cmd. 8269 viii 525.

3. Howarth and Ogilvie had met in the spring of 1915 when Dr Ogilvie visited Sheffield to prepare a report for the City Council on how the museum could be co-ordinated with other educational institutions in the city.

4. City of Birmingham, Report of the Museum and Art Gallery Committee, 6 May 1919.

5. *Ibid.*

6. City of Sheffield, *Report of the Museums and Mappin Art Gallery*, 1919.

7. City of Leicester Museum and Art Gallery, *Twentieth Report of the Committee 1912–24*, 1924.

8. Notes by Major Manners Howe, C/O Royal Defence Corps., Cromwell Gardens Barracks, on the 'war farm at South Kensington' in 'Notes on the British Museum (Natural History) and the war 1914–18', (unpublished pamphlet), 1920: BMNH CMA, CP/7461.

6. Educational uses of museums

1. Ogilvie's report came out in 1919. It commended the work of the curators as a 'good illustration of what can be done'. *Educational Pamphlet, No 34, Report on the Sheffield City Museums, HMSO*, 1919.

2. The advisory committee consisted of schools inspectors, representatives from the National Union of Teachers, the Head Teachers Association, the Class Teachers Association, and Ben Mullen, curator of the museum, following consultations with the chairman of the museum sub-committee (Mullen 1918: 21–5).

3. Ben Mullen (1862–1925). Assistant in Art and Ethnography, National Museum of Ireland, Dublin 1884–92. Director of Salford Museum from 1892.

4. *Report for the year 1915 on the Victoria and Albert Museum*, P.P., 1916, Cmd. 8280 vii 551.

5. Representatives from the following towns attended: Bolton, Derby, Dundee, Lincoln, Merthyr Tydfil, Newcastle-upon-Tyne, Norwich, Reading, Salford, Southport, Wednesbury, Bristol, Doncaster, Leeds, Manchester, Middlesbrough, Northampton, Preston, Rotherham, Sheffield, Warrington, York. Five representatives from the Board of Education were nominated to attend.

6. City of Sheffield, *Report of the Museums and Mappin Art Gallery*, 1919

7. *Reconstruction First (Industrial and Social Conditions) and Third (Libraries and Museums) Reports*, P.P., 1918, Cd 9107, ix, 319, 361. *Adult Education, Report of the Committee*, P.P., 1919, Cmd. 321, xxviii, 453.

7. Making do

1. Birmingham Museum and Art Gallery Minutes, 21 February 1921.

2. The National Gallery's committee reported principally on whether there should be mechanisms for the retention of art works in this country. They recommended that there should not be any form of restrictions on the export of works of art, and advised against export duties and any form of register of paintings in private ownership. They judged it was not desirable 'to grant rights of pre-exemption or option to the nation, or otherwise restrict the free enjoyment of such works'. *Report of the Committee of Trustees of the National Gallery*

on the Retention of Important Pictures in the Country and other matters connected with the National Art Collections, 1914–16 Cmd. 7878 xxix 317.

3. The grant was £2000 in 1915, £3,500 in 1916, and £3,000 in 1917 and 1918.

4. *Report of the Director of the National Gallery for the year 1915 1916/19 xivi, also for the year 1916, 1917/18 (11) xvii, 1 and the year 1917, 1918 (55) xii 389.*

5. *National Portrait Gallery Annual Report 1915–16*, 1916, Cmd. 8290 xiv 7.

6. *National Portrait Gallery Annual Report 1916–17*, 1917–18 Cmd. 8644 xvii 19.

7. *Report for the year 1914 on the Victoria and Albert Museum 1914–16* Cmd. 7947.

8. *Report for the year 1915 on the Science Museum and the Geological Survey and the Museum of Practical Geography 1916*, Cmd. 8269 viii 535.

8. Local war museums

1. Leicester Museums Accessions Register. Leicestershire Museums and Art Gallery Records.

2. Sir Guy Laking 1875–1919. Trained as an artist, then worked for Christies. Keeper of the King's Armoury. Keeper of the Armoury, the Wallace Collection. Keeper, Secretary and Accounting Officer for the London Museum from 1911.

3. Attenburg, Breslau, Chemnitz, Düsseldorf, Elderfeld, Godesburg, Goslar, Ludwigshafen, Mannheim, Nordhausen, Saarbrucken, Stettin, Weimar and Zerbst. There was a Hindenberg museum at Pasen and another in connection with the Katzbach museum at Bonau (*Museums Journal* 15: 376).

4. The committee included Lord Barbard, Sir Clement Kinlock Cooke MP, Sir Cecil Smith (Victoria and Albert Museum), Sir Guy Laking (Museum of London), Sir Whitworth Wallis (Birmingham), Bailie Charles Carlton, Dr F.A. Bather (BMNH), Captain Ackland and Herbert Bolton (Bristol), E. Ruskin Butterfield (Hastings), A.J. Caddies (Stoke), Carter (Kingston-upon Thames), T.V. Hodgson (Plymouth), E.E. Lowe (Leicester), Mould (Southwark), T. Renhie (Glasgow), O.S. Scott (Barnard Castle), Arthur Smith (Lincoln), and A.G. Wright (Colchester).

5. Note from Walcott to O. Murray, 6 May 1917: IWM C/F Walcott.

6. Imperial War Museum Committee Minutes, Vol. 0, 29 March 1917: IWM C/F.

7. Imperial War Museum Committee Minutes, Vol 0, 5 April 1917: IWM C/F.

8. Imperial War Museum Committee Minutes, Vol. 0, 12 April 1917: IWM C/F

9. The provisional General Committee had the following adherents (in addition to the Executive Committee). Lord Burnham, the Lord Mayors of Birmingham and Bristol, The Lord Provost of Glasgow, the Mayors of Burnley, Cheltenham, Dorchester, Gloucester, Hastings, Lincoln, Salisbury and Swansea, the Provost of Inverness, Dr W. Evans Hoyle (Director of the National Museum of Wales), Alderman J. K. Butcher (Bury), Lawrence Howard (Manchester), E. Howarth (Sheffield), John W. Howarth (Chelmsford), Councillor W. Howell (Reading), Sir William Lever (Bath), Mr Joseph Robinson (Kirkcudbright), A.G. Temple (Guildhall, London), Councillor F. Todd (Manchester), G.H. Wallis (Nottingham), Thomas Wallis (Inverness), and Alderman E. Whitehead (Burnley) (*Museums Journal:* 17:272). As impressive as this list sounds, there is no evidence that they ever engaged in activities on the LWMA's behalf, Whitworth Wallis excepted.

10. These appear in a pamphlet, Local War Museums Association (1917), which presumably was written by Grundy. City of Lincoln: museums archives.

11. Imperial War Museum Committee Minutes, Vol. 0, 24 May 1917: IWM C/F.

12. Local War Museums A3/4 IWM C/F.

13. The principal speakers were Dr W.E. Hoyle (National Museum of Wales), E. Howarth

(Sheffield), R.F. Rowley (Exeter), T. Sheppard (Hull), J. Bailey (London), J.A. Deas (Sunderland and West Hartlepool), R.E. Martin (London), E.E. Lowe (Leicester), H. Bolton (Bristol), W. Grant Murray (Derby) and C. Madeley (Warrington).

14. Imperial War Museum Committee Minutes, Vol. o, 19 July 1917: IWM C/F.

15. Curatorial and institutional representatives came from the following towns: Bolton, Derby, Dundee, Lincoln, Merthyr Tydfil, Newcastle-upon-Tyne, Norwich, Reading, Salford, Southport, Wednesbury, Bristol, Doncaster, Leeds, Manchester, Middlesbrough, Northampton, Preston, Rotherham, Sheffield, Warrington, York (Howarth 1918).

16. H. Bolton (d. 1936). Assistant Keeper, Manchester Museum. Victoria University 1890–98. Curator of Bristol Museum 1898–1911. Director of Bristol Museum and Art Gallery 1911–30. Reader in Palaeontology, Bristol University 1911–26. Member of the Advisory Council of the Victoria and Albert Museum 1920–33.

17. Imperial War Museum Committee Minutes, Vol. o, 14 February 1918: IWM C/F.

18. The principal speakers were Sir Cecil Smith (Victoria and Albert Museum), Sir Henry Haworth (President of the Museums Association), Dr Bather (Wimbledon), T. Sheppard (Hull), Sir Whitworth Wallis (Birmingham), F.R. Rowley (Exeter), Dr Hoyle (National Museum of Wales) and H.D. Roberts (Brighton).

19. Sheffield Public Museum Minutes for 13 February, 15 May and 17 July 1919: Sheffield City Museum Archive.

20. Leicester Museums Accession Register.

21. Sheffield Public Museum Committee Minute, 14 August 1919.

22. Swansea, Liverpool, Manchester, Leeds, Hull, Dundee, Aberdeen, Nottingham, Halifax.

23. *Second Annual Report of the Committee from the Imperial War Museum*, P.P. 1918–19, 1919 Cmd. 138 xxii 1187.

24. Aberdeen, Acton, Ashford, Ayr, Bangor, Berwick-on-Tweed, Bexhill, Birmingham, Blackburn, Blackpool, Bournemouth, Bradford, Brentwood, Brighton, Bristol, Broadstairs, Brondesbury, Buckingham, Cardiff, Carlisle, Chelmsford, Chingford, Chistlehurst, Cookstown, Coventry, Deptford, Derby, Devizes, Dinnington, Discharged Soldiers and Sailors, Doncaster, Dudley, Ealing, Eastbourne, Eastry, Edinburgh, Effingham, Englefield Green, Farnham, Faversham, Gillingham, Glasgow, Glasgow Red Cross, Glasgow YMCA, Grimsby, Guildford, Hackney, Halifax, Hammersmith, Harrogate, Harrow, Hastings, Hawick, Hoddesden, Huddersfield, Hull, Keastwick, Kidwelly, Kilmarnock, Knutsford, Leeds, Leicester, Lichfield, Lincoln, Liverpool, Liverpool Church Army, Loughborough, Maidstone, Maldon, Manchester, Midsomer Norton, Millom, Ministry of Information, Ministry of Munitions, Neath Red Cross, Newbury, Newcastle on Tyne, Newport Pagnell, Northampton, Northaw, Northwich, Northwick patriotic fund, Nottingham, Oakham, Oldham, Pembury, Petworth, Plymouth, Poplar, Portsmouth, Preston, Prestwich, Radcliffe, Reading, Rochester, Rotherham, Rugby, St Austell, Salisbury, Scarborough, Scottish Red Cross, Scottish War Savings Committee, Scunthorpe, Sevenoaks, Shanklin, Sheerness, Sheffield, Somerton, Southall, Southampton, Southend, Southgate, Southport, Stafford, Stepney, Stockton, Stoke on Trent, Sunderland, Sutton, Swansea, Taunton, Tottenham, Trowbridge, Tunbridge Wells, Wakefield, Walthamstow, Wantage, War Seal Foundation, Wealdstone, Wellington, West Hartlepool, West Leighton, Westminster War Savings, Weybridge, Weymouth.

25. Report of the Honorary Director, War Memorial Museum, January 1919: Birmingham Record Office.

9. Proposals for a national war museum

1. Quoted in Harries 1983 as Second Interim Report on the work conducted for the Government at Wellington House (1.2.16): IWM C/F.

2. Note Walcott to O. Murray, 6 May 1917: IWM C/F Walcott.

3. C. ffoulkes, 'Origins and beginnings of the National War Museum (copy of notes from my diary 1917)' dated 15 March 1917: IWM Committee Minutes Vol 0: IWM C/F.

4. Copy of letter from Ian Malcolm MP to Lord Harcourt, 20 February 1917: IWM Committee Minutes Vol. 0: IWM C/F.

5. Copy of letter from Ian Malcolm MP to Lord Stamfordham, 20 February 1917: IWM Committee Minutes Vol. 0: IWM C/F.

6. National War Museum. Memorandum by Sir Alfred Mond, First Commissioner of Works, 27 February. (CAB 24/6 GT83): IWM C/F A1/3.

7. War Cabinet Minutes 87, Minute 15, 5 March 1917 (Works 17/108): IWM C/F A1/3.

8. Conway of Allington papers, Cambridge University Library, Martin Conway's diary, 21 March 1917.

9. Lloyd George papers, Beaverbrook Foundation Library F/36/6/14, Letter from Lloyd George to Alfred Mond, 23 March 1917.

10. The establishment of the National War Museum

1. National War Museum, Second Committee Meeting Minutes, 5 April 1917: IWM C/F.

2. National War Museum, First Committee Minutes, 29 March 1917: IWM C/F.

3. National War Museum Committee Minutes, 5 April 1917: IWM C/F.

4. National War Museum (B72 7 9) 24 4/17: IWM C/F A1/2.

5. Memorandum on the Scope of the National War Museum. Sir Martin Conway to the First Commissioner, HM Office of Works (Cab 24/22 GT1650): IWM C/F A1/3.

6. 'Imperial War Museum', Notes: IWM C/F A1/3.

7. Letter to Field Marshall Haig from Sir Martin Conway, 23 July 1917: IWM C/F A1/3.

8. National War Museum Committee Minutes, 16 August 1917: IWM C/F.

9. Note from Walcott to O. Murray, 6 May 1917: IWM C/F Walcott.

10. National War Museum Committee Minutes, 29 March and 5 April 1917: IWM C/F.

11. National War Museum Committee Minutes, 7 and 28 June 1917: IWM C/F.

12. National War Museum Committee Minutes, 28 June 1917: IWM C/F.

13. National War Museum Committee Minutes, 3 May and 5 July 1917: IWM C/F.

14. National War Museum Committee Minutes, 7 and 14 June 1917: IWM C/F.

15. *First Annual Report of the Committee of the Imperial War Museum* 1917–18 P.P., 1918, Cmd.9061 xiv 761.

16. National War Museum Committee Minutes, 7 June 1917: IWM C/F.

17. National War Museum Committee Minutes, 17 May 1917: IWM C/F.

18. National War Museum Committee Minutes, 2 August 1917: IWM C/F.

19. National War Museum Committee Minutes, 19 April 1917: IWM C/F.

20. National War Museum Committee Minutes, 26 April 1917: IWM C/F.

21. Memorandum on the Scope of the National War Museum. Sir Martin Conway to the First Commissioner, H.M. Office of Works (CAB 24/22 GT1650): IWM C/F A1/4.

22. Memorandum on the National War Memorial and Museum by the First Commissioner of Works (CAB 24/22 GT1650): IWM C/F A1/4.

23. War Cabinet Minutes 221, Minute 2, 2 August 1917 (works 17/108): IWM C/F A1/4.

24. Conway of Allington papers, Cambridge University Library, Conway diary 21 August 1917.

25. National War Museum Minutes, 27 September 1917: IWM C/F.

26. National War Museum Minutes, 22 November 1917: IWM C/F.

27. National War Museum Minutes, 22 November 1917. IWM C/F

28. National War Museum Minutes, 4 October 1917: IWM C/F.

11. The Imperial War Museum

1. Lord Crawford Committee on the War Museum. Interim report, 14 December 1917 (GT3016): IWM C/F A1/3.

2. Minutes of the Cabinet Committee on the National War Museum, 2 October, 1 November, 13 December 1917 and 29 January 1918: IWM C/F A1/3.

3. Letter to Lord Crawford from H.A.L. Fisher, 20 September 1917: IWM C/F A1/3.

4. Imperial War Memorial and Museum. Report of Lord Crawford's Committee, 14 March 1918 (G202): IWM C/F A1/3.

5. War Cabinet Minute 383, 7, 5 April 1918: IWM C/F.

6. War Cabinet Committee Minutes, 5 April 1917: IWM C/F.

7. National War Museum Committee Minutes, 5 April 1917: IWM C/F.

8. National War Museum Committee Minutes, 2 August 1918: IWM C/F.

9. National War Museum Committee Minutes, 13 December 1918: IWM C/F.

10. Geoffrey Allfee, Philip Connard, Nelson Dawson, John Lavery, Ambrose McEvoy, Charles Pears, Glyn Philpot and Norman Wilkinson.

11. Walcott Memorandum c. 1917: IWM C/F Walcott.

12. *Second Annual Report of the Committee of the Imperial War Museum 1918–19*, P.P., 1919, Cmd. 138 xxii 1187.

13. Imperial War Museum Committee Minutes, 31 January 1918: IWM C/F.

14. The Imperial War Exhibtion, Burlington House 1918 IWM C/F.

15. IWM British Official War Photographs. Exhibition Catalogue, London 1918. IWM C/F.

16. Imperial War Museum Committee Minutes, 6 June 1918: IWM C/F.

17. Imperial War Museum Committee Minutes, 12 December 1918: IWM C/F.

18. Imperial War Museum Committee Minutes, 1 June 1918: IWM C/F.

19. Letter from Conway to R.P.M Gower, 6 March 1919: IWM C/F A1/3.

20. National War Museum Committee Minutes, 28 June 1917: IWM C/F.

21. Imperial War Museum Committee Minutes, 1 May 1919: IWM C/F.

22. Memorandum from Mond to Conway, 14 May 1919: IWM C/F A1/2.

23. Imperial War Museum Memorandum by the First Commissioner of Works, covering draft bill, 16 March 1920, CP880: IWM C/F A1/2.

24. Cottesloe Committee I–II 1921–30 distribution of Military Weapons and Equipment, IWM C/F A3/2.
Royal Commission on National Museums and Galleries, 1928–29.

25. Letter from Kenyon to Conway, 28 April 1928, IWM A/F A3/2.

26. Imperial War Museum Committee Minutes, 27 November 1919: IWM C/F.

27. C. ffoukes, report on the work and operations preliminary to the opening of the

Imperial War Museum by his Majesty the King nd: IWM C/F A3/2.

28. Letter from Beckles Willson to Mond, 2 July 1920: IWM C/F A!/2.

29. *Third Annual Report of the Committee of the Imperial War Museum*. P.P., 1919–20, 1920, Cmd. 844 xvciii 37.

30. Letter from Lord Robert Cecil to Sir Alfred Mond, 24 June 1920: IWM C/F A1/2.

31. Letter from Mond to Cecil, 1 July 1920: IWM C/F A1/2.

32. Oral evidence,memoranda and appendices to the final report Royal Commission on National Museums and Galleries, Question 4382, 13 December 1928.

33. *Fifth Annual Report of the Imperial War Museum* (Second Report of the Board of Trustees) 1921–22 , IWM C/F.

12. Memories, memorials and mementoes

1. A marble faced bronze tablet commemorating the soldiers and a bust of the donor were sited in the Entrance Hall of the Dorman Memorial Museum.Both have been removed and their present whereabouts are unknown. Portraits of the donor and his wife, Sir Arthur and Lady Dorman,have been removed to the art gallery.Only the bold relief letters, **Dorman Memorial Museum**, over the entrance door remind us that it was built as a memorial.

2. Sir William Grey fell ill and it was his son, Captain William Grey, in whose honour the gift was being made, who handed the house and contents over to the Mayor. Hartlepool's Book of Remembrance has recently been moved to the crematorium.

3. The collections of the Royal Artillery Institution had existed as a museum within the Rotunda, Woolwich, since 1778. The Royal Engineer's Museum was formed in 1885.

4. I am grateful to Tom Hodgson for the primary source on which this account is based.

13. Museums and the inter-war years

1. In November 1920, the Editor of the *Museums Journal* reported on the work of the Imperial War Museum, and having grumbled that the IWM 'do not favour us with their paragraphs', went on to observe:'It is obvious they know how and where to advertise for the public they desire.We may give one example of a method probably new in the museum world. There is a wooden model of the biggest gun used during the war. For the sum of one shilling, including postage, members of the public may have their photographs taken by the side of this terrible engine of destruction. Among the first so to be taken were Miss Daphne Pollard of the Hippodrome, and Miss Evelyn Laye of the Gaiety Theatre' (*Museums Journal* 20: 120).

2. Radio broadcasting had begun in 1922 and was initially under the control of the British Broadcasting Company.

BIBLIOGRAPHY

Alberge, D., 1991, 'Driven underground', *The Independent*, 1 October

Anon., 1935, *The Silver Jubilee Book. The Story of 25 Eventful Years in Pictures*, Odhams Press, London

Bather, F.A., 1914 a, 'Discussion', *Museums Journal*, **14**, 284

Bather, F.A., 1914 b, 'Museums and national service', *Museums Journal*, **14**, 121–7

Bather, F.A., 1914 c, 'Patriotism in the museum', *Museums Journal*, **14**, 249–53

Bather, F.A., 1915 a, 'Discussion on museums and the war', *Museums Journal*, **15**, 72–9, 106–11

Bather, F.A., 1915 b, 'Museums and the war', *Museums Journal*, **15**, 2–10

Bather, F.A., 1918, 'National work at the Natural History Museum', *Museums Journal*, **17**, 120–25.

Bather, F.A., 1919, 'National work at the British Museum and the advancement of learning', *Smithsonian Report of 1917*, 617–33

Bell, G., 1991, 'Museums as memorials', unpublished Masters Degree dissertation, University of Leicester

Board of Education, 1931, *Memorandum on the Possibility of Increased Co-operation between Public Museums and Public Educational Institutions*, No 87, Board of Education.

Bolitho, H., 1933, *Alfred Mond, First Lord Melchett*, Martin Secker, London

Bolton, H., 1917, 'Local war museums' in Howarth, E., *Educational Value of War Museums*, 71–7, William Wesley, London

Bond, B., 1983, *War and Society in Europe 1870–1970*, Leicester University Press, Leicester

Borg, A., 1991, *War Memorials*, Cooper, London

Boorman, D., 1988, *At the Going Down of the Sun. British First World War Memorials*, Sessions, York

Bourne, J.M., 1989. *Britain and the Great War 1914–1918*, Edward Arnold, London

Bray, M.I., 1981, *Bells Of Memory. A History of the Loughborough Carillon*, BRD (Publishing), Loughborough

Brears, P. and Davies, S., 1989, *Treasures for the People*, Yorkshire and Humberside Museums Council, Leeds

Briggs, A., 1983, *A Social History of England*, Weidenfeld and Nicolson, London

British Association for the Advancement of Science, 1920, Final report of the committee on museums in relation to education, *Report of the British Association for the Advancement of Science*, 267–80, British Association, London

British Museum (Natural History), 1922, *War Memorial Record*, British Museum (Natural History), London

British Museum, 1939, *Air Raid Precautions in Museums, Picture Galleries and Libraries*, British Museum, London

Brittain, V., 1933, *Testament of Youth*, Fontana, London

Butterfield, W.R., 1917, 'A national war museum', *Museums Journal*, **16**, 243–48

Caygill, M., 1981, *The Story of the British Museum,* British Museum, London

City of Leicester Museum and Art Gallery, 1924, *Twentieth Report of the Committee 1912–1924,* City of Leicester

Clewes, R., 1915, 'Military Curios', *Connoisseur,* **44,** 21–4

Condell, D. M., 1985, The Imperial War Museum 1917–1920: a study of the institution and its presentation of the First World War. Unpublished Master of Philosophy thesis, University of London

Cowper, L. I., 1935, 'British military museums', *Museums Journal,* **35,** 40–49

Daily Express, 1933, *First World War*

Dibdin, E.R., 1915, 'Presidential address', *Museums Journal,* **15,** 33–9

Dibdin, E.R., 1916, 'Presidential address', *Museums Journal,* **16,** 37–8

Durbin, G., 1983, A museum in the Great War: Norwich Castle Museum 1914–19, *Museums Journal,* **83** (2/3) :

Evans, J., 1966, *The Conways. A History of Three Generations,* Museum Press, London

ffoulkes, C., 1915, 'Belgian artwork', *Connoisseur,* **40,** 143–4

ffoulkes, C., 1939, *Arms and the Tower,* John Murray, London

Follett, D., 1978, *The Rise of the Science Museum under Henry Lyons,* Science Museum, London

Ford, B., (ed.), 1992, *Early 20th Century Britain. The Cambridge Cultural History,* Cambridge University Press, Cambridge

Fulford, R., 1957, *Votes for Women,* Faber, London

Fussell, P., 1975, *The Great War and Modern Memory,* Oxford University Press, Oxford

Gardner, J.S., 1915, 'War memorials', *Connoisseur,* **43,** 37–8

Gibson, E. and Ward, G.K., 1989, *Courage Remembered. The Story behind the Construction and Maintenance of the Commonwealth's Military Cemeteries and Memorials of the Wars of 1914–1918 and 1939–1945,* HMSO, London

Glover J. and Silken, J., 1989, *The Penguin Book of First World War Prose,* Penguin, London

Graves, R.and Hodge, A., 1940, *The Long Week-end,* Penguin edn, Harmondsworth

Green, J.A., 1914, 'The museums committee for the British Association', *Museums Journal,* **14,** 344

Griffiths, G., 1991, *Women's Factory Work in World War I,* Alan Sutton, Stroud

Grundy, C. R., 1915, 'A suggestion for war memorials', *Connoisseur,* **42,** 235

Grundy, C.R., 1916, 'Local war museums', *Connoisseur,* **46,** 168–70

Grundy, C.R., 1917, *Local War Museums: a Suggestion,* private publication

Harries, M. and S., 1983, *The War Artists: British Official War Art of the Twentieth Century,* Michael Joseph, London

Harrison, M., 1985, 'Art and philanthropy: T.C. Horsfall and the Manchester Art Museum', in Kidd, A.J., and Roberts, K.W., *City, Class and Culture,* 120–47

Haste, C., 1977, *Keep the Homefires Burning,* Allen Lane, London

Haywood, W., 1918, *The Development of Birmingham. An Essay with Designs and Drawings,* Kynoch, Birmingham

Higgs, J. W. Y., 1963, *Folk Life Collection and Classification,* Museums Association, London

Holdsworth, A., 1988, *Out of the Doll's House. The Story of Women in the Twentieth Century,* BBC, London

Hooper-Greenhill, E., 1991, *Museum and Gallery Education,* Leicester University Press, Leicester

Howarth, E., 1913, 'National Folk Museum', *Museums Journal,* **13,** 187

Howarth, E., 1913, 'Presidential address', *Museums Journal,* **13,** 33–52

Howarth, E., 1914, 'The museum and the school', *Museums Journal,* **14,** 282

Howarth, E., 1918, 'The co-ordination of museums with direct general education', in Howarth, E., (ed.), *The Educational Value of Museums and the Formation of Local War Museums: Report of Proceedings,* 6–20, William Wesley, Sheffield

Howarth, E., (ed.) 1918, *The Educational Value of Museums and the Formation of Local War Museums: Report of Proceedings* , William Wesley, Sheffield

Howarth, E. and Platnauer, H.M., 1911, *Directory of Museums in Britain and Ireland with a Section on Indian and Colonial Museums*

Howorth, Sir H.H., 1917, 'The legal status of the British Museum', *Museums Journal*, **17**, 116–118

Kavanagh, G., 1990, *History Curatorship*, Leicester University Press, Leicester

Kavanagh, G., 1991, 'The articulation of professional self-consciousness' in Kavanagh, G. (ed.), *The Museums Profession. Internal and External Relations*, 39–55, Leicester University Press, Leicester

Kenyon, F.G., 1934, *British Museum in Wartime*, Jackson, Wylie and Co., Glasgow

Keuren, D. K.Van, 1984,'Museum and ideology: Augustus Pitt-Rivers, anthropology museums and social change in later Victorian Britain', *Victorian Studies* , 171–89

Knightley, P., 1982, *The First Casualty. The War Correspondent as Hero, Propagandist and Mythmaker*, Quartet, London

Lasswell, H.D., 1927, *Propaganda Technique and Identity in the World War*, Kegan Paul, London

Leed, E.J., 1979, *No Man's Land: Combat and Identity in the First World War*, Cambridge University Press, Cambridge

Leeson, C., 1917, *The Child and the War, Being Notes on Juvenile Delinquency*, published for the Howard Association, London

Leetham, Sir A., 1918, 'Local war museums', *Museums Journal*, **18**, 93–7

Leney, F., 1916,'Wartime exhibitions at the Norwich Castle Museum', *Museums Journal*, **16**, 221–24

Lewis, G.D., 1984, 'Collections, collectors and museums to 1920/ Museums in Britain to 1920,' in Thompson, J.M.A. *et al.*, (eds), *Manual of Curatorship*

Lewis, G.D., 1989, *For Instruction and Education. A Centenary History of the Museums Association*, Quiller Press, London

Lowe, E.E., 1915, 'Infant welfare in the Leicester Museums', *Museums Journal*, **15**, 254–64

Lowe, E.E., 1918, 'Museum and art gallery finance', *Museums Journal*, **18**, 112–14

Lowe, E.E., 1920,'The transfer of museums to the educational authorities', *Museums Journal*, **19**, 105–11

Markham, S.F., 1938, *The Museums and Art Galleries of the British Isles*, CUKT, Edinburgh

Marwick, A., 1965, *The Deluge: British Society and the First World War*, Macmillan, London

Marwick,A. 1974, *War and Social Change in the Twentieth Century, A Comparative Study of Britain, France, Germany and the United States*, Macmillan, London,

Marwick, A., 1977, *Women at War 1914–1918*, Fontana, London

Marwick, A., (ed.), 1989, *Total War and Social Change*, Macmillan, London

Masterman, L., 1939, *C.F.G. Masterman. A Biography*, Nicholson and Watson, London

McKernan, M., 1991, *Here is there Spirit. A History of the Australian War Memorial 1917–1990*, University of Queensland Press in association with the Australian War Memorial, St Lucia

Miers, Sir H.A.,1928, *A Report on the Museums and Galleries of the British Isles*, Carnegie United Kingdom Trust, Edinburgh

Minihan, J., 1977, *The Nationalisation of Culture. The Development of State Subsidies to the Arts in Great Britain*, Hamish Hamilton, London

Moore, K., 1991,' "Feasts of reason?" Exhibitions at the Liverpool Mechanics Institution in the 1840s', in Kavanagh, G., (ed.), *Museum Languages. Objects and Texts*, 155–78

Mullen, B., 1918,'Scheme for scholars visiting the Salford Museums', in Howarth, E. (ed.), *The Educational Value of Museums*, 21–5

Munson, J., 1984, Echoes of the Great War, *Listener*, 16 August

Myre, J.L., 1919, 'Peace Museum', *Museums Journal*, **19**, 73–6

Norfolk Museum Service, 1984, *The Past Displayed*, Norwich Museum Service, Norwich

Oddy, A., 1992, *The Art of the Conservator,* British Museum, London

Ogilvie, F.G., 1919, *Report on the Sheffield City Museums*, Educational Pamphlet, No. 34

Paton, J., 1894, 'The education of a curator', *Report of the Proceedings of the Fifth Annual General Meeting of the Museums Association*, Museums Association, London, 95–105

Peel, C.S., 1929, *How We Lived Then. A Sketch of Social and Domestic Life in England during the War,* Bodley Head, London

Rathgen, F., 1913, 'Decay and preservation of antiquities', *Museums Journal*, **13**, 156–82

Rasmussen, H., 1966, *Dansk Folkemuseum and Frilandsmuseet,* Nationalmuseet, Copenhagen

Royal Commission on National Museums and Galleries, 1928, *Oral evidence memoranda and appendices 1928–9*, Cmd., 3192 viii 699

Royal Commission on National Museums and Galleries, 1929, *Final report Part 1. General Conclusions and Recommendations 1929–30*, Cmd.3401 xvi 431

Sanders, M. and Taylor, P.M., 1982, *British Propaganda during the First World War*, London

Sheppard, F., 1991, *The Treasury of London's Past*, HMSO, London

Sheppard, T. 1918, 'Notes on packing and removing a museum of geology and antiquities in wartime', *Museums Journal*, **18**, 79–82

Skinner, G. M., 1986, 'Sir Henry Wellcome's museum for the science of history', *Medical History*, **30**, 383–418

Spiller, E.M., 1918, 'The Children's Christmas Holidays at the Victoria and Albert Museum 1917–18', *Museums Journal*, **17**, 177–80.

Stallings, W.T., 1933, *The First World War: a Photographic History,* Daily Express Publications, London

Stearn, W.T., 1981, *The Natural History Museum at South Kensington. A history of the British Museum (Natural History) 1753–1980*, Heinemann, London

Stevenson, J., 1984, *British Society 1914–45*, Penguin, London

Taylor, A.J.P., 1969, *War by Time-table,* MacDonald, London

Teather, J.L., 1983, 'Museological traditions. The British experience, 1845–1945', unpublished PhD thesis, University of Leicester

Teather, J. L., 1990, 'The museum keepers. The Museums Association and the growth of museum professionalism', *Museum Management and Curatorship*, **9**, 25–41

Thwaites, P., 1992, 'From private corps to public museum: a history of the Royal Corps of signals Museum of Army Communication 1920–1992', unpublished Masters Degree Dissertation

Westrate, J.L., 1961, *European Military Museums: a Survey of their Philosophy, Facilities, Programmes and Management*, Smithsonian Institute, Washington

Wilkinson, M., 1991, 'Patriotism and duty: Women's work collection at the Imperial War Museum', *Imperial War Museum Review*, **6**, Imperial War Museum, London.

Williams, J., 1972, *The Home Fronts: Britain France and Germany 1914–1918*, Constable, London

Wilson, D.M., 1989, *The British Museum. Purpose and Politics*, British Museum Publications, London

Winter, J., 1986, *The Great War and the British People*, Macmillan, London

INDEX

Illustrations are referred to by number and in **bold** type